The business of risk

PETER G. MOORE
London Business School

CAMBRIDGE
UNIVERSITY PRESS

Published by the Press Syndicate of the University of Cambridge
The Pitt Building, Trumpington Street, Cambridge CB2 1RP
40 West 20th Street, New York, NY 10011-4211 USA
10 Stamford Road, Oakleigh, Melbourne 3166, Australia

First published 1983
Reprinted 1990, 1993, 1995, 1999

Printed in Great Britain by
Athenæum Press Ltd, Gateshead, Tyne & Wear

Library of Congress catalogue card number: 82-23594

British Library cataloguing in publication data

Moore, Peter G.
The business of risk.
1. Risk management – Decision making
I. Title
658.4'03'018   HD61

ISBN 0 521 24174 X hard covers
ISBN 0 521 28497 X paperback

U P

Contents

Preface

Risk is all pervasive. An individual faces physical risks from driving a car, career risks from the possible bankruptcy of one's employer, financial risks from investing his or her savings in equities. A company faces the risk of collapse of a traditional market, or of research failure for a new product. A government may face an unexpected strike or a foreign government's rebuff to a diplomatic overture. While in some areas, such as life assurance, risk is well understood and systematically handled in an accepted manner, this is not common in other areas of economic and social activity.

The proceedings of a 1980 Royal Society symposium on risk were published under the title *The Assessment and Perception of Risk*. Lord Ashby's introduction gave a commercial example concerning the damages involved from a collision between two ships. The fifteen papers in the volume dealt, however, almost exclusively with areas of personal physical risk. I hope this book will help to answer the kind of question posed by Lord Ashby and redress the narrow perspective given to the subject, no doubt accidentally, by the Royal Society symposium.

The three principal messages conveyed are: first, risk arises in some form or other in virtually all fields of endeavour; second, it is important neither to ignore risk nor to be frightened by it; third, systematic methods to assess and handle risks can be developed. After an introduction and four general chapters dealing with risk assessment, the book examines the progress that has been made in handling risk in seven distinct fields. While these fields are not exhaustive, they cover the more common risk areas. The appendixes provide some basic background material on risk handling of general relevance to the application orientated chapters. Only a rudimentary knowledge of mathematics and statistics is assumed for all except a few sections of the book.

Much confusion is caused over the terms *objective* and *subjective* as applied to risk assessment. The former is commonly linked to situations where a history of precisely similar situations exists, while the latter assumes that no such history exists on which to base assessments. Pundits argue that probability concepts can be applied in the first, but not the second, situation. This is to paint a black or white canvas that is unrecognizable in real life. Most situations mix objective and subjective inputs. Methods have necessarily to be developed to use the information available fruitfully, and this book aims to make a contribution to this end.

References are grouped together, by chapter, at the end of the book. This layout allows the references to form a select bibliography of recent work done in the area of risk. A set of thirty exercises is included at the end of the book, covering many of the concepts illustrated in the book. They should help readers to reinforce the concepts, whether or not they have the benefit of tutorial guidance.

The book draws material from many reports, research papers, magazines, journals and books – in some instances unpublished. The source of any material quoted is acknowledged wherever practicable and I apologize for any accidental omissions. Particular acknowledgement is made to Her Majesty's Stationery Office for Table 2.6, Coral Industries for the letter reproduced on page 146, Risk Measurement Service of the London Business School for Figures 8.1 and 8.3 and other tabular material, and to *The Guardian* with reference to Exercise 13 on page 225.

It is a pleasure to acknowledge the help received from many quarters, not least student groups who have wrestled with drafts or some chapters. My wife, Sonja Moore, has give me invaluable assistance with proof-reading of the text, and compilation of the index. Nevertheless, ultimate responsibility rests with the author and comments from readers will be welcome.

London   P. G. MOORE
March, 1983

1
Introduction

Tesman: But good heavens, we know nothing of the future.
Løvborg: No, but there is a thing or two to be said about it all the same.

Ibsen: *Hedda Gabler*

1.1   The background

Risk is about future happenings and enters everybody's lives at numerous points. A mountaineer going on an expedition can break a leg, or be killed. A business person keeping an appointment in Birmingham may be involved in a serious road accident. A traveller in Africa may contract dysentery. A gambler entering a casino could lose all his capital in a night. The company in which an individual has invested may go into liquidation. An entrepreneur starting a new business venture can lose his capital when an expected market fails to materialize. A government may be thrown off course when a major trading bloc operates a cartel against it.

Economic progress is impossible without taking risks; indeed it is arguable that even the maintenance of an economic status quo involves risk taking. Hence risk has about it an aura of achievement and progress, communities commonly rewarding those who handle difficult risk situations successfully. Effective handling of risks requires first their assessment and, secondly, their subsequent incorporation in the decision-making process. Exploring these themes in a variety of business, economic, political and social settings forms the primary objective of this book.

To take an action involving a risk is to take a chance or a gamble; it implies a degree of uncertainty and inability to control fully the outcomes or consequences of such an action. Sometimes the chances of benefit are low and it's only just possible the risk will pay off. At other times the chances are high: it's very likely the desired outcome will occur. Faced with a choice of courses of action, with differing levels of risks and possible rewards, a decision has to be made as to what to do. The more the precise nature and level of the risks faced can be revealed the better informed the decision made will be. But if hunches are followed – flying by the seat of the pants – then outcomes may occur that sometimes surprise both the decision maker and his colleagues.

1

Risk is a 'portmanteau' word. It describes a scenario in which possible losses are present: physical (such as death), disappointment (failure to climb a mountain), financial loss (as when a business person makes a poor investment in a new venture). Higher risk makes the loss more likely, lower risk makes it less likely. Sometimes risk has a different meaning as being the precise quantum of money that can be lost by undertaking some venture. For example, insuring household possessions against loss by theft for £5000 leads the insurance company (or the underwriter on its behalf) to regard the sum of £5000 as being *at risk*. To them risk is the maximum monetary loss the company can incur.

The word 'risk' is relatively modern, coming to England in the mid-seventeenth century from France as the word *risque*. The anglicized spelling began to appear in England around 1830 in insurance transactions, and for about 100 years the two spellings existed side by side. Only in the twentieth century has the derivative risqué become the word for a joke that risks offending. In earlier days, before the word risk existed, the word *hazard* appears to have had the closest meaning as in Shakespeare's *Merchant of Venice*:

Men that hazard all do it in hope of fair advantages.

Hazard and risk can both be used as either a noun or a verb and so both

Figure 1.1. Risk Levels

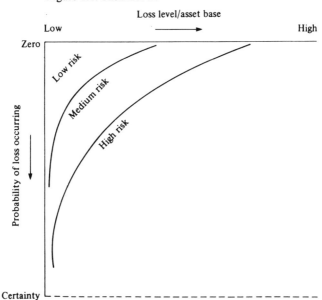

are capable of expressing two ideas: first, a danger located in some aspect of the external world and, second, the idea of acting in a way that involves the taking of a chance. But Shakespeare reminds us that risk is connected not only with the possibility of loss or harm, but also with the hope of some benefit or gain.

There are thus two basic components of risk: first, a future outcome which can take a number of forms, some of them commonly unfavourable; and, second, a non-zero chance that the less favourable outcome(s) may occur. Colloquially, risk is used to cover the combination of an unfavourable result and the non-zero chance of its occurring. However, when terms like 'high risk' or 'low risk' are used, the meaning commonly depends on the starting asset base and the consequences that the occurrence of the 'risk' would have for the asset base of the individual or organization concerned. The position can be viewed simplistically on an asset-free basis by postulating the loss level as being expressed as a multiple (or ratio) of the asset base. Figure 1.1 illustrates schematically the combinations of probability of loss against level of loss that lead to so-called high-risk situations and the duality implied by the use of the term risk in the two dimensions. The boundary lines are indicative of the kinds of situations colloquially labelled with the various degrees of risk.

The word *risk* is used in either sense in this book where its connotation is clear, but otherwise the words *probability* or *chance* are used for one dimension, with the words *value, payoff, gain* or *loss* for the other dimension.

1.2 Some thumbnail sketches

Brief thumbnail sketches illustrate the problems discussed in this book.

Oil exploration

An area of land or sea is to be allocated by the Government to the highest bidder, entitling them to explore for oil in that area. An oil company is deciding whether to put in a bid for drilling on the area and, if so, what level of bid to make. If oil is found they can develop the site and sell the oil, subject to various taxation provisions on the proceeds. Clearly the price bid for the area is linked both to the assessed probability of striking oil and, secondly, to the likely proceeds from raising and marketing the oil found. The chance of any individual borehole striking oil is low; furthermore, as more ground is explored, the chance of further successful boring diminishes, as the more promising areas will usually be the first to be explored.

The risk in drilling cannot be eliminated – and an area that has no oil cannot magically be given some – but the possibility of purchasing a dud area can be reduced in a number of ways, for example by a study of geological conditions already found in neighbouring blocks, seismic soundings, etc. If taxation of the financial proceeds is raised in real terms, exploration activity could be expected to diminish, and lower prices paid for areas. This feature is sometimes referred to as a lowering of the reward/risk ratio: a concept that seems to have been borne out in recent years when rises in the real level of taxation of oil revenues have led to a slowing down of exploration and development activity in the North Sea, albeit to the surprise of some politicians.

A lending decision

A finance house has a funding proposal from an entrepreneur interested in manufacturing and marketing a jig which enables any amateur do-it-yourself enthusiast to build wardrobes, kitchen units, bookcases, etc. to professional standards. The entrepreneur, a biologist by background, has run a textile retailing business for eight years and wishes to raise £100000 to set up his own company. The finance company is concerned with the safety of both capital and interest for any funds it advances. This involves assessing the risks centred around the production capabilities, the market potential, the financial structure, and the managerial potential of the entrepreneur and the team he either has, or proposes to recruit. Only when these assessments have been made will the finance company be in a position to make a decision as to the terms on which any financial backing could be given.

Pharmaceutical launch

A pharmaceutical company plans to launch a new drug on the market. The problem is the size and scope of the product launch. Various methods are available to generate publicity: advertising; television commercials; direct mail; free samples to doctors and others; special shop displays; doorstep promotion; etc. These may be used singly or in combination, and at differing intensities. The costs of alternative media are known and, while the effectiveness of each medium can be estimated from information on past launches, no two launches are precisely similar. The number of combinations of publicity options is immense, but for each there are differing degrees of uncertainty about their effectiveness. From all this information a launch plan has to be decided upon.

Fruit cargoes

The purchasing manager of a fruit-importing business is deciding what to do about forward dealings in grapefruit for next January. Only two cargoes of grapefruit, of different sizes, are due in London next January. He can purchase either cargo, but for cash reasons not both, provided he contracts quickly. He always has the opportunity of spot purchases, albeit at a higher price than for a full cargo. There are two big customers who will decide their contracted requirements in about a month, after the decision regarding the cargoes has had to be made. If the manager signs for one of the cargoes, and then fails to win a sales contract, he could sell small quantities at a good price, but larger quantities would have to be sold at clearance prices. What is his optimal strategy?

Tourism

An American property company is looking at the possibilities of various development schemes within the Caribbean area. With the rapid growth of tourism and the increasing wealth of the area, a number of options are identified:

(*a*) a mix of office and apartment development activity;

(*b*) residential developments: apartments and homes;

(*c*) hotel and leisure park developments.

The major uncertainties revolve around the inherent political risks, i.e. the likelihood of government stability, of revolution, of subsequent military takeover, of changes in laws and, ultimately, the chance of appropriation of assets. Quite apart from these crucial sources of uncertainty, the company is also concerned with the chances of obtaining suitable short-term and long-term financing, the likely development costs, the speed with which planning permission can be obtained, and the number of potential users of the proposed developments. In addition, the development of a good transport infrastructure and the degree of willingness of international airlines to route more airplanes to this area could affect the profitability of the operation considerably. Which option or options should be pursued?

Diagnosis

A doctor does not know whether his patient's sore throat is caused by streptococcus or by a virus. If it were strep, he would prescribe penicillin pills or an injection, whereas if it were a virus he would prescribe rest, gargle and aspirin. Failure to treat a strep throat by penicillin (or other drugs) may result in a serious disease, such as nephritis. However, penicillin must not be administered indiscriminately since it could result in a serious penicillin reaction causing extreme discomfort, while penicillin-resistant bacteria might later develop.

A throat culture can be taken to indicate presence or absence of strep but the test is imperfect. The doctor even then still has a variety of ways to treat the patient. He can prescribe penicillin pills, or rest and gargle. How should he decide among these alternatives?

Television series production

A United States film company is contemplating a new twelve-episode film series for television based on Abe Bayley's novel entitled *The Dollar Game*: an exposé of the workings of a finance house. The company has approached one of the major US television networks for financial backing.

The network concerned is considering whether, and how much, to invest in the series and faces a number of uncertainties in reaching its decision. These relate primarily to the costs of production, the availability of outside financial backing, the level of viewing audience that will be attracted, the pulling power to potential advertisers, the availability of artists to play the lead roles in the series, and the sales potential of the series to networks outside the United States.

Faced with such uncertainties, the network is considering yet another option, namely to contract for one or two pilot episodes only, using these to evaluate more clearly the likely viewing audience and the advertising potential of the complete series. The sums of money involved are large, combined with inherent high risks as to the return.

Road programme

A limited amount of money is available for spending on roads and road improvements over the next three years. Various alternative programmes have been put forward and it is necessary to choose between them. In making this choice, a number of possible considerations emerge. First, there are the general benefits to traffic flow, both for through traffic and for local traffic; second, the amelioration of bottlenecks; third, the reduction of accidents; fourth, the public reaction to the ways in which they perceive priorities being defined and their money being spent. By taking all these factors into account, with the various consequences, many of which are only quantifiable in terms of expectations, a specific programme has to be selected.

1.3   Substitution of risks

The examples described suggest that efforts should be made to reduce (or even eliminate) some or all of the risks involved. However, eliminating, or reducing, one risk can sometimes mean an increase in another risk. Numerous illustrations where this kind of trade-off has to be made occur in this book, so just two instances will be mentioned at this stage. The first relates to the insect killer DDT. Unlike some other insect killers, DDT does not decompose readily into harmless constituents. Rachel Carson wrote an emotive book *The Silent Spring* in the 1950s (Hamish Hamilton, 1963) about the potential dangers of DDT and other insecticides and weed-killers to human beings. Partly as a result, Ceylon (Sri Lanka) banned DDT. Shortly afterwards Ceylon had a raging and virulent epidemic of malaria, a disease transmitted by mosquitoes. At that time the disease could have been controlled, and possibly virtually eliminated, by DDT. Many people in Ceylon therefore died unnecessarily because it had become possible to develop ways of measuring as little as 1 part in 10 million of DDT and its use in some form to control malaria thus became possible. The pursuit of a no-risk society in one sense had increased the risks in another sense.

A second example relates to crash helmets for motor cyclists, for which a British Standard was introduced some 20 years ago. This standard was widely misunderstood initially on two counts. First, there was inadequate realisation that part of the protection when a crash happens comes from the absorption of shock by the breaking of the helmet on impact. A broken helmet is not proof of an ineffective helmet: indeed it could be the opposite. Second, it was insufficiently appreciated that, while a stronger and more rigid helmet could in theory protect the head better, it would mean there was a greater chance that the motor cyclist whose skull is saved would instead seriously dislocate his neck. Thus ameliorating one risk could expose another equally lethal risk.

1.4   Risk and probability

The word 'chance' has been used earlier in relation to some happening that cannot be predicted with absolute certainty. The more common way of expressing such chance is by means of the term *probability*. An outcome that must occur is given the probability value 1, while an outcome that cannot occur under any circumstances is given the probability value 0. All other outcomes have probabilities that fall somewhere between 0 and 1. Suppose that in taking some specific course of action a particular outcome is given the probability value 0.3. Subsequently this outcome either does or does not occur, and from the result one won't be much wiser as to whether the original probability value 0.3 was indeed 'correct' or not. Over a period of time, however, all situations where the probability value used was 0.3 could be put together and looked at as a set. In this set it should be found that in about 30% of the cases the named occurrences had occurred, while in about 70% they hadn't. A large number of 'probability 0.3' situations would have to be considered to achieve a precise match but, as the number of situations or trials increases, so should the closeness between the observed outcomes and the probability concerned.

The value of 0.3 for the probability in an individual situation can be reached in a variety of ways. Many of these are examined later in Chapters 2 to 4. But, however the probability is arrived at, it must always obey a number of basic rules of behaviour such as coherence and consistency. For example, suppose that an insurance company rates the probability of a male driver insured with them having an accident in a given year as 1 in 10 (0.1), with the equivalent probability for a female driver being 1 in 15 (0.067). Of the policyholders on its books, two-thirds are men and one-third are women. Then the overall probability of a policyholder chosen at random from among all the policyholders having an accident in a given year is equal to $\frac{2}{3} \times 0.1 + \frac{1}{3} \times 0.067$, or 0.089. This result does not depend on the processes used to determine the two probabilities. It simply states that, if these two separate probabilities are given, then the consequence derived above follows. If the consequence is untrue, this implies that one or other – or both – of the original probabilities must themselves be incorrect.

Appendix A demonstrates the basic rules that have to be obeyed by probabilities, and the ways in which appropriate probabilities for complex combinations of events be derived from the component probabilities if coherence and consistency is to be maintained.

1.5   Decision analysis

Decision analysis forces decision makers to carry out a thorough and logical evaluation of the alternative strategies open to them, so that the 'best' available strategy in terms of some stated preference criteria for choice among the alternatives is selected. It provides a framework for taking decisions in an environment of risk and uncertainty.

The decision maker goes through five stages in this process (see for example, Raiffa, 1968). The stages do not always need to be rigidly followed and, indeed, some may occasionally be redundant. The value of the step-by-step procedure lies in its power to force the decision maker to conceptualize the structure of decision problems in a coherent and meaningful way. The five stages are as follows.

Stage 1: Structuring through decomposition

The decision maker first decomposes a complex decision problem into a series of simpler and more individually manageable decision problems. Such a decomposition is commonly shown in the form of a kind of flow diagram known as a *decision tree*. Figure 1.2a shows a typical tree. The essence of it is that, no matter how complex the decision problem, the decision maker is forced to define the problem clearly, to consider all feasible alternatives and to clarify the nature of the outcomes that can arise from each alternative course of action. Structuring is both art and science, and cannot easily be taught as a series of rules. In practice, decision makers improve their structuring skills through 'learning by doing'.

Stage 2: Assessing payoff (or utility) values

The decision maker evaluates the payoffs for each end-position on his decision tree. These payoffs will commonly be in terms of the net gain (or loss) for the unique route along the tree leading to the particular end point concerned. This net gain will be income less expenditure although, if the project spans a substantial time span, both income and expenditure would be discounted to the same point in time (commonly the start date). When decision makers do not regard money on a linear scale (for example, they attach greater importance to increasing their assets from £1 million to £2 million, than in increasing them from £2 million to £3 million) then some utility scale has to be used in place of payoff. This need is discussed in Chapter 5, where situations whose outcomes are judged on more than one dimension, for example monetary return and maintenance of employment, are also considered.

Stage 3: Assessing probabilities for uncertain outcomes

Judgements about the chances of various outcomes arising from particular courses of action are quantified in terms of probabilities. Considerable evidence exists that decision makers use probability concepts effectively when assessing uncertainties for their analyses of decision problems, once they have had experience in the processes involved. Procedures for assessing probabilities in various forms are available (see Chapters 3 to 5). Much attention has been devoted in recent years to understanding the biases which occur in probability assessments, and to seeking approaches that simplify the assessment task.

Stage 4: The roll-back process

The solution procedure followed is based on the principle of optimality used in dynamic programming. It involves calculating expected values for each alternative course of action at the appropriate points on the decision tree, expected value being commonly referred to as *expected monetary value* (EMV), even when the payoffs are not expressed in strict monetary terms. Roll-back then operates by working from the end points (right hand side) of the decision tree and folding it back towards the start (left hand side), choosing at each decision point the course of action with the highest expected value. By repeated application of this principle until the start point is reached, all alternatives are eventually eliminated except the 'best' strategy. Decision analysis rests upon the principle that no other decision rule exists that will, used consistently over time for all decisions, achieve a higher payoff.

Stage 5: Sensitivity analysis

In any decision analysis the quality of the deduced strategy depends primarily upon the quality of the judgements both of probability and the outcome valuations on which the analysis is based. (This, incidentally, is true whatever decision-making approach is adopted.) To meet this concern the decision maker should examine the sensitivity of the derived strategy to possible variations in the judgemental inputs. The crucial factors in the decision situation can be readily identified in this way, and extra assessment effort concentrated on the more sensitive factors.

1.6   An illustrative example

The concepts of decision analysis are illustrated with an example of a company deciding whether or not to invest £130000 in a one-year research and development (R&D) project aimed at developing a new product. If the project is successful, the company can choose between building a plant capable of producing 100000 units per annum or one capable of producing 200000 units per annum.

Figure 1.2*a* shows the decision tree defining the situation. There are two kinds of node on the tree. The square-shaped *decision nodes* represent points in time where a choice has to be made between alternative courses of action. The circular *outcome nodes* represent points in time where the outcomes which occur from decisions already made are not completely within the control of the decision maker.

The first node at *A* is a decision node, and the two branches emanating from it indicate that the company can choose whether or not to go ahead with the R & D programme. If the company does not go ahead, there are no further decisions, and outcomes are unimportant. (Hence the 'not go ahead with R & D' branch leads to no further branches.) If the company goes ahead with the R & D, the tree shows at node *X* that there are then two possible outcomes: 'R & D successful' and 'R & D unsuccessful'. If the R & D is unsuccessful there are no further relevant decisions and the process terminates. If the programme is successful the company must, as the second decision node B on the tree shows, choose between a large or small plant. Whichever decision is taken at node *B*, the final branches on the tree at either node *Y* or node *Z* show that the market size is liable to be 'high', 'medium', or 'low'. This completes stage 1.

For stage 2 the payoff values are calculated corresponding to each

Figure 1.2 (*a*) Decision tree with probabilities and NPVs (£ thousands); (*b*) Roll-back procedure for analysis

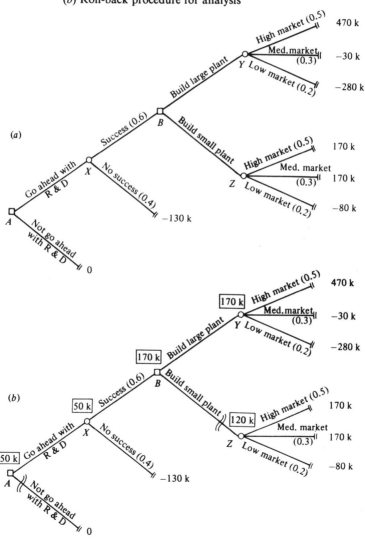

possible end point on the decision tree in the form of a monetary value (MV). This is the sum of money invested today that could produce the cash flows involved along the route to the end point concerned. Figure 1.2 shows a total of eight end points to be examined, for which the basic data are as follows:

(a) the present value of the cost of the R & D programme is £130000 (£130k for brevity)

(b) the capital cost, in present value terms, of a small plant is £200000 and of a large plant is £400000;

(c) a small plant can cope with a low or medium market size, but not with a high market size;

(d) the present value of the net cash flows corresponding to sales in a high market, medium market and low market over the life of the plant are £1000000, £500000 and £250000 respectively.

The end values can now be computed. For example, the end point corresponding to a medium market from node Z has a value of

$$-130k - 200k + 500k = +170k$$
$$\text{R \& D} \quad \text{small} \quad \text{medium}$$
$$\text{plant} \quad \text{sales}$$

Stage 3 of the process requires probabilities be assigned to each branch emanating from an outcome node. These are taken to be:

(a) the probability of the R & D programme being successful is 0.6 (for node X)

(b) the probabilities of there being a high, medium or low market for the product are 0.5, 0.3 and 0.2 respectively (for nodes Y and Z).

The analysis in stage 4 involves working from right to the left on the tree asking at each node reached (decision node or outcome node) the question: 'How much is it worth to be at this node?'

The first nodes encountered by this principle are at Y and Z. At node Y the tree indicates a 0.5 probability of an MV of 470k, a 0.3 probability of $-30k$, and a 0.2 probability of $-280k$. Hence the EMV if node Y is reached is

$$0.5 \times 470 + 0.3 \times (-30) + 0.2 \times (-280) = 170k$$

(This value is shown in Figure 1.2b adjacent to node Y.) Similarly the MV if node Z is reached is

$$0.5 \times 170 + 0.3 \times 170 + 0.2 \times (-80) = 120k.$$

Node B is a decision node which, if reached, gives a choice as to whether to move to node Y where the expected EMV is 170k, or to node Z where the expected EMV is 120k. Given the basic assumption underlying the analysis of maximizing EMV, the former route is chosen, and a double bar put on the other route to indicate its rejection. Hence the expected NPV associated with node *B* is 170k.

Consider next node *X*. At this node there is a 0.6 probability of reaching node *B* where the expected EMV is 170k, with a 0.4 probability of reaching a situation where the EMV is −130k. Hence the EMV associated with node *X* is $0.6 \times 170k + 0.4 \times (−130k) = 50k$. It is also the EMV to be associated with node *A* as the no-go option has zero EMV. Thus the optimal strategy is to go ahead with the R & D programme, with an overall EMV of 50k. If the R & D is successful, a large plant should then be built.

Stage 5 relates to the sensitivity of the proposed strategy to the assumptions made. Two major areas for study in this example are the success probability for the R & D, and the relative chances of the three sizes of market. Taking the former as illustrative, the probability of R & D success could be calculated for the position at node A where there is indifference between going ahead with the project or not. If this probability is *p*, then

$$170\,p - 130\,(1-p) = 0$$

or $p = 0.43$.

Thus the probability of R & D success has to fall below 0.43 for the previous decision strategy to be reversed, indicating that the sensitivity of the current decision to the assessed probability of 0.6 for R & D success is not very strong.

Another form of sensitivity requires that the information inputs be reviewed each time a decision node is reached. For example, suppose that R & D takes a year to carry out successfully, leading to decision node B. A check should be made at this time to verify that the incremental yields and the probabilities assigned to the outcome at nodes Y and Z still hold. If not, they should be changed on the remaining portions of the tree, and the calculations re-worked to check that building a large plant still remains the optimal strategy. For an extended discussion of the analysis of decision trees see Moore and Thomas (1976).

1.7 Structure re-examined

The first stage in the decision-analysis process determines the problem structure, which in turn requires a list of the possible actions and outcomes to be drawn up. Considerable attention must be paid to the compilation of this list, since the choices of action will necessarily be limited to the items contained in it. Sometimes one can be reasonably sure that all practicable alternatives have been included, but often one cannot be so sure that some attractive possibility hasn't been omitted: there is always the ingenious person who comes along with a good proposal that the decision maker has not considered. Indeed many effective decision makers derive their success and reputation not so much from their ability to select from a list, as from their ability to think of original ideas to include in the initial feasible set.

The menu concept is important, although many decision procedures do not start from this point. Two illustrations will suffice. In the 1960s a British Government Committee was set up to consider the suitability of Stansted to provide a third London airport, but without reference to any other possible locations. The report recommending Stansted aroused such fierce opposition that the whole matter was reconsidered and, as reported in *The Guardian* at the time, 'Lord Kennet [the Government Minister] was forced to admit that the planning procedure was unsatisfactory and is to be changed in future so that inquiries into major projects can consider the options instead of merely giving a "yes" or "no" to a particular scheme.'

A second illustration of a different kind concerns a promotional film that an organization planned to make for showing to potential buyers of its products. Four possible film companies were approached and these were narrowed to two on the basis of costs, with the choice finally going to P primarily on grounds of previous expertise in a related field. At this point, because of the personal doubts of some directors about the choice, company Q was given a further chance to show its paces and, after some false starts, produced a good potential scenario for the film. It was then awarded the contract, without P being given the equivalent opportunity. Thus the information and analysis input was biased even though all the alternatives had been on the menu.

In this book the preparation of the list of alternatives is not discussed in depth. Appendix B reviews briefly a number of alternative decision-making procedures and mentions some of the procedures that have been proposed for menu building. The emphasis here is concentrated primarily upon the risk inputs involved in selection from among a set of alternative options.

1.8   The plan of the book

The book divides into two main parts. In the first part Chapters 2 to 4 discuss various ways in which probabilities can be determined for a wide variety of situations. Chapter 5 then discusses the concept of utility, or value, to be placed on outcomes, when straightforward money values are inappropriate for the situations concerned. The second and longer part of the book, Chapters 6 to 12, discusses risk in a variety of applied fields: project appraisal; the operations of financial institutions; the management of investment portfolios; gambling; physical hazards; medical diagnosis; and finally a number of situations concerning public policy issues.

There is one major risk application area that is not dealt with in any systematic way. This relates to the specialized field of defence operations, for which an interesting general review and further references can be found in Coyle (1981).

References to some relevant books and articles for each chapter are given at the end of the book. Items marked with an asterisk are specifically mentioned in the chapter concerned; other items listed are for general background reading. The index does not include authors listed in the references.

2

The determination of probabilities

2.1 Introduction

In the next three chapters various methods used to determine the probabilities required for decision making are explored and four broad approaches distinguished:

(*a*) the enumeration (or theoretical) approach;

(*b*) the relative frequency or collective principle;

(*c*) the actuarial approach;

(*d*) the subjective (or personal) approach.

Items (*a*), (*b*) and (*c*) are covered in this chapter, item (*d*) in Chapter 3. Chapter 4 then looks at questions of bias in assessments, and how these can be ameliorated. Whichever approach is employed to determine probabilities, the basic rules for handling probabilities, summarized briefly in Appendix A, remain the same.

2.2 The enumeration approach

A coin is tossed to determine whether you or your opponent should have the choice to serve first in a tennis match. The coin has two sides which look evenly balanced. You consider them equally likely and consequently assign them both a probability of 1/2. The same procedure could be followed in a board game using an ordinary six-sided die, each face appearing equally likely and therefore assigned a probability of 1/6. In taking part in a roulette game it is again assumed without great deliberation that the 36 slots (or 37 including the zero) are all equally likely. In the local village fete, 500 tickets are sold in a raffle for an electric mixer. You hold five tickets and assume unconsciously that your chances of winning are 1 in 100.

In these instances the assessment is made on the grounds that, if there are m different outcomes whose relative likelihood of occurrence seem indistinguishable, and only one outcome is a 'success', then its probability is $1/m$. Thus no experience as such is called for; it is the physical set-up that determines the probability concerned. There are many examples where, without any further assumptions, such an approach has been useful. Indeed the most famous probability book of all time, namely Abraham de Moivre's *Doctrine of Chances* (1718), was based primarily upon such a principle. Whitworth's *Choice and Chance* (1897) provides a wealth of problems that have been solved by this principle, although many of them may today seem rather archaic. 'Four whist players cut for partners (i.e. each draws a card) the two with the highest numbered cards to play together, and the two lowest to play together. What is the chance that they will have to cut again?' (Answer 0.1107). This answer may not seem very useful, but some knowledge of how many spades your bridge partner is likely to hold, when you have two and dummy on the table is showing three, might well be helpful in playing your hand!

Not unexpectedly this kind of approach is only relevant to a limited number of fields: such as the development of various forms of gambling games. Nevertheless an assumption of a set of equally likely outcomes can be useful in many situations as a first approximation to some required probability. For example, a machine has made five rogue items among a large batch because some faulty material has been used. The factory supplies 100 customers, each of whom buys about equal quantities of that item from the factory. On an 'equally likely' principle the chance of any single customer receiving two or more of the dud items can be shown to be 0.001. This is very small indeed so that, while it is reasonable to expect five disgruntled customers each getting one rogue item, it seems very unlikely that any single customer would receive two or more rogue items. The 'equally likely' principle may not be entirely correct, but it provides an order of magnitude for the required probability.

A classic legal example involving this type of probability is the *People* v. *Collins* case in California, referred to by Zeisel (1978). Essentially a crime had been committed by a black male with moustache and beard, accompanied by a white female with blond ponytails, who then escaped in a yellow car. Two persons were found with these characteristics to which various probabilities were assigned on the bases of population numbers believed to be with or without the various characteristics. Calculations then showed that there was only one chance in 12 million of all these characteristics occurring simultaneously. In the event a conviction in the lower court was overturned by the California Supreme Court because

(i) there was little statistical support for the probabilities used by the prosecution, and (ii) the probabilities of individual characteristics had been assumed to be independent which was not necessarily true.

The 'equally likely' notion in both the latter examples had, however, been recognized as extremely restrictive even in ancient times. When the ancient Egyptians used astragali, the heel bones from sheep, as a kind of four-sided die they rapidly realized that the four sides did not come down equally frequently in a long series of tossings. Again, a newborn baby can be either a boy or a girl, but it does not follow that the two sexes are equally likely to occur (and indeed boys occur more frequently than girls). Hence something more than an assumption of 'equally likely' is needed.

2.3   The relative-frequency approach

The second approach to probability determination, the relative-frequency or collective approach, seeks to determine the appropriate probability for some uncertain event by assembling relevant information arising from a series of similar situations in the past, rather than by relying on the physical attributes approach. Thus to put a figure on the probability of a particular six-sided die giving the number six on a single throw, a long run of past tosses of this particular die is examined. Figure 2.1 illustrates the cumulative record of one such series of 250 tossings giving the proportion of sixes against the number of tosses (in steps of five tossings at a time). The shape, oscillating greatly at first, settles to a more stable shape, or limit, as the number of trials increases. After 1000 tossings it was found to be stabilizing at approximately 0.15. This limit, hypothetical as

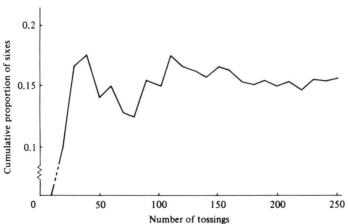

Figure 2.1. Cumulative probability limit

it may seem, is then defined as the probability of the event in question, namely that of getting a six on a single tossing of this particular die. Such a set of tossings, or *collective* as it is called, has been obtained by a simulation in the sense that it is based on a series of tossings, but is not (and cannot be) the actual tossing in which we are interested. Nor may it be the probability if different dice are used. But the historical series is assumed to provide relevant information for the determination of the appropriate probability for the die in hand.

The next example moves away from the simulated experiment. Table 2.1 gives the age distribution of full-time home undergraduates admitted to UK universities in October 1980. The final row expresses the numbers in each age group as a proportion of the total. For the probability that a home undergraduate entrant in 1980 picked at random was aged 19, this would seem an appropriate collective to use, giving the required probability as 0.22. (The word *random* means that each individual is equally likely to be selected: itself a tautology.) However, it should be noted that if the question had related to the probability of a home undergraduate entrant in 1981 being aged 19, the answer must then be more guarded. The collective is based on 1980 figures (perhaps the 1981 figures were not

Table 2.1. *Undergraduate entrants, October 1980*

Age (yrs, months)	Under 18,0	18,0– 18,11	19,0– 19,11	20,0– 20,11	21,0– 21,11	22,0– 22,11	Over 23	Total
Number	3145	47578	17615	3479	1596	1002	4524	78939
Proportion	0.04	0.60	0.22	0.05	0.02	0.01	0.06	1.00

Table 2. *Weights (g) of zinc coatings of galvanized sheets*

Weight of coating	No. of sheets	Cumulative number	Cumulative proportion
up to 13.0	1	1	0.013
13.1–13.5	5	6	0.080
13.6–14.0	6	12	0.160
14.1–14.5	13	25	0.333
14.6–15.0	8	33	0.440
15.1–15.5	17	50	0.667
15.6–16.0	14	64	0.853
16.1–16.5	7	71	0.957
16.6–17.0	1	72	0.960
17.1–17.5	3	75	1.000
Total	75	—	—

available at the time anyway) and it would have to be accepted as being relevant to the purpose in hand, for the same probability as that given before to be used. The actuarial approach discussed later makes the assumption that in many situations past data can indeed provide an appropriate collective for many purposes, but it is an assumption that needs continual testing.

A further example of a collective of a rather different kind is contained in Table 2.2. A factory makes galvanized sheets, and samples are examined to determine the weight of zinc coating on a standard area of sheet. The table gives the results from 75 such samples. The probability is required that a sheet being taken at random from the total output of the factory has a coating of 14 grams or less. From the final column of the table the appropriate probability would seem to be 0.160. However, it must be borne in mind that this collective does not relate to all sheets, but only to a sample of them. Another sample of 75 sheets might produce a different distribution of weights: maybe only marginally different. This indicates the need to consider the desirable size of the collective. Ten sheets might be considered too small for a precise determination of the probability, while 10 000 sheets would seem more than adequate. Hence the collective is not in this case *definitive*, but more of an *indicative* nature.

2.4   Mixed collectives

Homogeneity within collectives is important. Figure 2.2 shows the reported motor accident rates per 100 drivers at various ages in California

Figure 2.2. Reported accident rate as a function of age and sex

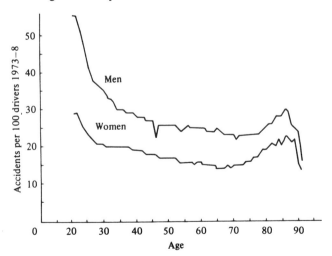

over the period 1973–8 for the two sexes separately (based on Jewell, 1980). The overall numbers involved are large and hence the difference in accident rates between the sexes is meaningful. A company offering insurance based on the overall combined accident rate would find men flocking to take up its policies, but no women. As a consequence its financial results would be somewhat adverse. Women on the other hand who went to an office offering policies based on female experience only would get better terms. (Legislation may try to make such a sub-division illegal, but its enforcement effectively implies that one group is subsidizing another.) Hence it would be desirable to use a separate collective rather than a combined collective on general competitive grounds. Of course, looked at in retrospect, significant overlap will occur in the distributions of accidents among individuals placed in these two separate classifications. This means that a substantial fraction of the 'worse' classification will in retrospect see themselves as better drivers than a large number of the 'better' classification.

Insurers attempt to correct for such perceived anomalies of the collective system through devices such as 'no claims bonuses'. The latter are at best crude and imperfect methods of adjustment and may still, even after some years of operation, give a substantial misclassification of motorists by premium. To illustrate this point suppose that there are in reality two categories of driver; 'good' who have a probability of 0.10 of an accident in any one year, and 'bad' who have a probability of 0.20 of an accident in any one year. There are 50% of each type of driver in the total population of drivers. All drivers start with the same premium but after five successive claim-free years they are entitled to have their premiums halved. The position in year 6 per 100 drivers can be calculated as:

	Premium paid		
	Basic	Halved	Total
'Good' drivers	20	30	50
'Bad' drivers	34	16	50
Totals	54	46	100

While almost half the drivers are paying the reduced premium, over one-third of these are actually 'bad' drivers. Similarly some 40% of the 'good' drivers are still paying the full premium.

A second illustration relates to fire insurance. Suppose the risk of fire (and the extent of damage) is linked to the structural type of the house.

Office Y offers a premium rate that is invariant with the structure while office Z quotes two premium rates, one for stone and brick structures, the other for wooden or thatched roof structures. The second premium rate for office Z would, on the collective principle, be higher than the first premium rate, while the single premium for office Y would lie somewhere between the two rates for office Z. The consequence, at any rate in a perfect market situation for insurance, is that those with thatched cottages would go to office Y while those with brick structures would go to office Z. This would imply that while office Z is taking on profitable business, office Y would lose money. This situation existed with the Vehicle and General Insurance Company, which collapsed in the UK some years back because it used for motor premiums a basis that attracted business much of which was not covered by the basic collective, i.e. the company was selected against by potential insurers, a process referred to as *adverse selection*.

While so-called objective probabilities depend upon the collective principle, i.e. the risk is assigned to an appropriate 'collective' of risks, there is not necessarily always universal agreement as to the 'correct' collective. The conceptual difficulties are exemplified by the following simplified example concerning drivers of motor cars. A total population contains 400 drivers with an annual (unvarying) accident rate of 25%. Insurance company A offers a common rate to all drivers based on the overall accident rate. Insurance company B decides that instead of a common premium for all drivers, it will split them into two categories according to whether they live in an urban or a rural area, and charge an appropriate rate for each of the two categories. Company C decides to base its premiums on whether the driver has had a previous driving conviction or not, and again offers two rates. Table 2.3 shows, in the two margins, the bases for the rates charged by each company and, in the body of the table,

Table 2.3. *Accident rate breakdown*

| | | Company B categories | | Company C rates |
		Rural	Urban	
Company C categories	No convictions	100 (0.1)	100 (0.3)	200 (0.2)
	One or more convictions	100 (0.2)	100 (0.4)	200 (0.3)
	Company B rates	200 (0.15)	200 (0.35)	400 (0.25) Company A rate

the numbers of drivers, with (in parentheses) the accident rates for each of the four categories of driver included in the total population, for example rural/no convictions, etc.

Each driver would, presumably, now take the lowest of the three premium rates on offer to him, which results in the following choices being made:

Rural/no convictions	Company B
Rural/convictions	Company B
Urban/no convictions	Company C
Urban/convictions	Company A

If motorists followed these conclusions the companies would have the following experience rates:

Company A	0.4 (against an assessed 0.25)
Company B	0.15 (against an assessed 0.15)
Company C	0.3 (against an assessed 0.2)

Thus, while company B's experience would be consistent with its assumed experience, the other two companies would have worse experiences than

Table 2.4a. *Length of life of electric light bulbs (hours)*

	1700–	1800–	1900–	2000–	2100–	2200–	⩾ 2300	
No. of bulbs	13	36	86	100	41	16	8	Total 300
Cumulative number	13	49	135	235	276	292	300	300
Cumulative proportion	0.043	0.163	0.450	0.783	0.920	0.973	1.00	1.00

Table 2.4b. *Length of life of electric light bulbs (hours) by type*

	1700–	1800–	1900–	2000–	2100–	2200–	⩾ 2300	
Type A bulbs								Total
No. of bulbs	8	16	36	80	36	16	8	200
Cumulative proportion	0.04	0.12	0.30	0.70	0.88	0.96	1.00	
Type B bulbs								
No. of bulbs	5	20	50	20	5	—	—	100
Cumulative proportion	0.05	0.25	0.75	0.95	1.00	—	—	

those originally assessed. However, each company has apparently provided an objective approach to the determination of the appropriate risk probability. If all the population insured with a single one of the three companies, then that company would in retrospect show the correct overall risk rate. Competition therefore tends to make insurers have a common system of breaking down overall collectives.

An example of a different kind concerns the lengths of life of electric light bulbs. A factory has inspected 300 of its incoming bulbs and finds that the fraction 0.163 have lives below 1900 hours (see Table 2.4a). On this, and the other fractions, a policy for regular total replacement of bulbs is based. However, in practice, this policy doesn't seem to work very well and further investigation is made. This shows that, among the bulbs bought and tested, there are really two types, from different makers, A and B, as shown in Table 2.4b. When the separation of bulbs is done, it is clear that type B has a very much higher proportion of bulbs below 1900 hours life than type A. Hence an effective replacement policy depends on being able to operate separate policies for the two types of bulb.

The importance of using an appropriate collective is paramount; there should be no other major source of heterogeneity in the collective that could be allowed for. In most practical situations a collective is being used that is not strictly the one to which the trial in which you are interested uniquely belongs (the principal exceptions being games of chance, lotteries, etc.) Hence there is always the implied assumption that the historical collective being used is appropriate for the future situation in hand. To this extent the collective approach contains a subjective element and is not quite as objective as is commonly claimed.

2.5   The life table

A particularly well-known example of a collective, analogous to the electric light bulb situation just discussed, is the *life table* used by actuaries. The aim is to demonstrate the mortality experience that has occurred in a large group of individuals over time. Suppose, for example, that in 1880 there were exactly 10 000 male births. Ideally, the history of these babies would be traced through life so as to establish that in 1890, 9300 were still living, in 1900, 9100 were still living, in 1910 8950 and so on. These data displayed in tabular form such as Table 2.5 provide a crude form of *life table*. It traces in effect a *cohort* of 10 000 male babies born in the year 1880 through life. Other tables could be established for female babies born in the same year, or for another country or another year. Such tables will differ in the manner in which the figures decrease from year to year (*the decrements*) but the process is carried out each time on the cohort principle.

From such a table a number of probabilities relevant to life assurance can be obtained. For example, the chance that a baby survives to age 30 is 8950/10000 or 0.895. Again, the chance that one of the babies who has reached the age of 30 then survives for another 30 years is 3800/8950, or 0.424.

If Table 2.5 is used to calculate the premium for an assurance policy involving a male baby born today, the figures obtained would be misleading. So much has happened since 1880 in the way of better diet, standard of living etc. that the mortality picture today is very different. But it is in turn not known what the next eighty years will bring and a compromise is sought with the most recent data to hand being used as a basis for the necessary mortality forecast. This is done by taking some recent year (or small run of years), calculating for that period specific death rates for each age, and using these to form a hypothetical cohort analysis. An age-specific death rate is calculated by obtaining, first, an estimate of the total number of males aged x in the relevant population on a given date and, second, the number of deaths occurring among this group in the succeeding year. The quotient of the latter to the former is then the age-specific death rate for age x. A series of such death rates is similarly calculated for each age x from zero to 100. These then form a life table of the type just discussed, the difference being that it is based on current mortality rates throughout.

Table 2.5. *Decremental table for males*

Year	No. living	Year	No. living
1880	10000	1930	7600
1890	9300	1940	3800
1900	9100	1950	1600
1910	8950	1960	700
1920	8500	1970	100
		1980	0

2.6   English life table no. 12

The death rates obtained in this way using male mortality experience of 1960–2 in England and Wales are shown, with some small adjustments, in the columns marked q_x in the extract from English life table no. 12 (ELT 12) shown in Table 2.6. The progression of these rates is of some interest. They fall at first, until they reach a minimum at x equal to 11 or 12. They then rise slowly but steadily, but the speed of rise is modest until x exceeds 50, after which the rates rise quite rapidly. The rates for

Table 2.6. *English life table no. 12: males*

Age x	l_x	d_x	q_x	Age x	l_x	d_x	q_x
0	100000	2449	0.02449	45	92433	369	0.00399
1	97551	153	0.00157	46	92064	412	0.00448
2	97398	96	0.00099	47	91652	463	0.00505
3	97302	67	0.00069	48	91189	520	0.00570
4	97235	60	0.00062	49	90669	584	0.00644
5	97175	55	0.00057	50	90085	656	0.00728
6	97120	51	0.00052	51	89429	736	0.00823
7	97069	47	0.00048	52	88693	825	0.00930
8	97022	43	0.00044	53	87868	923	0.01051
9	96979	40	0.00041	54	86945	1029	0.01184
10	96939	38	0.00039	55	85916	1144	0.01331
11	96901	37	0.00038	56	84772	1265	0.01492
12	96864	37	0.00038	57	83507	1393	0.01668
13	96827	40	0.00041	58	82114	1526	0.01859
14	96787	45	0.00047	59	80588	1664	0.02065
15	96742	57	0.00059	60	78924	1805	0.02287
16	96685	75	0.00078	61	77119	1947	0.02525
17	96610	96	0.00099	62	75172	2088	0.02778
18	96514	108	0.00112	63	73084	2228	0.03049
19	96406	113	0.00117	64	70856	2366	0.03339
20	96293	115	0.00119	65	68490	2499	0.03648
21	96178	113	0.00118	66	65991	2625	0.03978
22	96065	110	0.00114	67	63366	2745	0.04332
23	95955	104	0.00108	68	60621	2856	0.04712
24	95851	98	0.00102	69	57765	2959	0.05122
25	95753	95	0.00099	70	54806	3051	0.05566
26	95658	94	0.00098	71	51755	3130	0.06047
27	95564	96	0.00100	72	48625	3195	0.06570
28	95468	99	0.00104	73	45430	3243	0.07139
29	95369	104	0.00109	74	42187	3273	0.07759
30	95265	110	0.00115	75	38914	3282	0.08434
31	95155	115	0.00121	76	35632	3266	0.09167
32	95040	122	0.00128	77	32366	3225	0.09963
33	94918	129	0.00136	78	29141	3154	0.10824
34	94789	137	0.00145	79	25987	3054	0.11752
35	94652	147	0.00155	80	22933	2923	0.12747
36	94505	158	0.00167	81	20010	2763	0.13808
37	94347	171	0.00181	82	17247	2576	0.14934
38	94176	185	0.00196	83	14671	2365	0.16122
39	93991	201	0.00214	84	12306	2137	0.17366
40	93790	220	0.00235	85	10169	1897.4	0.18659
41	93570	242	0.00259	86	8271.6	1654.1	0.19997
42	93328	268	0.00287	87	6617.5	1414.1	0.21369
43	93060	297	0.00319	88	5203.4	1184.6	0.22765
44	92763	330	0.00356	89	4018.8	971.6	0.24177

Table 2.6. (*cont.*)

Age x	l_x	d_x	q_x	Age x	l_x	d_x	q_x
90	3047.2	779.9	0.25593	100	67.749	25.733	0.37983
91	2267.3	612.2	0.27003	101	42.016	16.349	0.38912
92	1655.1	470.0	0.28396	102	25.667	10.209	0.39776
93	1185.1	352.73	0.29764	103	15.458	6.2721	0.40575
94	832.37	258.83	0.31096	104	9.1859	3.7949	0.41312
95	573.54	185.74	0.32385	105	5.3910		
96	387.80	130.39	0.33623				
97	257.41	89.59	0.34806				
98	167.82	60.30	0.35929				
99	107.52	39.771	0.36989				

q_x are inserted into the life table shown in Table 2.6 by taking some arbitrarily chosen number of starters at birth (called the *radix*) and then applying the various age-specific death rates in turn to this radix. In Table 2.6 the radix used is $l_0 = 100000$. The figure for l_1 is then obtained by the formula

$$l_1 = l_0 - q_0 l_0$$
$$= 100000 - 0.02449 \times 100000$$
$$= 97551$$

In general

$$l_{x+1} = l_x - q_x l_x = l_x(1 - q_x) \tag{2.1}$$

and formula (2.1) is followed sequentially through the table until the final l_x values are reached. (Note that d_x, the number of deaths each year in the table, is equal to $l_x q_x$.) The table can be used for the same calculations as before. The probability that a man now aged 30 will live to at least age of 50 is

$$\frac{l_{50}}{l_{30}} = \frac{90085}{95265} = 0.946$$

The probability that a man aged 60 will die within the next 10 years is

$$\frac{l_{60} - l_{70}}{l_{60}} = 1 - \frac{l_{70}}{l_{60}} = 1 - \frac{54806}{78924} = 0.306$$

The age-specific death rates in ELT 12 do not precisely apply to any particular cohort of males. The age 30 death rate, for example, applies to males born in about 1930, the age 50 rate to males born around 1910 and so on. Hence, while the life table represents mortality rates for the period 1960–2, it does not represent the lifetime experience of any one particular group of males and in that sense is a fictional table. Actuaries are concerned with predicting mortality in the future and they use life tables based on current experience as the best forecast that is available to them. Nevertheless they recognise that the number of deaths derived from the life table are not likely to be fulfilled exactly: history rarely repeats itself. The past is a guide, but never an exact blueprint for the future. Knowing this, the actuary monitors current mortality experience and checks the continuing validity of the assumptions behind his projections. At intervals, perhaps every three years or so, the assumptions are formally revised with projected probabilities being recalculated on the new bases. In this way the procedure continually hones in on the unfolding future as the target. In newly formed pension funds, new classes of insurance, or new projects where data from past experience are scant, the degree of uncertainty is correspondingly greater and data must be sought from comparable organizations or situations. It is rare indeed that no relevant data are available, but for such situations re-appraisals may well be made more frequently perhaps at yearly intervals, until a satisfactory body of information has been built up to give confidence with less frequent appraisals.

The life table just discussed related to males, but a similar table could be compiled for females. The main differences in the figures would be that female mortality is generally lower, so that the q_x values are slightly less at each age, giving slightly higher l_x figures for an equal starting radix at age 0.

2.7   Appropriate actuarial collectives

Actuarial methods seek to place risks against their appropriate collectives. For example, if you want to insure your life the insurance company will normally use an established life table (possibly checking its appropriateness by asking for your birth certificate and arranging a medical examination). If they are satisfied that you belong to the particular collective on which their premium rates are based they will quote you a premium accordingly. They will not use a global mortality table covering everybody because of competition for the same reasons that occurred in the motor insurance illustration discussed earlier. A fit person of good stock might reasonably expect better rates in comparison with a person who is suffering from a severe debilitating illness. If company A used an overall table for all proposers, its rates would effectively average these two (and other) cases. If company B used a more select (i.e. lower mortality) table – ensuring that the proposer belonged to that select group – it could charge lower rates and attract the better risks, leaving company A to handle the worst risks. Hence company A would then find that its *average* experience was worse than that of the table they were using. They would thus be forced to raise their rates which would sharpen the differentiation between the two companies and the kinds of business they attract. Such a situation would occur if company A's table was based on males and females combined, while company B's was based on females only.

Pension schemes, which in the UK and elsewhere are now required by legislation to provide comparable benefits for men and women employees, illustrate one consequence of side-stepping the collective principle. With a pension payable at age 65 the mortality rate year by year from age 65 onward is lower for women than for men. Hence to provide an equal pension for both sexes from age 65 requires higher contributions during working life from, or on behalf of, women than from men. Alternatively, if the contributions are to be equal through working life, the pension should be higher for a man than for a woman. The UK Government compounds the felony in the case of state pensions by allowing women to draw a full pension at age 60 instead of 65 for men. Curiously, although this is felt to be socially divisive as well as fiscally unsound, the problem remains unsolved because of the political difficulties of effecting a cure.

How far individual circumstances should govern pension benefits is a moot point. An unmarried man with no contingent rights to a widow's pension might claim he should pay lower contributions, or get a higher personal pension, than if he were married. At present such nuances are commonly ignored and employees pay equal contributions (usually related to salary) into a common pot which provides a variety of benefits some of which specific individuals will never obtain. If the equity argument is pushed to its limit, there would be pressure for pension schemes to be based less on a collective basis and more on allowing each individual to make up his own benefit package for fixed levels of contributions from employer and employee. Since some or all of the benefits will be of an insurance type nature, individuals will benefit if they are easily insurable (for example, fit, residing in a good area, working in sedentary occupation, etc.) but lose if they are less easily insurable. Thus the collective principle of the firm will be lost and the burden placed on the individual to find an appropriate collective.

An interesting example of such difficulties on a macro-scale occurred in 1982 when the UK Government decided to amend the state sick pay scheme for all workers, requiring each employer to meet the cost of sick pay for the first eight weeks of any spell of employee sickness. As a corollary there would be a once-for-all reduction of 0.6% in the National Insurance contributions from firms. The effect, if we assume the arithmetic is correct, is to increase costs for industries where sickness is more prevalent and to lower costs where sickness is below average, for example in non-manual jobs. One consequence is that firms will have a pecuniary interest to avoid employing sickness-prone employees, because the fitter their workforce, the lower will be their costs. This could tilt employment prospects adversely for some. A way round the difficulty would be to keep National Insurance arrangements as currently proposed, but to allow firms to deduct sick pay benefits paid out against contributions paid by the firm. This neat solution has been (as at mid-1982) ruled out by the UK Government.

2.8   Other life tables

The life table concept applies in areas other than insurance. The following illustration relates to the turnover of male employees in a large firm. Some simple figures had been internally prepared which suggested that about one-third of the men taken on had left within a year, suggesting average service per man of about three years. With the expensive training involved, it was considered uneconomic to have such a turnover of labour.

The careers of men joining the firm in each of the years from 1965 to 1978 inclusive were extracted from the records. This showed the numbers who had left with under one year's service, those who had left with service of between one and two years, with service between two and three years, and so on. From these figures Table 2.7 was compiled showing in column 2 that, of the 731 men who joined during the period 1965–78, 229 left in their first year of service, 65 left having between one and two years' service, and so forth. Column 3 gives the cumulative numbers from column 2, while column 4 is column 3 expressed as a percentage of 731, the total entrants in the fourteen-year period.

The figures now suggest that only 48% of the men had left by the end of three years' service, and not 100% as previously implied! Furthermore

Table 2.7. *Distribution of length of service*

Leavers with service of (1)	Number of men (2)	Cumulative totals (3)	Cumulative percentages[a] (4)
Under 1 year	229	229	31.3
1–2 years	65	294	40.2
2–3 years	53	347	47.5
3–4 years	45	392	53.6
4–5 years	33	425	58.1
5–6 years	23	448	61.3

[a] Based on the 731 men who entered the firm in the period 1965–78

the rate of loss is apparently slowing down fairly rapidly by the end of the three years.

However, this is still an invalid picture (in the opposite direction from before) because the figures in the final columns of Table 2.7 are effectively weighted differentially. The more recent entrants have not had the chance to leave except after very few years' service, with the result that the longer-term leaving rates are being underestimated. This difficulty can be overcome by calculating separate leaving rates for each year of service using only those employees who actually entered the particular year of service, and then combining them. The detailed calculations are not given here, but summarized in Table 2.8. These rates relate to all those who began the nth year of service and then left within the year. The ratio of the latter to the former gives the leaving rate for the nth year shown in column 2. If these rates are applied to a radix such as 1000 as in column 3, a form of life table is obtained. It is now clear that, after three years 59%, and after six years 36%, are still employed by the firm. Guesses as to numbers over longer terms of service could be obtained by extrapolating the figures in column 2 and then applying these extrapolated figures to column 3.

Finally three other uses of the life table approach are briefly outlined. The first is similar to the light bulb replacement example and relates to a general problem surrounding the repair (or replacement) of plant and equipment. A large factory can either repair pieces of plant as they fail, which can be a tedious, costly and time-consuming activity, or it can overhaul each item after some defined length of service, irrespective of whether the item is still serviceable or not. The optimum point of time for a general overhaul, compared with breakdown overhauls, would depend upon the form of the life table for the lengths of service before breakdown of the items, coupled with the costs involved for breakdowns in service as opposed to routine overhauls.

Table 2.8. *An employee decremental table*

Year of service (1)	Leaving rate for year (2)	No. at start of year (3)
1st	0.313	1000
2nd	0.141	687
3rd	0.144	590
4th	0.160	505
5th	0.146	424
6th	0.140	362

The second illustration relates to a prediction of the number of students and graduates at the Open University in Britain (an institution that offers degrees by part-time home study). Students can take one or two courses a year (which they may or may not complete), they can work for an ordinary or honours degree, they can drop out (either temporarily or permanently), etc. Estimates are required, given a range of possible annual new student entry levels, of the number of active students for the year ahead, on a year by year basis, coupled with the numbers of graduates that will emerge each year. To make these estimates, assessments need to be made of the various rates concerned (finishing, dropping out, taking one or two courses, etc.) in order to graft them on to the assumed entry rates. From such an analysis it was clear in 1981 that, despite a proposed cut in the annual entry of new students, the 'stock' of students would continue to rise for many years to come.

The third illustration relates to possible changes in the structure of medical workforce within the British National Health Service (which is the principal employer of UK doctors) in the light of the rising number of entrants into medical schools and, with an interval of six years, of young doctors qualifying for registration. With a known current age distribution and assumed new entry rates, combined with estimates of the various wastage rates, an expected pattern of doctors by age and qualifications for the years ahead can be built up. Such an analysis shows, for example, that if the 1982 ratio of consultants to junior hospital doctors were to be held, a severe drop in the promotion rate into consultancies would occur by the late 1980s. This would probably lead in turn to a substantial rise in the average age (currently 37 years) at which this promotion occurs. One side effect might then be to make the profession less attractive to young doctors (or would-be doctors) and encourage alternative career paths such as private medicine or emigration.

3
Subjective risk determination

3.1 Risk and uncertainty

The collective principle for risks outlined in Chapter 2 can be applied to many situations inside and outside commerce. But in some circumstances no immediate relevant collective springs to mind. This chapter looks at such situations where probability estimates cannot be made by the collective approach on a basis that would necessarily command overall agreement. Such situations are sometimes labelled 'uncertainty' and differentiated from 'risk' situations.

The separation of uncertainty from risk is a frequent practice in industrial circles. Examples cited in this context are political uncertainties such as nationalization, economic uncertainties such as forthcoming rates of inflation, or changes in the rates of interest. Many statisticians argue cogently that there is no real distinction between risk and uncertainty as defined in this way. The distinction really being made, it is argued, is between repeatable and non-repeatable events. Thus games of chance such as roulette are repeatable, just as the actuary of an assurance company regards death as a repeatable event, in the sense that a large population is at risk and alternative events 'death' or 'no death' are repeated for each person in the population each year. Although one cannot be dogmatic about a single person dying, one can be reasonably specific about the number of persons dying from among a large group in a specified period. But the outcome, 'the next President of the United States will be a woman' is not of the same category. To count up the number of eligible voters who are women (W) and men (M) respectively and express the chance as the proportion $W/(M+W)$ and apply it to the next presidential election on an empirical probability basis would be fallacious. Hence the idea of dividing situations into two types, risk and uncertainty, looks promising. There are, however, two drawbacks. First, it can be difficult to decide into which category some events fall and, second, to have available statistical risk probabilities only is not helpful in many situations.

To illustrate the first drawback consider the case of a man having to decide on his stock of ice-cream and beverages for the month of July in a large outdoor amusement park. He has the long-range forecasts, the statistical weather records for past Julys, his sales in past years, his knowledge of the economic conditions and so forth. Can he just put these together in a straight statistical sense? The event is strictly non-repeatable, but most people would agree that among the many input factors in the total problem some are of a probabilistic nature and differ in kind from other factors, and that elements of both risk and uncertainty are contained within the decision framework.

The second drawback can be illustrated with the actuarial example of death. To the company actuary the event appears undoubtedly statistical but, to the individual who is contemplating taking out an insurance policy, the classification is not so obvious. The individual is concerned with the possibility of his own death, not with the overall behaviour of the group insured with the company. To him the event is non-repeatable, and his circumstances differ from those of everybody else. The actuary, on the other hand, considers the masses, and practical difficulties arise should he try to separate out the various risks into smaller sub-sets, such as different ethnic groups. Another example, already cited, is car insurance which in theory is related to 'exposed to risk', and yet is commonly charged on a per year basis without strict reference to the exposure to risk (i.e. factors such as mileage and the type of driving carried out, etc.) except indirectly in ways such as no-claims bonus discounts. The same is true of Industrial Injuries Benefit in the UK where the so-called insurance contributions are fixed at a level rate not necessarily linked to the different risks of the various industrial employees concerned, but to the population as a whole.

A similar situation arises with games of chance. The gambling house can rest content with the long-run fairness of the roulette wheel which, combined with the different odds offered for the various combinations, gives it a positive expectation of gain. It can therefore suffer short-term losses in the knowledge that the long term will be in its favour. The player's capital is limited and he cannot take a wholly 'repeatable' view. He is interested in one particular spin, or a relatively small set of spins, and not with the generality of spins. Hence he is not concerned with repeatable outcomes but with a single outcome. In bodies such as the insurance market at Lloyd's of London this grey area between repeatable and non-repeatable events is even more pointed. Here opera singers can insure their voices against damage, trout farmers against disease in their stock, a village fete against rain, a fisherman against lack of rain, and an auctioneer against the loss in transit of a valuable shipment of old master paintings, etc. All these are, from the point of view of *both* the parties concerned, in the grey middle area. Thus to attempt a rigid distinction between risk and uncertainty may be helpful in concept, but not in reaching meaningful decisions for a wide range of very real problems.

3.2.   Assessment by words

When separating out uncertainty in business situations where appropriate collectives seem to be lacking, the probability is sometimes expressed in verbal terms rather than as a number. This approach can be challenged because words are useful to convey meaning, only provided that the writer and the reader (or speaker and listener) agree on the meanings to be ascribed to the words. However, in the realms of describing uncertainty, words do not have a generally accepted and agreed meaning. As an illustration, the following lists of ten expressions were all culled from the same substantive article which was discussing, in a literary rather than numerate style, some forecasts that had been made in the consumer durables field:

Probable	Hoped	Expected
Quite certain	Possible	Doubtful
Unlikely	Not unreasonable that	Not certain
		Likely

Some 250 executives, on middle and senior general management programmes at the London Business School and elsewhere, were asked to rank these ten words or phrases in decreasing order of uncertainty. Table 3.1 summarizes the results obtained, the expressions being re-ordered in the

Table 3.1 *Ranking of uncertainty expressions*

Expressions	Average rank	Range of ranks
Quite certain	1.10	1–3
Expected	2.95	1–6
Likely	3.85	2–7
Probable	4.25	2–9
Not unreasonable that	4.65	3–7
Possible	6.10	3–9
Hoped	7.15	3–10
Not certain	7.80	3–10
Doubtful	8.60	7–10
Unlikely	8.75	3–10

table in descending order of average rank. The final column, giving the range of ranks given to each of the ten expressions, illustrates the considerable overlapping of ranks for many of the expressions among the respondents and thus the inconsistent use being made of these words. Indeed, only three out of the 250 respondents produced precisely the same rankings. A further experiment, with a smaller group of respondents repeated the ranking process after an interval of about three months, and demonstrated that individual respondents are not even consistent over time in their ranking of the same expressions.

3.3   Need for scale

There is clearly a need for an agreed and acceptable scale for measuring and describing uncertainty. A number of possibilities arise, but only two have been seriously entertained in practice, namely probability and odds. These are effectively the same scale expressed in a different form. In the former the scale goes from 0 (absolute impossibility) to 1 (absolute certainty). In the latter, uncertainty is presented in the form of 2 to 1 against, 3 to 1 against, 10 to 1 against, etc., a format familiar to all who have followed the turf or other sporting occasions.

Odds are directly translatable into probability: for example, odds of 3 to 1 against are equivalent to a probability of $1/(3+1)$ or $\frac{1}{4}$ of the event occurring. Table 3.2 shows the conversion of odds to probabilities and vice versa over a wide commonly used range of quoted odds. It is a matter of personal choice as to which form is used. Probability has the advantage of being mathematically more tractable, and it also gives a more complete use of the entire scale for most people. Odds used tend to be of the form 3 to 1 against, 4 to 1 against, etc. as shown in the table, i.e. using whole numbers only, and, while covering some of the probability scale well, they do not cover the other parts so delicately. Thus statisticians prefer to work with the probability scale, as do most executives once they have become used to the scale and its handling.

Odds, however, can be useful for two situations that arise in probability assessments. First, because odds are readily interpreted as bets, analysts in decision theory often use them to check probabilities that have been expressed on the 0–1 scale. For example, if an assessor believes that the probability of no devaluation in the next six months in the UK is 0.9, then he believes that the odds against devaluation are 9 to 1. The assessor should be willing, if he is risk-neutral, to be indifferent between the following two bets offered to him by an opponent on a single opportunity basis.

Bet A: The opponent pays the assessor ten times this stake if there is a devaluation; otherwise he loses the stake

Table 3.2. *Conversion of odds to probabilities*

Probability (%) when odds are odds **on**	Odds	Probability (%) when odds are odds **against**
50.0	1–1	50.0
52.9	9–8	47.1
53.3	8–7	46.7
53.8	7–6	46.2
54.5	6–5	45.5
55.6	5–4	44.4
60.0	6–4	40.0
63.6	7–4	36.4
65.2	15–8	34.8
66.7	2–1	33.3
68.0	17–8	32.0
69.2	9–4	30.8
70.4	19–8	29.6
71.4	5–2	28.6
73.3	11–4	26.7
75.0	3–1	25.0
76.9	10–3	23.1
77.8	7–2	22.2
80.0	4–1	20.0
81.8	9–2	18.2
83.3	5–1	16.7
85.7	6–1	14.3
87.5	7–1	12.5
88.9	8–1	11.1
90.0	9–1	10.0
90.9	10–1	9.1
91.7	11–1	8.3
92.3	12–1	7.7
93.6	100–8	7.4
92.9	13–1	7.1
93.3	14–1	6.7
93.7	15–1	6.3
94.1	16–1	5.9
94.7	18–1	5.3
95.2	20–1	4.8
96.2	25–1	3.8
97.1	33–1	2.9
97.6	40–1	2.4
98.0	50–1	2.0
98.5	66–1	1.5
99.0	100–1	1.0
99.5	200–1	0.5
99.8	500–1	0.2
99.9	1000–1	0.1

Bet B: The assessor pays the opponent ten times the stake if there is a devaluation, otherwise he keeps the stake

If the assessor is willing to take bet A but not bet B, then he really believes the probability of devaluation is greater than 0.1. If he is willing to take bet B but not bet A, then he is placing the probability of devaluation at less than 0.1. By putting the degree of certainty in the form of odds or a bet, the assessor is given a different psychological viewpoint to judge it. The bet specifies a definite act implied by his assessment, and he is often thereby more able to judge whether he would be willing to act that way than he would have been able to judge whether his original assessment was accurate.

The second way in which odds are useful is that they permit comparison of multiple probabilities. For example, suppose an analyst assesses the following probabilities concerning inflation:

P_1 the probability that inflationary conditions will deteriorate by at least 1% in the next three months

P_2 the probability that inflationary conditions will remain within $\pm 1\%$ in the next three months

P_3 the probability that inflationary conditions will improve by at least 1% in the next three months.

With $P_1 = 0.6$, $P_2 = 0.2$, $P_3 = 0.2$ as the assessed probabilities, then $P_1 : P_2 : P_3 = 3 : 1 : 1$

As a check the analyst can ask himself if it is really three times as likely that conditions will deteriorate markedly as it is for them to improve markedly, i.e. $P_1 : P_3 = 3 : 1$. There are similar questions that the analyst could ask himself. Only when he is satisfied with all the comparative odds thereby obtained can he be sure that the probabilities represent his true degree of uncertainty.

Sometimes the probability assessments given are mutually inconsistent and are therefore technically incoherent. In such instances the assessor must be asked to amend the assessment. To illustrate this consider the three categories of natural death: H heart failure, C cancer, D any other form of natural death; and let N denote all causes of natural death ($\bar{N}$ denotes the complement, similarly for the other categories). Suppose assessor X makes the following assessments regarding the ultimate death of another individual Y:

$$p(H) = 0.33, \quad p(C) = 0.27, \quad p(D) = 0.23, \quad p(\bar{N}) = 0.12$$
$$p(H/N) = 0.41, \quad p(C/N) = 0.31, \quad p(D/N) = 0.28$$

These assessments are incoherent in two senses. First

$$p(H) + p(C) + p(D) + p(\bar{N}) = 0.95$$

instead of unity as it should, since Y must either die from one of the three categories of natural deaths or else die unnaturally. Secondly, the conditional probability ratios do not coincide with the ratios of the corresponding unconditional probabilities. For example

$$\frac{p(H/N)}{p(C/N)} = 1.324, \quad \text{while} \quad \frac{p(H)}{p(C)} = 1.22$$

The two ratios should be equal because H and C are both sub-sets of N. Assessor X must reconsider his assessments, but even so may still produce inconsistencies (just as, for example, the linear measurements and angles provided by a surveyor may still remain inconsistent after repeated experimental work). If the inconsistencies cannot be ironed out by assessor X, other methods be used to introduce coherence; a discussion of some possible methods is given by Lindley, Tversky and Brown (1979).

3.4 Discrete and continuous variables

In assessing uncertainties there is one other dichotomy of importance that affects the approaches followed. Situations can be of a discrete type (the 'either does or does not occur' variety) or of the continuous type (what will be the temperature at noon tomorrow?).

As an example of the discrete type, a particular piece of research can, by the end of a twelve-month period, either have succeeded or failed. This is a two-category situation. The assessment may alternatively be in a position where there are three or more categories of interest of which one and only one can occur; for example a lawsuit could be withdrawn, be settled out of court, go to court and be won, go to court and be lost. In these instances the assessor has to assess probabilities for 'yes' in each of the four categories, with the implication that it is 'no' for the other three categories. There must be consistency as before, with the probabilities for the total range of possible events summing to unity.

The other type of situation is when the outcome is measured on some continuous scale. Here estimation of a total probability distribution is required for the uncertain outcome of a future action. For example, the event might be the demand for some product in the following twelve months. The complete distribution may be required, rather than merely the probability of demand reaching some defined level, because of the need to decide upon levels of equipment, manning, raw material purchases, etc. In the following sections we discuss methods used for estimation in these two cases.

3.5   The EQU method

The equivalent urn (or EQU) method is well known in principle, and dear to the hearts of many statisticians. Suppose the probability is required of the successful development of a new product expected to net £100 000 by the end of eighteen months. The assessor is offered the choice between gamble A or gamble B shown in Figure 3.1. Gamble A is to take up the development of the new product, receiving £100 000 if the development succeeds, nothing if it fails. Under gamble B one ball is drawn at random from an urn at the end of eighteen months, the urn containing 700 black balls and 300 white balls. If a black ball is drawn the assessor receives £100 000, if a white ball is drawn, nothing. If the assessor chooses A the assessment is repeated, but with more black balls (and correspondingly fewer white balls) in gamble B; if he chooses B the assessment is repeated with fewer black balls and correspondingly more white balls.

The process is repeated until the proportion of black balls in gamble B is such that the assessor is indifferent between the two gambles. The required probability is then taken as being the final proportion of black balls in the urn for gamble B. At no time in this process is it necessary to ask a more difficult question than 'do you prefer this gamble, or that one, or can't you say?'. Numerical measurement of the individuals' degree of belief can thus be obtained by asking a series of simple questions of preferences.

Other standard devices besides urns with coloured balls can be used to simulate variations in probability levels, for example a roulette wheel with a pointer rather than a ball and the outside rim divided into two coloured

Figure 3.1. Choice of gambles

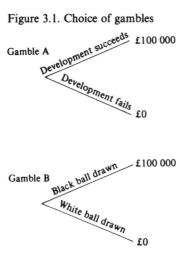

sectors, the relative sizes of the two sectors being capable of adjustment. Adjustments are made until the indifference point is reached when the relative sector sizes at this point represent the appropriate probabilities.

Such methods are quick and easy to use, although care must be exercised to ensure that the assessor does not give a quick and possibly ill-considered judgement. Many executives who carry out this form of assessment nevertheless feel uncomfortable about it. The main reason seems to be the implication that business risk is akin to gambling of the casino type. Furthermore, for a complex problem with many probabilities to be estimated, they find that the discipline imposed on them is tedious: they get stale and hence are not so certain that later assessments are realistic.

Research has also demonstrated that the form the reference devices take (for example, the total number of balls in the hypothetical urn, or the size of the winning bets used) can affect, albeit only marginally, the assessments. In general, reasonably large amounts of money should be used, but not so large that the amounts become virtually meaningless to the individual.

3.6 CDF assessments

Where a decision involves considering the probabilities of several different levels of demand (say) it is more realistic to assess the complete distribution by the CDF (cumulative density function) method described below, and then to read off the required probabilties, rather than to proceed by the EQU method of the previous section for each separate probability, a method which carries with it serious dangers of inconsistencies.

Much experimental work has been carried out to determine the optimum way in which to proceed with the CDF approach. Two possible methods are described below. The first, proposed by Raiffa (1968), has the following steps:

(a) The assessor chooses a value for the unknown quantity X (for example, sales in the next month) such that he thinks it equally likely that the true but unknown value will fall below or above it. (Call this value X_{50}.)

(b) The assessor next considers only those values above X_{50} and is again asked to repeat the process of judgementally sub-dividing the range above X_{50} into what the assessor considers are two equally likely parts. (Call this dividing point X_{75}.)

(c) The procedure in (b) is now repeated for values below X_{50} and a value X_{25} obtained.

(d) The procedure in (b) is repeated again for each of the four intervals now available, so that in all seven assessed values of X are obtained. The values X_{50}, X_{25} etc. are referred to as the 50th percentile, the 25th percentile, etc.

(*e*) Finally, a graph of the cumulative percentage probability ($12\frac{1}{2}$, 25, $37\frac{1}{2}$, 50 etc.) is plotted against X and a smooth curve drawn by eye through the plotted points. A typical CDF is shown in Figure 3.2 from which any required probabilities can be read off.

An alternative procedure, proposed by Barclay and Petersen (1973), is based on the view that some assessors find it easier to judge when they are indifferent between two quantities, rather than to judge the absolute magnitudes of the two quantities. Suppose the problem involves an individual estimating a CDF for the population of Brazil. Then a possible procedure would be to ask the person to assess, as a start, levels of population that it is essentially impossible to be below or, alternatively, above. Suppose these levels are put at 50 million and 250 million respectively. A scale is now marked from 50 to 250 and two cardboard pointers placed on the scale. The assessor adjusts the position of the pointers so that he considers the population is equally likely to fall in the three alternative ranges: i.e. from 50 million to the first pointer, between the two pointers, and from the second pointer up to 250 million. The four points now available can be plotted and a smooth CDF curve drawn through them freehand as before. The object of trisecting the range, rather than bisecting it, is to give more points on the scale as well as to overcome a tendency for assessors to give too narrow a range in their assessments.

While the general shape of a CDF curve will always be of signoid form,

Figure 3.2. Cumulative density function (CDF)

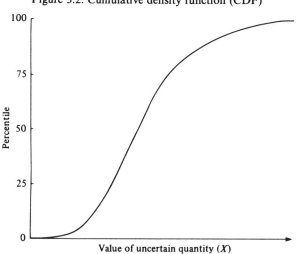

Value of uncertain quantity (X)

its general slope will, of course, vary according to the information available and the technical skill deployed by the assessor in its handling. Gustafson (1971) has reported some experiments for estimating the length of stay of individuals in hospitals for operations for various causes, such as hernia. The assessments were made by different groups such as medical students, junior hospital doctors and consultants. Although the distribution of 'actual time minus assessed time' had a mean of approximately zero for all three groups, the variability of the discrepancies (as measured by their standard deviations) showed considerable differences, the consultants having a smaller standard deviation than that of the junior hospital doctors, which was in turn smaller than that of the medical students. Similar (unpublished) results have been found in assessments made of the time necessary to repair electrical failures in a large UK region, where the more skilled and experienced engineers showed a much 'tighter' estimation of the final figure than those achieved by the less experienced.

3.7 Components of risk

In some situations the required risk may relate to a total project, although the risk may in reality be an amalgam of a number of risks. For example, a firm deciding whether or not to design, manufacture and launch a new product is concerned with the ultimate chance of success. This overall chance is made up of a number of steps, each of which has its own probability of success or failure. The first step could be whether the research is successful (probability p_1 say). The second is whether a successful prototype can be made, given the research success (probability p_2). The third is whether the prototype can be turned into a successful mass manufacturing process (probability p_3), while finally there is the chance of a successful market launch, given a successful manufacturing system (probability p_4). If these were the only factors or components, then the overall probability of a successful product is the product of these four factor probabilities or $p_1 \times p_2 \times p_3 \times p_4$. Since the formation of probabilities is commonly done through the assistance of experts, who may have knowledge of just one part of the total process, this breakdown into components can be helpful. Without it there is the danger that the overall assessor, with his varying knowledge levels of the various components, will be biased one way or the other regarding those components of which he is ignorant: 'those marketing boys always mess up a good product launch' etc. The probabilities used are conditional in form, i.e. provided there is success to stage k, what is probability of success in stage $k+1$. Such an approach is generally preferable to seeking cumulative probabilities, since the latter require assessors to assimilate and allow for the assessed cumulative probability of each stage up to the current stage.

3.8   Group assessments

Attention has so far concentrated on the individual assessor. Frequently, however, a group assessment is to be made. In these circumstances the *Delphi technique* is a proven vehicle for obtaining probability estimates. The technique consists of a series of questionnaires, with each questionnaire constituting a 'round'. The responses and information yielded by individuals to the first questionnaire are circulated to all assessors and become the basis for the second questionnaire and feedback. The process is repeated, usually for a predetermined number of rounds or until the results obtained converge to a settled pattern. Any set of information available to some experts and not to others is effectively passed on to all concerned, enabling the experts jointly to have access to all the information available between them for assessment. Such a technique aims to eliminate the bandwagon effect of majority opinion.

An example of its use involved estimating the optimal price at which a new instrument should be sold on the market. Ten separate decision makers, comprising marketing or R & D personnel, were asked to make estimates ϕ (optimistic), ML (most likely) and P (pessimistic) of the mature sales volume in units per month, for each of a range of prices for the instrument. This comprised the first stage of the exercise. From this information the mean value of mature sales and the standard deviation about this mean value for each level of sales were then calculated using the following formulae:

$$\text{Mean} = \tfrac{1}{6}(\phi + 4\,ML + P) \tag{3.1a}$$
$$\text{Standard deviation} = \tfrac{1}{6}(\phi - P) \tag{3.1b}$$

For a discussion and derivation of these formulae see, for example, Appendix 1 in Battersby (1965).

Table 3.3. *Iterations of Delphi technique*

	First iteration		Second iteration	
Price (units)	Mean sales (rounded)	Standard deviation	Mean sales (rounded)	Standard deviation
5	29	6.9	29	4.4
6	25	7.0	25	3.2
7	20	5.7	21	3.1
8	14	5.4	14	2.3
9	10	5.5	11	2.4
10	7	5.7	7	3.8
11	5	4.1	4	2.9
12	3	3.5	3	2.6

The values for the mean and standard deviation at each price were now presented to the ten decision makers, who were asked to repeat the exercise of estimating sales levels, ϕ, ML and P for each price level. The recalculated means and standard deviations are given in the right hand side of Table 3.3 There is a regression of decision makers towards the mean with a substantial reduction in the magnitude of the standard deviation at all levels of price. The particular approach adopted here was suggested by Brown and Helmer (1962), but differs from their approach in using the mean and standard deviation, rather than the median and interquartile range to describe the estimates.

The Delphi technique is useful in handling the consensus problem, but it can be criticized for giving false validity to the mean 'guesstimates' of a number of decision makers. The final consensus might be achieved through pressure from the most forceful decision maker or from the existence of a bandwagon effect. A wide-ranging discussion of the uses that have been made of the Delphi technique in a number of fields is given in Linstone and Turoff (1975).

While the Delphi method provides one approach for handling the problem of a group probability, it is clear that it is only partly successful. Winkler (1968) suggests that the final consensus should be a weighted average of each relevant decision maker's evaluation. This is a reasonable procedure but leaves open how to determine the weights. Winkler suggests four approaches: equal weights, self-weighting, subjective weighting by a third party, or weighting based on past performance experience of the individuals. The last three suggestions all have potential for bias, so that the first alternative wins in practice by default rather than intrinsic merit. However, the problem is to some extent an artificial one because the onus is on the investigator to locate the relevant decision maker for a given project, and then to use that person's weighting for the evaluation process.

3.9 Further illustrations

Experience shows that individuals can improve their probability assessment reliability, even when the events concerned are not of a directly repeatable variety such as tossing coins, or playing with roulette machines, or estimating the deaths occurring among the policyholders in a large life assurance company. In an industrial company the routine monthly forecasting ability of sales managers was dramatically improved over a year or so by asking for the 10th and 90th percentiles as well as the median. Every month a comparison was made of actual with forecast sales for each product, with a follow-up discussion to determine the cause of discrepancies between forecast and actual. After a time the differences between actual and median forecasts were considerably reduced, as were the differences between the 90th percentile and the 10th percentile.

Among published studies Hoerl and Fallin (1974) studied the reliability of subjective estimates of probabilities in a high-incentive situation using data comprising the totalizer betting outcomes for all thoroughbred horseraces (some 1825 races in total) run in 1970 on two United States race courses: Aquaduct and Belmont Park. A comparison was made between the subjective probability of winning as derived from the total amounts of money bet on each horse, and the actual frequencies of wins as a function of odds rank for races with each of 5 to 12 entries. The results demonstrated good agreement between expected and actual values and indicated a surprising ability of backers to be able to discriminate between small variations in the probabilities of success.

Weather forecasts of levels of precipitation have been routinely expressed in probabilistic terms in the USA since 1965. Small runs of forecasts may reveal moderate, or occasionally even large, departures from complete reliability, which can generally be explained by sampling fluctuations and/or forecaster inexperience. Such discrepancies usually become quite small as the number of forecasts increases. Table 3.4 gives a summary from Murphy and Winkler (1977) of one forecaster's results for successive 12-hour periods at Chicago over a four-year period. Each 12-hour period was labelled with one of thirteen forecast probabilities of precipitation, the

Table 3.4. *Weather forecaster's data*

Probability assessed	Number of occasions	Number with precipitation	Proportion with precipitation
0.0	161	4	0.02
0.02	146	5	0.03
0.05	282	8	0.03
0.1	575	39	0.07
0.2	589	89	0.15
0.3	259	72	0.28
0.4	172	63	0.37
0.5	203	108	0.53
0.6	147	87	0.59
0.7	159	120	0.75
0.8	82	61	0.74
0.9	38	38	1.00
1.0	9	9	1.00
Total	2822	703	0.25

third column giving the number of such occasions on which it actually rained, and the final column the achieved probabilities for comparison with assessed probabilities in the first column. The results achieved indicate that such a weather forecaster can broadly quantify the uncertainty inherent in his forecasts in a skilful and reliable manner. Since these forecasts involve individuals rather than an aggregation of estimates, they provide stronger and more direct evidence concerning the reliability of subjective probabilities in practice than the previous horserace results, which were based upon aggregated information. However, it must be pointed out that the analysis only tests reliability; for greater relevance one would look for more forecasts to be in the two ends of the table with no diminution in the reliability factor.

An example of a successful repetitive application of subjective probabilities in the banking world was described by Kabus (1976) in relation to work done by the Morgan Guaranty Trust Company. The company had been using, over a six-year period, group subjective probability assessments to forecast the 90-day certificate of deposit interest rate, both 90 days hence and also 180 days hence. Making such estimates is of some importance since the bank has various options, for example of borrowing now for 180 days, or borrowing initially for 90 days and renewing the loan in 90 days time. The experience over the six-year period showed excellent results both in forecasting performance (which had improved with regular feed back of performance) and in terms of decision (i.e. money) making.

Turning to industrial situations, Souder (1969) described how the Monsanto Chemical Company assessed the validity of subjective probabilities made in forecasting technical success by a study involving eleven projects that aimed to define or develop new products or processes. The conclusion reached was that the subjective probability approach appeared to be a valid and reliable means of indicating future technical success, as well as being superior to the narrative status reporting methods more typically used to control R & D projects.

Industrial work over a more extended period has been described by Balthasar, Bosch and Menke (1978) relating to Sandoz, a pharmaceutical company where the time horizon is such that it frequently requires five to ten years to achieve technical success, and an additional five to eight years to realize full commercial potential. The authors describe forecasts made over a seven-year period and the comparisons made with the subsequent actual outcomes. They find that the actual success results have been well predicted by the prior expected values. Furthermore, the consequential effects for forward planning have been immense.

Subjective assessments also enter into legal judgements. Downton (1982) quotes part of a judgement in the English Court of Appeal in the case of *Mitchell* v. *Mulholland*:

> The average man has an expectation of life of a certain number of years. This is a matter of probability, but for purposes of actuarial calculation it has to be treated as a certainty. Yet nobody can say whether an individual plaintiff is an average man, or that he will live for the expectation of an average man of his age. Any actuarial calculation must, therefore, be discounted to allow for the chance that he may only live for a shorter period. The chances, and not the probabilities, are what the judge has to evaluate in any given case. It is true that there is also a chance that the individual plaintiff may live longer than the average expectation of life. The chances are equal either way, but as a matter of calculation it can be shown that the impact of the chance of shorter life is of greater significance than that of longer life.

The judgement illustrates graphically a basic difference between legal and statistical thinking. Apart from the curious distinction drawn between chance and probability, the judge apparently saw an expected value as describing the 'average man'. Since, almost by definition, individuals appearing in court are not average, it was necessary to make some adjustment to the expected value to take account of the individual. Thus the judge is apparently aiming to use some overall collective approach to obtain a starting point, and applying judgement to determine a narrower collective to fit the particular individual case with which he is concerned.

4
Calibration and training

4.1   Introduction

Two major difficulties arise in formulating risk assessments: first, a faulty or incomplete information base from which to make the assessment and, second, the limited and varied ability of individuals to process information presented to them. The faulty information base is discussed in Chapter 10 when looking at risk perceptions in situations of physical danger. In this chapter we consider the information-processing problem familiar to readers from situations which require the assembling of complex probabilities from a mass of simple probabilities. For example, in whist or bridge, some players consistently play against the odds, apparently being unaware of them in situations where their form is relatively complex.

4.2   Availability of information

The ease with which specific relevant instances can be recalled from memory affects markedly our judgement of relative frequency of events. The frequency of well-publicized events is commonly overestimated (for example, deaths due to cancer, deaths due to fires in offices or factories) while the frequency of less well-publicized events is underestimated (for example, deaths due to car accidents, or to diabetes). Moreover the chance availability of particular key pieces of information can affect the overall judgement. Most people have at some time been at a meeting where a member has thrown in a single isolated scrap of information which has then had a marked effect on the estimate of some uncertain quantity and affected the subsequent decision taken; the other members present at the meeting may well have found it difficult to put the piece of information in proper perspective.

A second feature of availability is that of selective perception. Anticipation of expected information colours one's thinking and directs attention to information which seeks to match that expectation. In contrary fashion, assessors tend to play down or disregard what they believe to be conflicting evidence. Moreover, assessors tend to put more emphasis on frequency than on relative frequency. Anybody hearing about the prevalence of wrong telephone calls will recognize this phenomenon: the more calls we make the more likely it is that we shall sometime get a clutch of wrong numbers. In the same vein, the absolute number of failures is given more weight than the proportion of failures. Again concrete evidence of a personal nature is weighted very heavily; for example, when purchasing a car, the positive or negative experience of one acquaintance is liable to weigh more heavily in judgement than more valid statistical evidence, for example from general consumer reports in magazines such as *Which*.

More generally there is a tendency to concentrate on quantitative data to the exclusion of qualitative data, or vice versa. Thus an expert's assessment based on quantitative evidence to hand may be overturned by a senior executive acting on a 'hunch' about some aspect that is not susceptible to quantitative assessment. Conversely, a series of general beliefs based on the experience of a number of people may be overturned by a single piece of quantitative evidence. It is thus desirable to ensure that qualitative evidence is turned in some way, however crudely, into quantitative evidence, so that all evidence can be considered on a common scale.

4.3   Overconfidence of estimators

Individuals tend to believe that they are more certain than they really are. This is demonstrated by two forms of experiment. In the first a series of different questions (say about 100) of the following form are asked:

Which is the longer river?

(*a*) Amazon

(*b*) Mississippi

Instead of ticking the perceived correct answer the assessor is first asked which answer he prefers, and then the probability he places on the correctness of that answer on the scale 0 to 1.0. If he is certain that (*a*) is correct, he marks 1.0 against (*a*); if (*b*) is thought to be certainly correct, he marks 1.0 against (*b*). If he thinks (*b*) is the more likely to be correct, but only just, he might mark 0.6 against (*b*) etc. The assessor is then given a score by counting for each probability level used for the preferred answer, the proportion of the answers so marked that are correct. A perfectly knowledgeable assessor would score a proportion 1.0, as he would always put 1.0 against the correct answer. An assessor whose knowledge level is lower, but who understands perfectly his limitations on the various questions would spread his assessments from 0.5 up to 1.0 and analysis would show that, of all questions marked 0.8 (say), the proportion where he was correct would be 0.8, etc. When such an exercise is carried out with a large number of untrained assessors on a battery of such questions the 'hit rate' was generally found to be below the theoretical expected hit rate all the way from 0.5 up to 1.0 as shown by line *M* in Figure 4.1. Perfect agreement would fall along the diagonal line. Thus, assessors basically seem to believe themselves to be more certain than they really are.

However, calibration or a better understanding of the assessment mechanism can improve performance in exercises of this form. The data

Table 4.1. *Responses to 500 Yes/No questions*

Probability stated	Number of questions	Number correct	Proportion correct
0.5	289	190	0.657
0.6	78	52	0.667
0.7	42	31	0.738
0.8	22	19	0.864
0.9	29	28	0.966
1.0	40	38	0.950

Figure 4.1. Responses to Yes/No questions

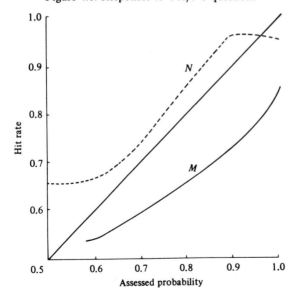

Assessed probability

in Table 4.1 due to Sarah Lichtenstein, and quoted in Lindley (1982), relate to a trained subject's performance with 500 questions of this Yes/No type. He was, as above, asked first which answer he preferred, and then for the probability he placed on that answer. This subject's curve is shown by line N in Figure 4.1 and indicates a marked difference from that of the untrained subjects, indicating now a slight tendency to underestimate rather than overestimate uncertainty. There is however, an unexpected effect when the subject chooses an answer but only rates its probability as 0.5 (indicating indifference between the two answers), and then has nearly two-thirds correct.

4.4   Some experimental results

The ensuing discussion is based on some experiments concerning the assessment of various unknown qualities carried out with the aid of post-graduate students in business studies at the London Business School. Some eighty students were involved, with an average age of about twenty-seven years and all studying for degrees in business studies; virtually all the students had some business experience and understood the basic statistical concepts concerning distributions, medians, quartiles, etc. They were each given a questionnaire (reproduced at the end of this chapter) which asked in part A for some information of their own habits and views and then in more detail, for their assessments of the percentiles of the particular probability distributions.

The questions used in part B of the questionnaire were selected so that, except for numbers 1 and 3 where the respondents as a group provided the answers themselves from part A, virtually all the respondents would have some background knowledge but few, if any, would have complete knowledge and actually know the correct answers. Respondents would, accordingly, have to assess the required quantities based on varying amounts of information. The questions were also such that the correct answers were ascertainable, and could be made available immediately the exercise was completed.

Each question in part B asked the respondent to assess five percentiles, namely the 1st, 25th, 50th, 75th and 99th. These five percentiles divide the whole range of possible values for the uncertain quantity concerned into six categories:

Category 1. All values below the assessed 1st percentile
Category 2. All values between the assessed 1st and 25th percentiles
Category 3. All values between the assessed 25th and 50th percentiles

Category 4. All values between the assessed 50th and 75th percentiles

Category 5. All values between the assessed 75th and 99th percentiles

Category 6. All values above the assessed 99th percentile.

When the respondent has specified his five percentiles for the eight questions, the category into which the true value falls can subsequently be ascertained for each question. For example, suppose that Jones gave the following percentiles for question 5 on the National Debt (£ million):

Percentile	1st	25th	50th	75th	99th
Assessment	5000	10 000	20 000	30 000	40 000

The true value (at the time) was 36 070 (£ million), and hence Jones' answer is in category 5. The results for each question for all respondents are shown in Table 4.2, the numbers in each row expressed as percentages.

In aggregate, as many true values should have fallen in categories 3 and 4 as fell in all the others combined, since these categories refer to the range from the 25th to the 75th percentile. However, the bottom row shows that rather more than twice as many fell outside than inside. Moreover, the top percentiles were seriously underestimated by a lot of the respondents. There were substantial differences from question to question, and also (although not shown by the table) between individuals.

The results of the experiment, which broadly agree with other experiments carried out (for example, as reported by Raiffa and Alpert (1969) and Wallace (1975)) suggest that respondents without training tend to underestimate the degree of uncertainty which exists in their knowledge

Table 4.2. *Summary of assessment results*

Question	Category						Total
	1	2	3	4	5	6	
1	0	0	12	22	41	25	100
2	6	3	16	34	32	9	100
3	6	9	12	22	29	22	100
4	31	9	25	16	0	18	100
5	0	3	6	19	9	63	100
6	6	13	9	19	28	25	100
7	12	12	6	17	13	40	100
8	0	3	3	6	6	82	100
Total	8	7	11	19	20	35	100
Theoretical percentages	1	24	25	25	24	1	100

of the quantities which they seek to estimate. As a result, assessors not only make errors of location but may also incur substantial errors of dispersion, giving overly narrow confidence intervals. This form of bias is shared by naive as well as sophisticated assessors and demonstrates the need for training.

A further experiment carried out with a group of executives asked them to draw their CDF (cumulative density function) for the number of motor cars per 100 persons in (*a*) the UK and (*b*) the remainder of the EEC as it then was. The group was divided into three sets of individuals. The individuals in set *A* were given no further information; those in set *B* were given some skeleton data about the UK and the EEC, while those in set *C* were given rather more data, but still not enough to make a definitive estimate. All executives were given 15 minutes to construct their CDF curve and the results then compared. In general, the slopes of the CDF curves were steeper in set *C* assessments than in set *B* assessments, which in turn were steeper than those in set *A*. There were discrepancies in the location of the CDF curves but the most immediate deduction was that, while the executives were aware of the broad value of increased information and gave relatively tighter distributions, they were unaware of the extent of their ignorance and consistently tended to draw distributions that were too 'tight'.

4.5   Value of additional information

Assessors commonly demonstrate an inability to revise accurately and consistently their initial assessments in the light of new information that becomes available. Observation suggests that assessors are polarized in this respect, some placing more weight on the extra information than would be justified by the use of Bayes' theorem (see Appendix A) while others ignore it in favour of earlier information. Two examples are given to illustrate this feature.

The first involves an experiment using two apparently identical canvas bags labelled A and B respectively inside. Each is filled with a large number of similar-sized small beads. Bag A is known to contain 7000 white beads and 3000 red beads, while bag B is known to contain 7000 red beads and 3000 white beads. The beads in each bag are well mixed and the two bags are moved around so that the assessor does not know which is which. The assessor now chooses one of the bags at random. Imagine you are the assessor.

   (*a*) What probability do you assign to the proposition that the bag chosen is the predominantly white bag, i.e. bag A?

   (*b*) Before making the probability assessment as in (*a*), you are allowed to draw out 50 beads one at a time from the chosen bag, replacing the beads after each drawing. 27 of these beads drawn are white and 23 are red. What is now the probability that the bag selected is the predominantly white bag?

(c) Instead of drawing 50 beads as in (b), a sample of 4 beads is drawn in the same manner, and all 4 are white. What is now the probability that the bag selected is the predominantly white bag?

For case (a) you would presumably say $\frac{1}{2}$ using the enumeration approach. But what of the other situations? Experiments with a large number of executives suggest answers in the range 0.6–0.8 for (b) and 0.7–0.95 for (c). The true probabilities can be obtained using Bayes' theorem (see Appendix A) and for case (c) the probability is

$$\frac{(0.7)^4}{(0.7)^4 + (0.3)^4} = 0.97 \tag{4.1}$$

while for case (b) it is

$$\frac{K(0.7)^{27}(0.3)^{23}}{K(0.7)^{27}(0.3)^{23} + K(0.7)^{23}(0.3)^{27}} \tag{4.2}$$

where K is a constant, representing the number of different orderings of 50 beads, of which 27 are white and 23 are red, in a row. This latter expression (4.2) reduces on cancellation of terms to

$$\frac{(0.7)^4}{(0.7)^4 + (0.3)^4}$$

which is the same as (4.1) derived earlier. The high level of the probabilities surprises many, and the equality of them even more so. The latter feature arises because it is the difference (white − red) in the number of beads that matters, not the proportion of reds and whites in the sample drawn from the bag.

The experiment was repeated with three bags A, B and C. Bags A and B were as before, while bag C had the same composition as B. One bag is again chosen at random. Most assessors reduced the probability they gave for picking bag A fairly sharply but the probability for both (b) and (c), calculated along the lines of Bayes' theorem as before, only reduces from 0.97 to 0.94. In other words the sample information is an important ingredient and must be very carefully assessed.

The second example is drawn from the medical field. A patient visits his doctor with some ailment. Talking with the patient, before any detailed physical examination or tests have been carried out, the doctor believes that he could be suffering from one of three diseases D_i ($i = 1, 2, 3$) and he allocates, from past experience of the apparent symptoms the probabilities 0.5, 0.4 and 0.1 respectively to the three diseases. Thus diseases D_1 and D_2 are both relatively common on the basis of the symptoms described and visible, while disease D_3 is not so common. Disease D_1, on the face of things at this stage, appears to be the most likely.

The patient is then given a detailed clinical examination and medical tests, as a consequence of which a certain symptom S is noted. Past experience shows that the probabilities of the patient having symptom S, given that he had each of the diseases concerned are 0.1, 0.3 and 0.8 respectively. In other words, the observed symptom S occurs only rarely with D_1, but is very common with D_3. Thus, as is commonly the case, the symptom is not unique to a particular disease. How should this affect the doctor's assessments of the diseases? Commonly the assessments made do not change very markedly. Using Bayes' theorem the revised, or posterior, probabilities of the three diseases for the particular patient concerned can be calculated as

$$D_1:0.20, \quad D_2:0.48, \quad D_3:0.32$$

These three posterior probabilities add, as they must, to 1.00. Comparing them with the original prior probabilities shows that the effect of including the information contained in the symptom S has changed the relative likelihood of the diseases considerably, making the intermediate disease D_2 the most probable. Disease D_1, originally the most suspected, has dropped to bottom place and the disease with the apparent outside chance is now much more likely than before.

4.6   Insensitivity to sample size

In addition to inconsistencies in the use of additional information as a whole, there is commonly insensitivity to considerations of sample size. To illustrate this feature suppose a factory inspects large batches of incoming components by taking a sample of 50 components and applying an enhanced test. This test is expected to result in a 50% failure rate for individual components in batches of satisfactory quality. Although not more than 25 components on average will fail the test, for some batches this number rises to 30 or more (i.e. 60% sample failure rate) which is regarded as a flash point. The management then decide to reduce the sample from each batch to 20 components and find that the percentage of sets in which 12 or more fail (i.e. the 60% flash point again) has risen. This is judged a sign that the quality of the output has fallen. Yet probability theory shows that, with unchanged quality of components, the expected proportion of samples with over 60% failures in the first case is 0.10, while in the second it is 0.25. This arises because a large sample is less likely to stray far from the 50% norm than a small sample. Such a fundamental notion of probability is evidently not part of people's repertoire of intuitions, and the assessment of a change of quality can be erroneously made on a basis that is broadly independent of the sample size involved.

A second illustration is drawn from the field of market research. A survey is carried out in which 1000 households were asked whether they would purchase a certain commodity over the next year. Of the 1000 households, 200 said yes, a 20% positive response. Standard statistical analysis techniques suggest that the possible 'error band' about this point estimate is plus or minus 3% giving an overall $20 \pm 3\%$ response. Subsequently one of the managers suggests examining regional differences and, working backwards from the individual survey forms, divides them up into those from each of three regions A, B and C with the following results:

Region	Number surveyed	Positive responses	Percentage
A	400	100	25
B	300	40	13.3
C	300	60	20

The final column shows variations between the regions, and the manager naively assumes that the 'error band' of $\pm 3\%$ still applies to each region, indicating some real differences between the regions. However, this is no longer the case; the sample size per region is much smaller and the error bands for the three regions can be calculated as

A: $\pm 7.5\%$, B: $\pm 6.3\%$, C: $\pm 7.8\%$

On this basis the information does not, by itself, indicate any definite clear cut differences between the three regions. It is, indeed, a general statistical rule that the precision of sample estimates improves proportionately to the square root of the sample size. Thus to halve the 'error band', a quadrupling of the sample is required and conversely as indicated by this particular illustration.

4.7 Anchoring

Probabilities of uncertain outcomes are often made by anchoring on a value suggested by past experience, and then adjusting to allow for the particular circumstances of the current situation. A sales forecast may be made by taking last year's actual results and adding 5% for next year.

Experiments made show that the departure point – or anchor – used can affect the final prediction fairly markedly. This implies that it is not necessarily optimal to assess probabilities by judging an 'add on' or 'knock off' factor from a fixed starting point. If such a process is adopted it should be at least paralleled by, and set against, a further approach made from first principles.

An illustration of how this procedure may be dangerous can be demonstrated from a sales forecast system. Across the previous year, sales had been more or less uniform, but had dropped 10% in the final month. A judgement is then made that overall sales for the next year will be 5% down on the previous year. But the 10% fall in the final month was, in reality, the permanent withdrawal of one large customer. Hence, with no other changes, the following year's sales will be a fraction

$$\frac{90}{\frac{11}{12} \times 100 + \frac{1}{12} \times 90} = 0.908 \text{ of the previous year's sales}$$

Thus this single change alone gives sales 9% down, so that a predicted fall of 5% is actually predicting a rise of 4% in other sales.

Estimates subject to the anchoring effect can have some far-reaching knock-on consequences. For example, the overall probability of a conjunctive event (i.e. one where a sequence of sub-events must each occur) is lower than the probability of each separate sub-event. Thus if each sub-element is assessed by anchoring and there is a consistent downward bias, the overall probability has a markedly greater downward bias. Again the overall probability of a disjunctive event (i.e. one where at least one of a sequence of sub-events must occur) is higher than the probability of each separate sub-event. Anchoring with downward bias in the individual probabilities would result in the overall probability being underestimated but not so seriously.

Such biases can be significant in planning situations. The overall completion of a project commonly requires the successful completion of each of a series of steps, with the consequence that any tendency to overestimate the probability of conjunctive events can lead to unwarranted optimism in assessing the probability that the project will be successfully completed. Conversely, disjunctive structures are typically encountered in the evaluation of failure risks. A complex system (for example a nuclear reactor) will malfunction if any one of its essential components fail. Even when the probability of failure in each component is slight, the probability of an overall failure can be high if many components are involved. Because of anchoring, people tend to underestimate the overall probability of failure in such complex systems. Thus the direction of the possible anchoring bias can sometimes be inferred from the structure of the event, with the chain-like structure of conjunction leading to overestimation, while the tree-like structure of disjunction leads to underestimation.

Anchoring also plays a part in the assessment of probability distributions (as opposed to the probability of single events). Such distributions serve to summarize an assessor's total knowledge or belief with respect to specific uncertain quantities, for example the price of gold thirty days hence. To select X_{90} for the price of gold a month ahead, for example, it is perhaps natural to begin by thinking about one's best point estimate of the price X_{50}, and to adjust this value upwards to obtain X_{90}. If this adjustment – like most others – is insufficient, then X_{90} will not be sufficiently extreme. A similar anchoring effect will occur in the selection of X_{10} which can be likewise obtained by adjusting one's best estimate downwards, but not by enough. Consequently, the confidence interval between X_{10} and X_{90} will be too narrow, and the assessed probability distribution as a whole will be too tight, a phenomenon which has already been commented upon.

Subjective probability distributions for some unknown quantity, such as the *Financial Times* index three months hence, can be obtained in two different ways: first, by asking the assessor to select values for the index that correspond to specified percentiles of his probability distribution; or alternatively by asking the assessor to assess the probability that the true value of the index will exceed a series of specified values. The two procedures are formally equivalent and should yield identical distributions. In the first procedure the assessor states his answer in units of the assessed quantity; the natural starting point is his best estimate and the assessments are likely to be too tight as described earlier. In the second procedure the assessments are stated in terms of odds or probabilities, and the natural starting point is even odds or a probability of $\frac{1}{2}$. Anchoring on the starting point in the latter case will tend to yield conservative estimates of odds, i.e. odds that are too close to 1:1 and probability distributions that are too flat.

To contrast the two procedures, Tversky (1974*a*) describes an experiment in which a set of 24 quantities (for example, the air distance New Delhi–Peking) was presented to a group of assessors who assessed X_{10} (or X_{90}) for each question posed. A second group of subjects were given the median assessments of the X_{10} values of the first group for each of the 24 quantities. They were then asked to assess the odds that each of the given median values exceeded the true value of the relevant quantity. In the absence of any bias, the assessors in the second group should retrieve the odds specified to the first group, i.e. 9:1. If the assessors in the second group are anchored on even odds, however, their stated odds should be less extreme, i.e. closer to 1:1. Indeed, the median odds given by this group, across all problems, were 3:1. When the assessments of the two groups were tested for external calibration, it was found that the assessments of the first group were indicative of overly tight probability distributions, in accord with earlier results, whereas the odds stated by the second group were indicative of overly flat probability distributions.

4.8   Importance of training

Overall it seems important to undertake training sessions for assessors to make them aware of potential biases and to help them eliminate such effects in their assessments. To this end it is essential that, whenever assessments of uncertain quantities are made, a retrospective comparison is carried out between actual and predicted to see what can be learnt from the inevitable divergencies. In this way performance over time can be improved whether it be for sales forecasts, the times for repair of breakdowns, or the incidence of faults. Greater confidence in the consistency, reliability and coherence of probability estimates can avoid the twin perils of underreaction or overreaction to individual risk elements in a complex problem situation. Formalized training programmes for assessors and potential assessors are used by many organizations on a regular basis for developing their executives.

Questionnaire

Questionnaire for assessments of probabilities

The purpose of this exercise is to see how well you, as an individual, and the group as a whole, can assess probability distributions for uncertain quantities. We list below eight items and you are asked to assess the median, the lower and upper quartiles, and the first and ninety-ninth percentiles for each item. Because of the type of items used, we will subsequently be able to compare your assessments with the true values, and be able to see if you tend to be 'too tight', 'too loose', or biased upwards or downwards on certain types of questions. Part A asks you to give your own answer to three questions. In Part B you are confronted with certain unknown (to you) quantities. Answer each question as best you can with your present knowledge.

Part A

(1) Do you take sugar with coffee?

(2) Do you currently favour Britain's withdrawal from the Common Market?

(3) Would you personally accept a 50:50 gamble where you could lose £30 or win £60?

Part B

Estimate the percentiles shown on the answer sheet for the following quantities:

(1) The percentage of students (excluding those who never drink coffee) who take sugar with coffee.

(2) The percentage of students who favour withdrawal from the Common Market.

(3) The percentage of students who would accept a 50:50 gamble to lose £30 or win £60.

(4) The distance (directly in miles) from London to Karachi.

(5) The size (in £ million nominal) of the British National Debt.

(6) The population of Brazil (in millions).

(7) The number of full-time students in British universities in the current academic year (in thousands).

(8) The number of qualified doctors on the Medical Register in Great Britain (in thousands).

Answer Sheet

Part A. Please check one response for each question.

(1) Coffee   Yes   No   Never drink coffee

(2) Common Market   Favour   Oppose
(3) Gamble   Accept   Refuse
(For questions 2 and 3, the answer 'Don't know' is not acceptable)

Part B. Please assess all five percentiles for the eight questions. The highest number on each line will be on the right. Decimals are acceptable, but note the units given. Where a percentage is required, write 27.5 for 27.5%, not 0.275, etc.

	Percentile				
	(1)	(25)	(50)	(75)	(99)

(1) Coffee
(2) Common Market
(3) Gamble
(4) Distance
(5) Debt
(6) Population
(7) Students
(8) Doctors

5

The concept of utility

5.1 Introduction

The EMV (expected monetary value) approach to insurance discussed earlier suggests that nobody ought to pay more for an insurance policy than its strict actuarial value. Since insurance companies could not reduce their premiums to this level and survive, insurance would become impracticable. A policyholder is normally willing, however, to pay a premium above the straight actuarial value given to a risk which suggests that potential insurers do not take the strictly EMV view implied in Chapter 2.

Consider house insurance and imagine that the risk of destruction by fire in a given year is assessed (correctly) as 1 in 1000. Your house is valued at £50000 and your total assets at the beginning of the year (including the house) are equal to A. The pure premium for the risk is $(1/1000) \times 50000$, or £50, but the lowest premium actually quoted by insurance companies is found to be, say, £100. Would you accept this offer of insurance? The asset tableau showing the end-year position is as follows:

	Outcome		
	Fire (probability 0.001)	No fire (probability 0.999)	Expected end-year assets
Insure	$A-100$	$A-100$	$A-100$
Don't insure	$A-50000$	A	$A-50$

From the final column the expected assets at the end of the year are maximized if there is no insurance, but not many readers – legal mortgage requirements apart – would actually follow this rule and not take out insurance. Presumably it is because of concern with the consequences of falling into the bottom left hand box situation. Note that this attitude could well depend on the value of A. If A was £10000, the wish to insure would be strong. If A was £100 million it probably wouldn't be. Somewhere in between a switch occurs from insuring to not insuring. Thus a premium excess is paid to avoid the possibility of the financial loss situation occurring, although this acceptable excess would reduce as A increases until a level of A is reached at which it vanishes. This concept is sometimes expressed in the form that the *utilities* of different outcomes are not directly proportional to their monetary consequences.

This analysis is reinforced by noting that large firms with hundreds, or even thousands, of houses on their books do not always take out fire insurance. The cause of the difference lies not in different assessments of risk, but in the firm's attitudes to the outcomes: the individual householder does not wish to be in the asset position of $A - 50000$, even though its probability of occurrence is small. The firm, on the other hand, can allow itself to be in such a position with regard to the insurance of a single house because its value of A is large relative to that of the individual house. In other words, the big firm may be satisfied with expected assets as its criterion, while the householder is not. But even the latter would be satisfied with expected assets for some purposes as it is the size of the possible loss relative to the asset base that governs the approach. The decision maker effectively maximizes his expected utility, while utility in turn may not always be linearly linked to money.

5.2   Background to utility

Utility is based upon a series of assumptions and properties that flow from them. The discussion below is worded in terms of an individual making a decision, but could apply equally to a corporate body.

Assumption 1. An individual when faced with two alternative outcomes B_1 and B_2 is able to decide whether he prefers B_2 to B_1.

Assumption 2. If an individual regards B_1 at least as well as B_2, and B_2 at least as well as B_3, then B_1 is regarded at least as well as B_3.

To any outcome B_j, a number $u(B_j)$ is attached which is called the utility of the outcome B_j. Then to accord with the first two assumptions the initial property of utility is that

$u(B_1) > u(B_2)$ if and only if the individual prefers outcome B_1 to outcome B_2 (5.1)

Suppose next the individual is given the opportunity to take a gamble involving outcomes B_1 and B_2. This is referred to as a mixture of outcomes.

Thus one possible mixture might be the outcome denoted by the prospect of outcome B_1 with a probability of 0.8, and outcome B_2 with a probability of 0.2. If B_1 is preferred to B_2, mixtures which give higher probabilities to B_1 are the more attractive. If the probability of outcome B_1 is close to 1, the mixture is almost as good as B_1 itself and vice versa. This suggests the next two assumptions:

Assumption 3. If B_1 is preferred to B_2 which is in turn preferred to B_3, then there are some mixtures of B_1 and B_3 which are preferred to B_2, and also some mixtures of B_1 and B_3 over which B_2 is preferred.

Assumption 4. Suppose the individual prefers B_1 to B_2, and B_3 is another prospect. Then the individual is assumed to prefer a mixture of B_1 and B_3 to the same mixture of B_2 and B_3.

These two assumptions lead to a second property for utilities, namely:

If B is the situation where, with probability p, an individual faces outcome B and, with probability $(1-p)$, he faces outcome B_2, then

$$u(B) = p\,u(B_1) + (1-p)u(B_2) \qquad (5.2)$$

Thus, once the utilities of any two prospects have been fixed, those for any other mixed prospect involving just those two prospects can be computed using formulae (5.1) and (5.2). Indeed the utilities for the two 'markers' can be fixed quite arbitrarily, giving the higher utility value to the more preferred prospect. (This is no different from fixing 0 to 100 on the Centigrade scale for the temperatures corresponding to freezing and boiling respectively; the Fahrenheit scale is different, but this is irrelevant as long as it is clear which scale is being used.)

In general terms, the aim is to select the prospect B which maximizes the value $u(B)$ computed according to equation (5.2). Individuals (as companies) differ in their attitudes towards risk and these differences will influence their choices. Rationality does not (in the sense used here) mean that all people faced with the same risks will do the same thing. However, an individual (or company) facing situations of equivalent risk, at different moments of time, and an unchanging attitude towards risk expressed by the utilities, should make the same decision each time, i.e. they should be consistent.

To illustrate this precept, imagine two colleagues each of whom owns a lottery ticket which gives, on the single spin of a coin, a 50:50 chance of prizes of zero or £500. They are each asked to state the lowest amount for which they would sell their lottery ticket before the spin takes place. After due reflection the first colleague comes up with a figure of £50, the second of £200. Probing to ensure that the two colleagues both understand the rules only serves to reinforce their answers: the first is overtly risk averse, the other rather near to being risk neutral. This has nothing to do with the accuracy of the information concerning the chances or outcomes, but it could be affected by their own personal financial position. Faced with a decision problem that involves an element of risk, the two colleagues can perfectly rationally behave differently. The same kind of situation applies as forcibly to industrial or commercial problems, both between companies and for different individuals within the same company.

5.3   Measuring utility

A utility function is linked to the individual or group of individuals who devise it. Widely different attitudes towards risk exist within most organizations. Some of these variations reflect legitimate differences of view concerning the company, others may reflect different interpretations of company policy. Without reconciliation, decisions made in relation to opportunities arising can vary according to which manager handles each particular proposition.

Two methods used to assess points on utility curves both depend upon the concept of the *certainty equivalent*, i.e. the sum of money the individual would pay (or accept) to avoid being exposed to some opportunity with an uncertain outcome. If we define

risk premium = certainty equivalent − EMV of opportunity

(5.3)

the risk premium can then either be positive or negative. For an individual it will generally be negative if the EMV is positive, or positive if the EMV is negative.

The first method asks the individual, for a series of hypothetical opportunities usually expressed in the form of 50:50 two-way gambles, to give his certainty equivalents (from which the risk premiums can be directly derived). The answers given can be made self-checking by using the results of one gamble as part of the input into another and directly using them to construct a utility curve. The second method is similar, except that the certainty equivalent is fixed and the assessor gives the $P/(100-P)$ gamble ratio for which he would just accept the particular gamble involved. Both methods presuppose that the individual starts from a defined net asset level, and curves constructed with different initial asset levels may differ.

Figure 5.1 gives an illustration of a utility curve constructed using the first method for a situation in which the two extremes were a gain in net assets of £60000 (£60k) or alternatively a loss of £10000. These were labelled 0 or 100 utility units respectively. For the first step the assessor gave his evaluation of the certainty equivalent between a 50:50 chance of a gain of £60000 or a loss of £10000. Suppose the value given was £15000. The assessor then looked at a 50:50 chance between £60000 and £15000 for which he gave the value £32000. Finally he looked at a 50:50 gamble between £15000 and −£10000 for which the value −£500 was given. From the five points now available a free-hand utility curve is drawn.

Misunderstanding sometimes arises through the common use of a utility scale going from 0 to 1 (or 0 to 100) and talking about 'the utility for money'. Managers find it easier to understand the principle if the argument is made in terms of 'change in net asset level' and the utility value goes from negative to positive with unlimited bounds. Thus an opportunity with expected zero change in net asset level would normally have a utility value around zero. Different decision makers would have varying shapes for their utility curves but all going approximately through the (0,0) point on the curve.

Swalm (1966) gives a number of illustrations of the utility curves obtained from individuals in the same organization using the second method given above. The curves obtained varied greatly, demonstrating the different ways in which managers would view proposals put to them. More disturbingly, managers' utility curves appeared to be related to the sums of money with which they are accustomed to deal as individual managers, rather than to the company's overall financial position.

The formulation of a corporate utility curve raises further difficulties. If we follow Spetzler (1968) the best route to take seems to be to assess the curves appropriate to each individual, and for the group to use these as a basis to formulate a corporate curve. A series of experiments carried

Figure 5.1. Construction of utility curve

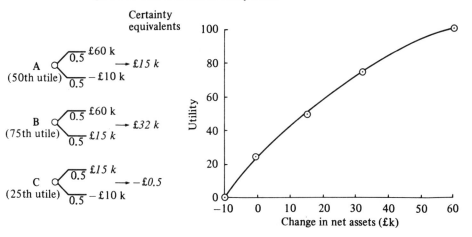

out with a group of a dozen managers from a merchant bank, used the following general procedure:

(a) each manager was presented with a series of hypothetical investment decisions along the lines of the first method described above and a utility curve plotted (one for each manager);

(b) a mathematical form (for example, logarithmic) was agreed upon to fit the utility plots (the same functional form, but with different parameters for each manager);

(c) each manager was re-interviewed to determine his parameters for the functional form adopted;

(d) the results were presented to top management for discussion with them to select the best parameters for a corporate utility function.

The group utility curve derived in this way was effectively linear from a net asset change of £1.5 million upwards, but extremely convex below that figure. It was less conservative than that for the individual managers concerned, where the curvature continued beyond £1.5 million, and was more pronounced on the downward side. This finding has been replicated in a number of other experimental determinations of utility curves and is a particular example of the 'risky shift phenomenon', i.e. the willingness of a group to be more risky than individuals, a phenomenon which has been commented upon by psychologists (for example, Wallach, Kogan and Bern, 1962).

5.4   Utility and insurance

The excess premium paid by householders in Section 5.1 can now be examined more formally. To assess the excess premium assume that the householder's net assets are S, while C is the cost of restoring the house if it is destroyed by fire. Further let $u(X)$ represent the householder's utility for assets of amount x. If he does not insure for the coming year, the utility of his assets in a year's time will be either $u(S)$ or $u(S-C)$. Let p be the probability that the house is destroyed by fire during the year. Thus his expected utility if he does not insure is

$$(1-p)u(S)+pu(S-C) \qquad (5.4)$$

If he insures for a premium R his final utility will be $u(S-R)$, whether there is a fire or not.

Suppose, first, that the householder's utility function between asset levels of S and $S-C$ is strictly linear as shown by line AB in Figure 5.2. He would then insure, provided that

$$u(S-R) > (1-p)u(S)+pu(S-C) \qquad (5.5)$$

The right-hand side of equation (5.5) corresponds, because of linearity, to the value of $u(S-pC)$ and hence R must not exceed pC (or the pure premium) if the householder is to insure. Thus, in practice he would not insure as the insurance company necessarily charges more than pC to cover its administrative and other costs.

Alternatively, and more plausibly, the householder's utility function can be risk averse as implied by line XY in Figure 5.2. The utility values for assets of S and $S-C$ are the same as before, while the point W represents the maximum pure premium that the insured would be willing to pay on the linear utility assumption. With the utility function represented by the line XY, the value of the right hand side of the equation (5.5) is now achieved at point V on the utility curve and the distance $LQ(R'$ say) represents the maximum premium that the insured is willing to pay. The difference $LQ - MQ = LM = (R-R')$ is the maximum excess (or risk premium) over the pure premium that the insured is prepared to carry.

For the insurer, his total assets are generally large in relations to C, and he is likely to be operating at a point on his utility function that is effectively linear in relation to a change of an amount C. He is accordingly willing to accept the pure premium (i.e. $R-pC$) plus an expense and profit loading and, provided that the latter is less than or equal to $(R-R')$, it is possible to meet the insured's requirements. It is thus the convexity in $u(x)$ for the insured that primarily accounts for, and defines, the maximum risk premium that the insured is willing to pay and hence makes insurance an economic possibility.

One way in which large-scale risk situations can be handled is through re-insurance, the obverse of the problem just discussed. If the insurance for a possible loss L is such that a firm would find it impractical to quote

Figure 5.2. Insured's utility function

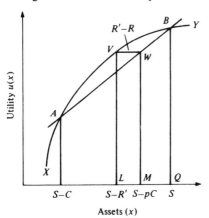

an acceptable premium because of the effect that the loss could have on its current asset level S, then it may still be willing to undertake some fraction q of the risk. This arises because the utility function of the insurance company may be effectively linear over the range from S down to $S - qL$, whereas it was not so from S down to $S - L$. The injection of further capital provides another way in which the company can be moved to an asset position where its utility function is more nearly linear over the appropriate range.

Life assurance companies are similarly concerned with utility. Their mean traditional uncertainty has been with mortality risks. Assessable from past data, year by year changes in these risks over time have been small. Until 25 years ago uncertainties regarding their investment returns were virtually non-existent since the vast bulk of the investments were in fixed interest securities. Moreover, the existence of with-profit policies has always provided a cushion against adverse effects of uncertainty, enabling any bias that develops to be corrected through bonus adjustments without any need for changes in the underlying structure. For this reason risk theory, or the probability of ruin notion, while popular with actuaries in some continental countries (see Borch, 1967 and Beard, Pentikainen and Pesonen, 1969), has had limited impact on UK life assurance companies. It can be argued however that, as a consequence, future generations of UK life policyholders are in effect being favoured at the expense of present policyholders.

Recent events have changed these views in two directions. First, taxation legislation has led to new forms of life insurance being devised whereby high regular income payments are made to the insured for a limited number of years, coupled with guaranteed surrender values. Such policies, with little dependence on traditional mortality consideration, can form the bulk of the business of a company. Secondly some companies have invested heavily in equities and property in contrast to the more traditional debenture and gilt-edged investments. These changes introduce new types of risk and, moreover, a single risk can represent a substantial proportion of the assets. In one case, a single property investment that failed formed about 20% of the assets of an insurance company; in another company a deposit with a secondary bank that formed 10% of its assets failed. In each case, having no other substantial cushion built into the system, the companies become insolvent in a technical sense. The utility functions of such companies may indeed not be linear over an indefinite range and hence cannot cover these forms of activity on bases previously considered reasonable.

It is somewhat ironic that the UK Government's reaction to the consequences of these changes has not been to nationalize (which would transfer the risk to the community as a whole), or to stress the 'caveat emptor' principle, or even to put strict operational controls upon such companies. Instead it charges all solvent companies up to 1% per annum of their premium income to bail out failed companies up to 90% of their liabilities through the Policyholders' Protection Act. (A single first call of 0.25% of premium income was made a few years ago in order to provide £1.25 million to bail out a failed company, Capital Annuities. A second company, Fidelity Life, that subsequently failed needed no levy to meet its basic liabilities.)

An unfortunate feature of the legislation is that the company has to be put into liquidation before the Act is operative and hence there is no way that the company can work its passage back. More generally, there is opposition to the basic principles behind the Act along four lines. First, the individual's responsibility for choosing a sound company in which to place his insurance is lowered. Secondly, it increases the temptation of brokers to recommend policies with high promises, for example of future bonuses. Thirdly it increases offices' temptations to declare high immediate bonus rates or make 'riskier' investments; and fourthly, the Department of Trade may not be so watchful over individual companies as it would otherwise. Thus the Act, which tries in a public way to modify the 'caveat emptor' principle, may unwittingly encourage companies to be more reckless, and force the more prudent policyholders to pay for that extra degree of recklesness.

5.5   Multi-attribute utility

For many projects the desired outcome attributes are multi-dimensional, and not simply the conventional net present value or return on investment. Thus an individual choosing a house for purchase does not consider only price but location, journey convenience for the office, amenities such as schools, shops, etc. The Roskill Commission enquiry (1971) into the location of a third London Airport was a notable attempt – albeit ill-fated – to reduce a large number of separate outcome dimensions into a single monetary scale on which a rational decision on location could be based. The problem is essentially the trade-off to be made between achievement on one attribute against that on another attribute. This often becomes a personal value question for each decision maker and there may be no unique answer to the question because, naturally enough, individuals can have different value structures. This is important when the decision maker is an agent (possibly a delegated agent) for somebody else since, unless there is some agreed explicit formalization of the value structure, there is no guarantee that the delegated decision maker will behave in the way his superior would expect him to do, or as the superior would himself.

One way in which this situation can be probed is to set aspirational levels for all the attributes involved bar one. For example, suppose there are n attributes and that the decision maker selects aspirational levels x_2°, $x_3^\circ, \ldots, x_n^\circ$ for attributes 2 to n. He then seeks a course of action A that satisfies the imposed constraints

$$x_i(A) \geqslant x_i^\circ \quad \text{for} \quad i = 2, \ldots, n \tag{5.6}$$

and maximizes $x_1(A)$. This form of optimization problem can be solved by standard programming procedures. If there is no feasible solution for x_1 then the set of aspirations $x_2^\circ, x_3^\circ, \ldots, x_n^\circ$ has to be changed as being incompatible.

Even if a feasible solution does exist, it may be desirable to iterate. If M_1 is the maximum value of $x_1(A)$ subject to (5.6), then the rate of change of M_1 with respect to changes in each constraint can be established. The decision maker then singles out one index, j say, and investigates whether the gain in x_1 is worth the loss in x_j. The cost of such additional analysis is small, and can be repeated again and again. Such a probing procedure is ad hoc, and dependent upon the skill of the decision maker. It is an incremental process of continuing interaction between what is achievable and what is desirable, and the decision maker has to decide when to stop the process.

The development of multi-attribute utility theory is mainly recent, and has been primarily based on deriving an appropriate functional form of utility function from assumptions concerning the decision maker's preferences. To assist, some preliminary assumptions are commonly made about the possible structure of the utility function. Two particular simplifications, namely those of *independence* and *additivity*, are found to permit simple but realistic applications to a wide range of problems. Moreover, they necessitate the decision maker making only a relatively few assessments of the trade-offs between the various attributes.

Independence allows the utility function $u(x_1, x_2, \ldots)$, where x_i is the value corresponding to the ith attribute, to be collapsed into an amalgam of a series of single attribute utility functions $u_1(x_1)$, $u_2(x_2), \ldots$ the assessment for each of which can be made by one of the methods discussed earlier. By using additivity the overall utility is given by an expression of the form

$$u(x_1, x_2, \ldots, x_k) = \sum_{i=1}^{k} u_i(x_i) \tag{5.7}$$

The implication is that the rate of trade-off between any two attributes may depend upon the values of those two attributes, but will not depend upon any others. For example, a corporate decision maker is establishing preferences for alternatives in terms of three attributes: asset position, market share and turnover. Additivity would imply a series of statements of the form:

> 'Whatever my turnover, increasing my market share from 10 to 11% would always have the same value to me as increasing my asset position from $2.0 million to $2.4 million.'

If utility functions are mutually independent, Keeney (1972) shows that the overall utility functions are specified completely by assessing conditional utility functions for each attribute separately, with adequate scaling contents to ensure consistency. Setting the relative scales may, however, be difficult and Keeney discusses a possible sequential approach to doing this through the use of a series of 50:50 gambles.

A further, and more far reaching, simplifying assumption is that of *linearity*, implying that each attribute can be quantified in terms of a common scale of measurement, say money. Formally, linearity states that

$$u(x_1, x_2, \ldots, x_k) = \sum_{i=1}^{k} a_i x_i, \tag{5.8}$$

where the a_i are constants. This assumption defines a constant rate of trade-off between attributes and implies a series of statements of the form:

> 'No matter what the value of my asset position, market share and turnover I would always consider a 1% unit increase in market share as valuable as a £100 000 increase in assets.'

Although conceptual advances have been made in multi-attribute utility, operational procedures have lagged far behind. Observation suggests that, with multi-dimensional attributes, the managerial approach is generally to select one attribute as being dominant and to satisfice (see Appendix B) on the other attributes. The weakness of this approach appears when no single attribute is obviously dominant. This applies increasingly to capital investment proposals, particularly in the public sector (which now accounts for over half of UK investment expenditure). In an analysis made some years ago of the various alternatives for a Heathrow Airport rail link to central London (Report, 1970), the two dominant items among the five considered in the evaluation were capital costs and the value of time saved by prospective passengers. The rankings of the alternative courses of action on these two particular characteristics differed considerably, so that the method chosen for their combination could be decisive.

As a further example of multi-attribute utility a study made on the development of airport facilities at Mexico City (De Neufville and Keeney, 1974) had sixteen alternative options and six outcome attributes. The former were whittled down to five by application of a dominance procedure (alternative X is ruled out if alternative Y dominates in expected value on all six attributes separately). For each of the five remaining alternatives a rank order was established on the various attributes, but it proved impossible to reduce the attributes any further by any agreed procedure. The authors comment that 'Whilst the approach defined the set of utility functions, it did not in itself provide a mechanism to resolve the legitimate conflicts between groups with different expectations or perceptions as to how they viewed the public interest.'

5.6   Use of hypothetical gambles

Critics of decision analysis often attack the use of hypothetical questions in the assessment procedure, and this is particularly so in assessing multi-attribute utilities. It has been suggested that observing how a particular decision maker *does* make decisions, reveals his preference structure. For these 'revealed preferences' to be used for normative purposes is to assume that the decision maker has indeed made 'optimal' decisions in the past. A further assumption is that the decision maker's perceptions (i.e. probabilities) can be separated from his preferences (utilities). In combination these two assumptions are unlikely to be met so that 'revealed preferences' alone do not generally provide enough information to specify a decision maker's preference structure, especially when interdependent uncertainties and multiple objectives are involved. If structured analysis of the general preference function is required, hypothetical questions have necessarily to be asked concerning the probabilities of various outcomes, preferences, and the like. It is the degree to which hypothetical questioning can be pursued that has to be resolved, not the principle.

An interesting example of the possible use of hypothetical questions to establish preferences is discussed in the report of the Committee on Policy Optimisation (1978):

> Optimal control theory is not necessarily ruled out if the Chancellor of the Exchequer is not good at mathematics. One method is to put him on a couch and ask him a series of hypothetical questions. For instance he might be asked whether, at a stated level of unemployment and rate of inflation, he would prefer a 1 per cent decrease in the rate of inflation to a 1 per cent decrease in the level of unemployment. With replies to a series of such questions, the technicians in the Treasury would be able to construct the Chancellor's criterion functions.
>
> A number of objections can be raised to such a scheme, the most serious

being that Chancellors would not, in practice, commit themselves on hypothetical questions. It is easy to see why. If the Chancellor's criterion function became known, as it easily might, his actions could be anticipated, and argument about the appropriateness of the criterion, in the Cabinet, in Parliament, and in the country at large, could inhibit its use without replacing it by anything equally decisive. Such consequences help to explain the reluctance of politicians to take positions on hypothetical questions, and their desire to maintain flexibility until it is essential to choose.

A little later the report reads:

> A second approach is to confine the questioning of the Chancellor to his attitude towards alternative feasible configurations of the economic future. In this case the technicians construct only that part of the criterion function which could – given the constraints of the economy – be realised. The policy analysts would present the Chancellor with a projection for the coming period and ask him how he would like to see it improved. For instance, would he like to see less unemployment or a healthier balance of payments? In the light of these comments, the analysts would produce another simulation of the future which tried to meet these objectives. The new projection would result in further comments which, in turn, could be incorporated in a third projection. Under fairly normal assumptions, the process of simulation and comments would converge on the Chancellor's optimum economic policy.
>
> The Chancellor's preferences have in some way to reflect national goals and setting these is commonly difficult. In the space programme, the criterion was to get a rocket from earth to moon using as little fuel as possible. In industrial applications, the criterion might be more ambiguous, but nevertheless it will normally be a fairly straightforward function of the plant's net output. If we are devising a corporate plan for a firm, the criterion function could be some version of profit maximisation or growth maximisation, or perhaps involve the maximising of employee satisfaction. In moving from an individual to a corporation we have at once become less certain of the objectives. One reason for this is that more than one person is involved in the corporate decision-making process, and those involved may have different preferences as to the way the company should develop. More importantly, there are now different interest groups, the shareholders, the managers, the workforce, and the community who can have conflicting goals.

5.7 The group utility function

The foregoing discussion centres primarily around a single decision maker concerned to optimize his perceived utility function. Two other cases merit brief discussion: first, when the decision maker wishes to incorporate systematically the views of others into his own decision making framework and, second, when the decision comes from a group as a whole.

For the former let u represent the decision maker's utility function, with u_i ($i = 1, 2, \ldots, n$) the utility functions of the n individuals (or groups) whom the decision maker wishes to consider in making his decisions. These individuals have no authority as such in the decision-making process; it is the decision maker who will make the interpersonal comparisons of utilities. The decision maker must consider the trade-offs among the impacts of various courses of action on the n individuals. Various approaches have been considered, for example additive or multiplicative models. Each has advantages and disadvantages with respect to the equity or fairness to the individuals concerned, both models assuming that the appropriate utility functions can be established for the individuals concerned. This may be reasonable if n is small, and perhaps still possible with elaborate questionnaires for moderate-sized groups. However, in government and many large private organizations, benevolent dictators are routinely making decisions which affect a large number of people. In such situations, it may be necessary to use representative experts to formulate the impacted preferences.

In the second situation the group formulates its own group utility function jointly. It is necessary to decide how to verify the assumptions, whose utility functions are to be used, and who will assess the scaling constants. In practice it is possible to use each individual's utility function, but group consensus and agreement is required for the assumptions and the scaling constants. Agreement on scaling constants is commonly difficult since the larger the weight for individual i, the smaller it will be for the other individuals and the more power individual i has in influencing decisions. Compromise can sometimes be reached if there are two groups among the individuals within each of which there is consensus but between which there is not. The objective can then be to maximize the overall utility of the two groups.

Finally some situations combine the two cases. Thus, members of an executive board of management responsible for different parts of an organization may each want to include the attitudes of the other members within the company in their decisions. Here each member when acting alone has a 'benevolent dictator' problem, while collectively they are involved in participatory group decisions.

5.8   Delegation

It is a generally accepted tenet of administrative theory that overall efficiency is enhanced by a determinate hierarchy (see, for example, Simon, 1957). Most large organizations are forced by the sheer scale of their operations to delegate decision making on a wide variety of issues.

But the ability of the manager to whom delegated powers are given to act rationally is limited in three directions: first, by his personal skills and habits; second, by his values and conception of purpose; third, by the extent of his knowledge and information concerning the delegated decision.

The second of these limitations is relevant to the present discussion in that the delegated manager will only be able to pursue consistently correct courses of action if he is fully appraised of the corporate utility function. This is not commonly the situation. What is more usual is a system of delegation with checks and balances that will, it is believed, bring decisions into line with company policy. For example, a number of management levels may be defined; the bottom level is allowed to approve a capital proposal provided that (a) it has a forecast rate of return greater than 20% per annum, (b) the capital expenditure involved is below £50000 and (c) a total annual capital allowance of £200000 to that level of management is not exceeded. If the proposal meets (a) but fails either (b) or (c), the project goes to a second level where it is re-appraised. If it now still meets (a), and falls within higher limits, say £100000 and £500000 respectively for (b) and (c), it can be approved. If it fails because of either of the latter tests, the proposal goes to a third level for similar consideration and finally to the board who can, at any rate in theory, approve up to any limit they care to impose.

This system does not incorporate a utility function as such, and relies on acceptance or rejection of opportunities at the lower levels on the basis of expected return. This can be counter-productive to the success of the enterprise as a whole owing to the way in which managers formulate the inputs to meet the expected criteria placed on them.

The following example from Moore (1977) illustrates the kind of situation that can arise. Consider two decision makers, A and B. A is the owner of a large public company, B the managing director of one of its divisions. The current net assets of the division concerned is £1.5 million whereas those of the total company are £30 million. A business opportunity arises in the division which will either give the company a net gain of £1 million with probability p, or a net loss of £1 million with probability $(1-p)$. How large must be the value of p for the opportunity to be accepted?

Suitable forms for a utility function for B, starting with assets of £1.5 million and considering net changes of the order envisaged in this opportunity, might be either the exponential form

$$u_B(x) = a(1 - e^{-b(x-c)})$$ (5.9a)

or the logarithmic form

$$u_B(x) = k \log (x+m) \qquad (5.9b)$$

where a, b, c, k and m are constants and x represents the assets held. Both functional forms reflect a risk-avoiding attitude.

On the other hand, A's utility for changes in assets of the order concerned, starting with net assets of £30 million and considering a similar range of changes is likely to be of a linear form

$$u_A(x) = r+sx \qquad (5.10)$$

where r and s are constants, over the relevant asset range of x for this particular project. Figure 5.3 illustrates the form that the various utility functions might take. Taking zero as the starting point for presentational ease, the possible changes in circumstances are as follows:

Expected utility of status quo	$u(0)$
Gain in utility if option successful	$u(1)-u(0)$
Loss in utility if option unsuccessful	$u(0)-u(-1)$
Expected change in utility of opportunity	$pu(1)+(1-p)u(-1)$

Figure 5.3. Decision makers' utility curves

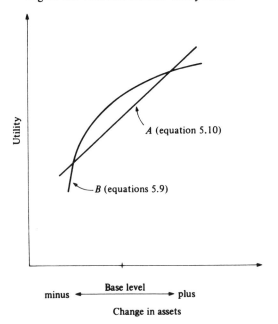

A (equation 5.10)

B (equations 5.9)

Utility

minus ◄─── Base level ───► plus

Change in assets

Hence B would take the opportunity, if he were making the decision, provided that

$$pu_B(1)+(1-p)u_B(-1) > u_B(0)$$

or

$$p\{u_B(1)-u_B(0)\} > (1-p)\{u_B(0)-u_B(-1)\} \qquad (5.11a)$$

or

$$p > \{u_B(0)-u_B(-1)\}/\{u_B(1)-u_B(-1)\}.$$

A, if the decision were made by him, would take the opportunity provided that

$$pu_A(1)+(1-p)u_A(-1) > u_A(0) \qquad (5.11b)$$

and by substituting from equation (5.10) this gives $p > \frac{1}{2}$. If we revert to B, the p value in (5.11a) will be less than $\frac{1}{2}$ if the form of $u_B(x)$ is concave with respect to $u'_B(x)$ (where u' is the rate of change of u), or more than $\frac{1}{2}$ if $u'_B(x)$ is convex as is the case for both forms of equation (5.9). Hence the required p value here will be more than $\frac{1}{2}$. Thus B will tend to be more risk averse than A with regard to such opportunities. Since a number of such opportunities will be rejected by subordinates that would, if taken to the centre, have been accepted, the consequence for the company is that delegation will lower the overall expected gain. This reinforces the need for delegation to be accompanied by a full delegated understanding of the levels of risk the enterprise is prepared to take.

6
Project investment risks

6.1   Basic assessment

Discussion of investment risk is frequently clouded by the word *investment* being used in two different senses. The first sense is the buying and selling of securities, say gilt-edged Government stock or ordinary shares in the XYZ Company. This sense is referred to as *financial investment*. The second sense is where a company (nationalized or private) or an individual decides to put some money into, say, building a factory and equipping it with machines and raw materials to make and market some new product or service. This is referred to as *project investment*. The processes involved, and the way risk is assessed and handled, are very distinct. Project investment is considered in the present chapter; financial investment is discussed in Chapters 7 and 8.

The normal limited liability company quoted on the Stock Exchange has a capital structure designed to handle the risks inherent in the development of new ideas or products. Debenture loans are commonly linked to company ownership of land, buildings and machinery and equipment; ordinary shares, or equity, are linked to the development costs of new products. Bank loans and overdrafts cover working capital, stocks, etc. Debentures and bank overdrafts carry defined rates of interest, while ordinary shares (equities) have a variable rate of dividend dependent on profits. The market value of the shares likewise varies with the current, and anticipated, levels of dividend payments.

A company seeking to acquire substantial fresh capital for risk investment purposes will basically do it in two ways, frequently in combination. First, it will retain a proportion of its profits each year, i.e the dividends paid will not be at the maximum possible level. (On average, British companies retain about 50% of their profits for re-investment.) Secondly, the company may issue new shares through a rights issue, allowing existing shareholders to purchase fresh shares at a discount on the current market price. (Occasionally a further general public issue of shares is made, but this is relatively rare.) An existing company raising money through a rights issue will do it on a general prospectus basis, and commonly does not spell out in great detail the precise purposes for which the money is required. The floatation of a new company, however, requires a rather more detailed description of company plans and abilities; moreover its launch is commonly based on a single product or process. A more established company would probably be diversified into a number of products, many unrelated in any direct way, making the rights issue approach a more appropriate vehicle for raising fresh funds.

Let the return obtainable from a risk-free investment (for example, a gilt-edged Government stock) over the same planning horizon as the project concerned be G. Then the project will aim for an increased expected yield above G for three reasons.

    (*a*) Unless the return is greater than G, it would be simpler and safer to invest the capital concerned in gilt-edged stock. Suppose the uplift required for this factor is set as a proportion g of the gilt-edged return of G.

    (*b*) Special taxes may be levied (for example, the special petroleum tax on North Sea oil developments). Suppose such tax is at a rate of t $(0 \leqslant t \leqslant 1)$.

    (*c*) There is a risk factor (i.e. probability of the project failing). Suppose such probability is assessed as r and it is assumed for simplicity that the project either succeeds or fails completely.

Overall the minimum expected rate of return, before the project is undertaken, would then have to be

$$\frac{G(1+g)}{(1-t)(1-r)} \tag{6.1}$$

Hence the risk, r, is the vital assessment factor in the project evaluation since the other three factors could normally be readily agreed.

Internal project risks come from items such as research and development success, time taken to complete a project, costs incurred, standard of work achieved, etc. These items of risk can, both individually and collectively be extremely important and the Anglo-French *Concorde* development saga over some twelve years provides an object lesson in this direction, and a pointer to the need to break a large project up into its components if effective risk control is to be achieved. In addition there are commonly substantial external project risks.

6.2   Environmental risk

Investment in the private sector occurs when a marketing opportunity is perceived and a way of meeting it profitably devised. The
opportunity may be an obvious one, as when equipment needs to be
replaced, or growth in the economy increases the demand for an existing
product. It may alternatively require the flair which sees a new possibility
for satisfying an existing need, as with package holidays; or which detects
a new mood in fashion, as with jeans; or notes a deeper social change, as
with convenience foods. Alternatively, it may rest on a new invention, as
with electronic pocket calculators. In all these situations an individual, or
group of individuals, feels they have found a need which their firm, or
possibly a new firm, can satisfy profitably.

Perceived industrial opportunities depend largely on what is happening
in the economy generally. Growth in the economy, changing consumer
preferences, the climate for labour relations and most technological
progress are exogenous, part of the external environment to which the
business reacts and which it does not fully control. In a world which is
changing rapidly and unpredictably the perception of opportunities for
investment is simultaneously more widespread and more difficult. There
is also much greater uncertainty about the returns to be expected from
taking such risks.

For a business to succeed, entrepreneurs require the ability to seize the
opportunities identified and avert the threats presented by the outside
world. They only do this successfully if their ideas suit the most important
element in the external environment, the market. Beyond changes in
consumer desires, the most obvious risks are technological and the
inevitability of being outdated by scientific advances increases steadily with
time. The UK machine tool industry in the 1960s and 1970s is an example
of a mature industry outdated by scientific advances.

With steady growth in the demand for existing products, most industrialists perceive the opportunity. If the consumers' buying habits are
changing, the trend may be misinterpreted, and investment misdirected.
With cyclical growth there is a fear that investment with its time lag will
come on-stream just as the market flattens off, or turns downward. If
Government policy on taxation and investment grants keeps changing, it
affects confidence in calculations of future cash flow, with the risk that
competitors entering later may be able to expand on more favourable
financial terms. If the rate of inflation is very volatile, there is no means
of calculating the real cost of that part of capital which is raised as debt,
and no certainty that future price controls may not affect profits to a level

where most of the after-tax profits are required merely to keep the substance of the business intact, with little left over for new capital investment.

Replacement investment is affected by the external environment as it usually involves replacing old machinery with more productive modern equipment, requiring less labour to produce the same output. Whether it will be worth installing depends on whether man hours can actually be reduced, or output increased to justify the existing labour force, and on any changes agreed in wage rates. Moreover, re-equipment often presents an opportunity for altering the range of products sold, and this too is conditioned by the market.

Finally, the decision to invest to satisfy any such identified needs depends heavily on the encouragement offered by the business environment generally. Evidence on this aspect commonly stresses tangible factors such as the availability of finance, the curbing of inflation, the reduction in public expenditure, and other aspects of the external environment. But it also includes intangibles such as the social esteem given to a successful business person.

Risk and uncertainty have effects beyond just their arithmetical probability. It would not be right for the management of a business on which a large number of people depended for their livelihood to invest in a project involving a considerable risk of bankruptcy, or of turning in results so poor that the business might no longer be able to obtain finance for investment, even if success could boost profits substantially. A large firm can, however, take big risks and withstand a high measure of uncertainty, provided that each individual risk, however considerable it may be in absolute terms, could not threaten the existence or the money-raising power of the firm. It is also conditional on different projects being sufficiently diversified to act as an insurance. The RB 211 engine development debacle of Rolls Royce in the late 1960s was an illustration of a situation where the probability of project failure was extremely small, but the loss when failure did occur was such as to threaten the firm's future. If a firm has ten substantial projects and each involves truly independent risks, the successful can pay for the unsuccessful and the firm may be able to hedge its bets effectively. But if the ten projects are dependent upon the same basic risk, so that if one project goes wrong they all do, then however big the firm it is basically in the same position as a small business with its future dependent on a single project. There have been some recent examples of this kind of danger. The Crown Agents in the early 1970s started to lend on property and subsequently suffered a bloody nose (which the taxpayer had to redeem). The subsequent enquiry concluded 'they drifted into acting on their own account without themselves properly appreciating what was involved, without adequately considering the risks and the reserves available to cover them... '. The collapse of Laker Airways in early 1982 was a further example of risk activity (such as currency fluctuations) being covered by loans rather than equity so that, when the risk occurred, the company found itself unable to redeem the loans.

The effect of tax is commonly said to reduce willingness to take risk, but this effect is in practice rather more complicated. For a project which is small in relation to the size of the firm and where any losses are therefore likely to be well below the profits generated from other activities, tax reduces the effective risk, because losses can be offset against profits elsewhere. In other words, the state is a partner for about one half of the risk even though it has not provided half of the capital. However, in so far as there are sufficient profits elsewhere in the business to permit taking a full depreciation allowance in the first year, or if the project attracts an investment grant or help under the Industry Act, a considerable part of the capital may effectively come from the state. While the small businessman is putting at risk his own money and the future of relatively few people, the board of a big business is using other people's money and may have to think of thousands of employees. Responsibilities of this sort must, and should, make for some measure of risk aversion.

The state can be a partner in the risks of the small business, but is quite likely to be a partner on whom it is not possible to draw, since there may not be sufficient profits elsewhere in the business to set off against the losses for tax if the project goes wrong. Indeed, if the project is of any size, it is equally unlikely that there will be sufficient profits in the rest of the business to permit taking full advantage of the 100% depreciation allowance against tax in the first year.

The small businessman is much more influenced by personal as well as corporate taxation. Risk-taking includes for him the possibility that, if the risk does not come off, he may lose his home or, in extremity, go bankrupt. To take such risks on board he needs the prospect of a high reward if he is successful.

Finally, there is political risk both at home and abroad. An investment may require taking a view up to fifteen years ahead, which in the UK covers at least three full Parliaments during which economic policy can well change several times. An isolated and disastrous political event abroad, such as the 1973 oil crisis or the 1979 Iranian revolution, can also occur. While these catastrophes may help particular firms (the Iran crisis certainly benefited some firms involved in North Sea oil), those making capital investments are bound to worry about the possibility of disasters that will harm them, rather than about the off-chance that something unexpected rebounds to their advantage. In Section 6.10 we look at some of the factors involved in political risks of this kind.

6.3   Project diversification

Chapter 8 discusses the issue of diversification of share portfolios showing how the investor can, through diversification, minimize the level of risk for any given level of expected gain. For shareholders in an active stock market it is unnecessary for the firm to diversify its risk activities; indeed diversification would, of itself, be unlikely to improve its share price. The motivation for diversifying within the firm primarily concerns risk to its management and employees, not to its shareholders.

In general there should be a higher expected rate of return from a project that contains an element of risk than for a risk-free project. Firms recognize this and commonly use a test discount rate (TDR) to determine which projects should go ahead, the minimum acceptable TDR being set somewhat higher than the risk-free rate of return (for example, the return on dated gilt-edged stock of the same length of time as the project). If the unbroken line in Figure 6.1 represents the relation between return and risk expected by the stock market, then to use the broken line as a single cut-off TDR for all projects that are not risk-free is erroneous since project A (indicated by a dot on the diagram) would be erroneously refused, while project B would be erroneously accepted.

It is important to consider the degree of risk, and a better approach is to base the test discount rate on the risk level of each individual project. This may be infeasible, however, as it would imply each project being examined in detail on its own and a TDR set to meet its individual circumstances. Many companies, therefore, adopt instead a general risk classification scheme. One such scheme classifies all projects into four

Figure 6.1. Capital market opportunities and the test discount rate

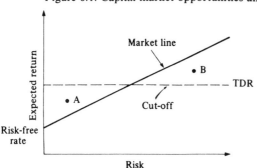

categories (A–D) according to their anticipated risk, the categories being broadly described as: fixed expense reduction, scale expansion, new products, research and development. A risk premium is assigned to each class and added to the appropriate after-tax interest rates as shown in Figure 6.2. The premia used are somewhat subjective, but endeavour to represent the past experience of the four types of risk in a typical industrial situation, although individual firms should formulate their own premia based upon their individual experiences. (For a fuller discussion see Broyles and Franks (1973).)

A portfolio of such risks, if we assume them to be independent of each other, can be diversified in the same way as can be done for a portfolio of stock market shares. The benefits to employees, suppliers and others will not beneficially affect shareholders who have available to them other forms of diversification that may be more effective. Indeed, if all firms diversified sufficiently within themselves to become 'average', then investors would be unable to construct a portfolio other than an average one with equal risk and equal expected value. Note that the criteria to be adopted for the risk classification should relate to systematic risk, i.e. that part of risk related to macro-economic uncertainties that cannot be diversified away by the firm. The risk premia to be used should thus be set by the central authority of the firm, not by the individual project manager, and reviewed from time to time.

Figure 6.2. Required rates of returns and risk classes

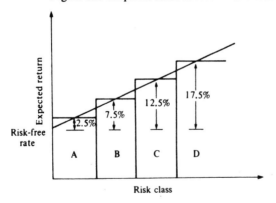

6.4   Risk profile

An alternative form of checking on the acceptability of a project can be made through the formation of a *risk profile* for the project. Under such an approach the decision maker first makes subjective probability assessments of those input variables which are important to the rate of return to be achieved by the project. These are then combined to derive a probability distribution for the achieved rate of return. The steps involved are:

(i) identify the key factors for the investment decision concerned;

(ii) obtain probability estimates in cumulative density function (CDF) form as in Chapter 3 for each key factor;

(iii) select by some random procedure a value for each of the key factors from the appropriate CDFs in step (ii);

(iv) calculate the return for the project corresponding to the value of the factors determined in step (iii);

(v) repeat steps (iii) and (iv) a large number of times and hence obtain a probability distribution for the project return.

The whole procedure is sometimes referred to as the *simulation* or *Monte Carlo* method. The procedure, and its business use, is described in more detail in Hertz (1964).

The decision maker can use the probability distribution determined in step (v) above to answer some of the typical questions that might be asked.

(*a*) What is the probability of making a loss? (i.e. a rate of return less than the risk-free cost of capital)

(*b*) What is the expected or mean rate of return? (i.e. the return that should be obtained on average)

(*c*) What is the probability of a rate of return greater than the appropriate test discount rate? (i.e. a rate of return greater than required rate of return for the appropriate risk class)

(*d*) How risky is the project? Is the variability or spread of returns large in relation to the mean?

Criteria (*a*) and (*b*) are of great importance to the company as these two figures encapsulate the risk alongside the expected return. For this reason risk analysis in this form is superior to the straightforward risk-class analysis which tends to ignore the variability factor inherent in each factor.

6.5 A legal decision

The risk examples quoted in this chapter have so far all related primarily to exploration, production or marketing or a combination thereof. A project risk of rather different context, although not of form, is described by Higgins (1982) and concerns a food company involved in litigation over a factory it had leased. The litigation arose partly because of possible extra costs for road access and partly because of construction deficiencies in the newly built warehouse. After efforts at an out-of-court settlement had proved nugatory, the company faced the prospect of either going to court or dropping each of the two contentious issues.

To evaluate the four options open to them, estimates had to be made of the costs involved in each option, the possible benefits and the probabilities of achieving those benefits. On the warehouse issue, by the time the final decision had to be made the contractor had paid into court a sum of £127500 and the lawyers estimated that the legal costs of a further hearing on this issue would be £25000. Lawyers are not accustomed to estimating probabilities but, with their help, the figures in Table 6.1 were drawn up. Because of the form in which the lawyers gave their probabilities, it was only possible to compute a maximum expected net benefit. Since, however, this was less than the amount that the contractor had already paid into court, the best solution seemed to be to settle out of court as quickly as possible, which was done. A similar form of analysis was used for the other issue.

Table 6.1. *Estimates of probabilities and benefits (costs)*

	Benefits		Costs		
Course of action	Proba-bility	Value	Proba-bility	Cost	Expected net benefit
Go to court on warehouse issue	0.05	£150000 −£225000	1.00	£25000	Maximum of £123250
	0.70	£130000 −£150000			
	0.05	£127500 −£130000			
	0.20	less than £127500			
Drop warehouse issue	1.00	£127500	—	—	£127500

6.6   Effects of incrementalism

The assessments of value (or utility) commonly made when considering projects are of changes or differences, rather than absolute final positions of the business. This method is widely practised in most large public and private organizations for it provides a means to cope with complexity and facilitates delegated decision making. Decision makers can then isolate the effects of the incremental change by examining *differences* in outcomes between the status quo (the 'do nothing' option) and the possible new situation that could be produced by adopting a new policy or alternative. Evaluation involves comparisons at the margin, and the value judgements are made, and conflicts resolved, at the margin. Comparison of the total terminal value of the business with one new alternative included, as against the status quo, is difficult and often impossible given the limits to human rationality and the costs of analysis. The general business position (status quo) therefore tends to be legitimized before analysis begins, and increments or decrements are estimated on the complete context in which an alternative would be embedded.

Ideally, the general business position (final end states) ought to be the criterion for the valuation of consequences. For this the reference point in the scale of wealth (i.e. assets) should be set to zero and not to the current wealth position (status quo). Decision analysts have advocated this principle. Organizational choice, however, is normally conducted in terms of differential effects on the current assets position which may lead to biases. Valuation depends on the context (i.e. current position) which forms the reference point for defining increments or decrements.

The danger of using incrementalism is that the delegated decision maker may effectively have a different utility function than that of the firm as a whole. Consider the simplified situation of a project which is generally agreed to have the following characteristics:

a profit of 2000 with probability 0.8, or
a loss of 1000 with probability 0.2.

The expected value, if the project were to go ahead, is $+1400$. The managing director of the firm would certainly accept such a project (if indeed such a project came up to him for decision) because such a project, in relation to the assets of the whole firm, would be in a region of its utility function that is effectively linear indicating that expected monetary value is an appropriate decision mechanism. The delegated decision maker, on the other hand, may well have a personal utility function that is somewhat concave which, on an expected utility basis, will lead him to reject the project (the concavity implying that he is more concerned with the possibility of loss than was the managing director). Hence incrementalism and zero-based approaches will not always coincide unless all decision makers in a business, whether delegated or not, are using the same utility function.

6.7 Small-business risks

Small businesses pose two kinds of risk problem. The first relates to the start-up problem, the second to the small company that already exists but which seeks funds to expand its scale of operations. Few new businesses have any substantial source of equity other than that provided by the proprietor himself, or his immediate family. Loan finance, as against specific security, may well be available from banks, but this is of little avail in situations where there are few assets to pledge, or where the new venture is not capital intensive in the conventional sense. The demise of Aunt Agatha, who in the past provided much of the equity for small local businesses, but now channels her savings through large financial institutions (possibly with tax advantages to herself) has left a gap. An alternative approach that has been much publicized recently is for innovators to try to persuade an established company to take up and develop their idea. The project then has a lower chance of failing through lack of financial backing or management expertise. Moreover, if it does fail, the cost can be offset against profits earned elsewhere in the enterprise, and the burden thereby effectively shared with the taxpayer. The difficulty with this approach is that individuals are naturally reluctant to allow others to benefit substantially from their ideas. They may also fear that an existing company will not commit the attention and drive to a project's development that they themselves would. Indeed, for many companies, management time is their major constraint anyway. The innovator is then thrown back upon himself and is caught between the need for capital on the one hand, and the reluctance to give up any substantial part of his equity rights on the other.

In the UK, new ventures are commonly unable to raise risk finance through a Stock Exchange listing because listed companies have to be able to demonstrate a record of success covering at least five years. An attempt to raise £3 million of equity from the public for a new company (Thermo-Skyships) in 1980 was an example of an attempt which failed, possibly because it had to be made outside the Stock Exchange mechanism. A further requirement for a wide spread of shareholders may also be a barrier. Issuing houses can, however, raise venture capital from their institutional and private clients for a new venture on the basis of a Companies Act Prospectus, and the Stock Exchange does allow shares in such companies to be dealt in under Rules 163 (2) and (3).

In addition to the institutional finance available in this way, there are specialist institutions who aim to provide venture or high-risk capital. Most of them are reluctant to invest in totally new ventures, demonstrated by the difficulties many small firms specializing in computer software or micro-electronics have experienced in generating funds. Of course, estimating the level or risk involved in any such venture is commonly a contentious issue. While the progenitor of the proposal may, not unnaturally, seek to minimize the risk involved, the potential lenders will be more cautious. Borrowers commonly complain that lending institutions often do not have – nor seek – the level of technical expertise to make realistic risk judgements in new areas of development in the way that they did for large-scale developments such as North Sea oil (discussed in the next section).

Virtually all institutions that specialize in providing high-risk finance, including those in the public sector, report regularly that they are not constrained by shortage of funds in supporting projects they regard as viable at the prevailing cost of capital. Of course, as they candidly accept, there may well be cases where their judgement of viability could turn out in retrospect to have been wrong. For this reason a plurality of institutions operating in this part of the market is desirable and to be encouraged. More could be done to reduce the risks attached to particular propositions by the institutions encouraging, or themselves implementing, greater research into the risks and hence the viability of the project. This might require institutions to re-appraise the amount and scope of industrial and technical expertise available to them, and for the specialized investment media to spread risks by diversifying their investments into a number of different projects within the same specialized area. It has been suggested (Wilson Committee Interim Report, 1979 b) that the formation of a Small-Firm Investment Company and a publicly underwritten loan guarantee scheme would provide two further means of encouraging the development of new enterprises. The former proposal has not been taken up, but the latter proposal has been.

6.8   High-risk projects

Companies prefer to finance risky projects out of retained earnings because it avoids the need to convince outsiders of the project's viability. A large established company with a proven track record is likely to have sufficient access to capital markets on the strength of its balance sheet to finance all reasonable propositions. Large companies are also more likely to have the experience and resources to take advantage of the various techniques for reducing risk including, for example, market and other forms of research (see Appendix C). Large companies may not, however, be particularly interested in small projects attached to high risks on the grounds that, even if successful, the absolute level of the cash returns would not be commensurate with the managerial time and skill absorbed by them. Again, when profits are low, companies are both less willing and less able to undertake risky projects.

Where the potential gain is sufficiently attractive, large-scale high-risk projects will still occasionally be undertaken by a company acting on its own. But the more usual pattern is for such projects to be undertaken through joint ventures with other companies. This has happened to a considerable extent with North Sea oil and in some European aerospace projects. Such ventures allow the pooling of expertise as well as the costs and risks. In some cases one company may contribute most of the expertise, while another puts up most of the finance. Clearly, in the event of success, profits will also be shared as there is always a cost to risk reduction.

The developments in the North Sea concerning the exploration and exploitation of oil reserves provide an illustration of a situation with high-level commercial risks. A full account of these risks and the way that they have been handled is given in the North Sea Oil research report of the Wilson Committee (1978).

The work involved in oil exploitation can be conveniently divided into two parts: exploration and appraisal, and development. Exploration is both risky and expensive. A single well costs over £3 million (in 1977 terms) to drill and the success rate is below 10%, although it was initially higher. By the end of 1977, some 600 exploration and appraisal wells had been sunk in the United Kingdom portion of the North Sea. Such drilling results basically in a *yes* or *no* outcome. Equity-type financing is therefore desirable, rather than loan or bank finance. This must either be raised directly from the market for such purposes or be provided out of a company's own resources. Most of the companies have obtained their exploration money from internal sources – retained profits akin to fresh equity financing – but approximately £100 million had been raised directly by 1977 through equity issues made for such purposes, spread over some eighteen companies. Initially this equity capital was provided mainly by institutional investors, but public issues later made a significant contribution. Smaller companies have commonly attempted to spread their risks by using their capital to participate in a number of consortia, and hence in a number of different drillings. Nevertheless, because the probability of success is low and variable, some financial participants have inevitably gained high rewards, while others have earned nothing.

Even when exploration has been successful and a decision has been made to proceed with development, substantial risks still remain. Such development risks can be divided into seven broad categories:

(a) *Reservoir risk*. The quantity of oil present in the reservoir is uncertain. Technical resources and expertise available for the evaluation of reservoirs reduces this risk, but reserves in more difficult geological formations cannot always be determined accurately.

(b) *Consortium period risk*. This risk occurs in two ways. The *first* is capital losses which can be substantial and inadequately covered by insurance. For example, the platform rig in the Frigg Field in the Norwegian sector sank while being towed into position, at a cost of around $85 million. *Second*, delays in completion have an immediate effect on cash flows.

(c) *Consortium structure risk*. Risks attach to the technical, managerial, and financial competence of the field operator, whether or not he is also the financial borrower. In a consortium, the capabilities of all its members must be considered as others would have to cover for an individual failure.

(d) *Product marketability risk*. North Sea crude oil is expensive to procure. It is priced at international crude levels, and attracts a premium because of its low sulphur content and relatively higher light end yield. The world price of crude oil is a key variable in evaluating the return.

(e) *Political and fiscal risk*. Investment in an oil-producing country involves exposure to fiscal risks. Governments of all the producing nations – including the UK – are constantly reconsidering their tax and control policies to ensure their domestic economy gains appropriate benefits from the development of a scarce natural resource.

(f) *Legal risk*. Legal problems in financing North Sea projects stem primarily from the mix of new legislation, the physical location of the fields outside territorial waters, and the body of historical case law built up to deal with some unusual situations.

(g) *Unforeseeable risks*. The residual class of risks includes some very low probability risks such as war, or disastrous accidents such as blow-outs, fires, or collisions. While these risks are in principle insurable, it is not necessarily easy to obtain suitable forms of cover at acceptable premia.

The experience of North Sea oil suggests that neither the size of the project, nor the magnitude of the technological risks, nor the period before which substantial profits can be expected are necessarily insuperable barriers to obtaining finance, provided the projects concerned are believed to have sufficient potential profitability. The exploitation of North Sea oil has presented risks that were technologically new to Britain, and on a relatively large scale in relation to the total economy. No substantive evidence has appeared of any significant handicap to development through lack of finance. Adequate risk capital, some of it provided through the Euromarkets, was available both to the companies engaged in exploration and development, and for those providing off-shore supplies and services. These latter companies were typically much smaller and presented even higher risks than the development companies. The risks involved were real, with several examples of financial failure within a generally successful picture. However, there were undoubtedly special factors operating in North Sea oil which would not necessarily be repeated in other sectors of the economy. For example, the extent of international involvement and the development of special in-house expertise by the banks and other financial institutions was justified by the magnitude of the overall financing operation required.

6.9   The creaming process

It is usual for exploration, whether it be for oil, gas, or minerals, to follow a form of creaming process that is common to all major companies engaged in these kinds of activities. In such a process the better apparent prospects are pursued first. The initial probabilities of success (and the size of the deposits found) are relatively high while, conversely, as time goes on, further exploration has a smaller chance of success and lower yields. Figure 6.3, adapted from Meisner and Demiren (1981), illustrates this effect for oil exploration in a Canadian province in the early 1970s. The horizontal axis represents the 220 oil wells sunk in chronological order, while the vertical axis gives the cumulative total yield from the oil wells in billions of barrels. The general declining trend in the size of the discoveries with advancing exploration in the province is clearly visible

Figure 6.3. Cumulative discoveries against number of exploration wells

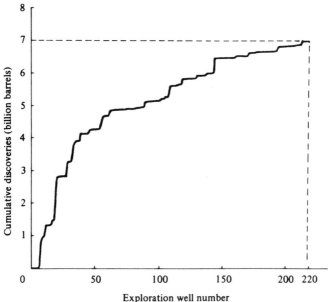

Exploration well number

from the shape of the step-graph. Figure 6.4 shows additionally how the probability of a successful drilling diminished as the rank order number of the drilling rose. The relationship has been plotted by taking successive groups of 10 drillings and calculating the proportion of successes among that group. The rate of success on this basis fell from about 0.4 to 0.15 over the 220 drillings. (The curve drawn through the points is of logistic form and has been fitted by the statistical principle of maximum likelihood.)

Methods have been suggested by Meisner and Demiren to project forward both the probability of success and the size of fields still awaiting discovery, using maximum likelihood estimates for the regression equations for the two variables concerned (success probability and size). This is an illustration of 'projecting' a collective forward and is akin to making trend projections of mortality rates over time.

6.10 International political risks

International operations such as exploration commonly involve serious political risks. Events in Iran provide a vivid reminder of this, while a paper by Jodice (1980) estimated that about 12% of all foreign capital investment made in 1967 was nationalized in the subsequent nine years. Assessing the risks of foreign direct investment there are first those elements specific to the project itself, many of which are comparable to those discussed earlier, and, secondly, the political risks of a more aggregate or countrywide nature. The latter can be grouped under three headings.

(a) *Domestic climate.* The variables considered here for risk assessment might include the levels of physical violence, the existence of

Figure 6.4. Decline of probability of success with advanced exploration

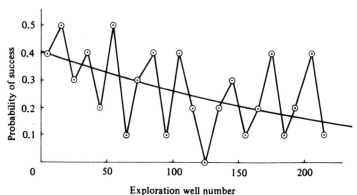

Exploration well number

extremist tendencies among political parties, and any recurring governmental crises.

(*b*) *Economic climate.* Major factors here are the likelihood of government intervention in the economy, the historical rate of inflation, the pattern of balance of payments deficits, external debt levels and the rate of gross fixed capital formation.

(*c*) *Foreign relations.* Some relevant factors are the size of the defence budget in relation to gross national product, any evidence of an arms race, and the incidence or otherwise of conflict with neighbours.

Most companies would aim for higher return on investment (ROI) the greater the political risks involved, and may indeed negotiate with governments to vary their tax policies on profits earned to reflect the incidence of such risks. Nevertheless companies will always be looking for risk-reduction measures in these kinds of situations, trying to combine risk reduction with increased political leverage (see Hoskins, 1970). Companies can do this in a number of ways: financing sought on a broad international basis rather than from a single country; joint-venture projects mounted with foreign companies or foreign nationals; joint-venture operations with local companies; or with local stockholders being encouraged to own a sizeable portion of the investment.

Substantial political risk with overseas investment does not necessarily imply an insurmountable obstacle to going ahead with a project. Although such risks can never be entirely eliminated, their systematic assessment and careful management can substantially reduce their impact. Hence, firms with a substantial overseas component should develop in-house expertise both to identify political risks and to be able to monitor and evaluate political developments, always making sure that current information is being fed to all decision makers concerned.

7
Risk and financial institutions

7.1   Types of financial institution

Financial institutions in the United Kingdom divide into three broad categories: (i) the deposit-taking institutions such as banks and building societies; (ii) institutions such as insurance companies and pension funds which collect and invest longer-term savings; and (iii) the specialized financing agencies, such as Finance for Industry and the National Enterprise Board.

The common feature of the first category is that they take deposits that are generally highly liquid, i.e. of a short-term nature, and use them to make loans or to acquire other assets with longer average maturities. In 1981 it was estimated that UK banks accounted for about 47% of all sterling assets of the financial institutions, a further 43% being held by building societies. The latter are mutual organizations whose prime function is to lend on mortgage for house purchase. Their loans are long term, commonly 25 years, although the average life of individual mortgage agreements in practice is only around seven years. The lending business of commercial banks is more broadly based, loans varying in size and terms from an overdraft of a few hundred pounds or less, to term loans of several hundred million pounds to multinational companies or sovereign governments for a number of years. A loan too large for one bank to take on can sometimes be provided by a number of banks acting as a syndicate.

A notable characteristic of insurance companies and pension funds is that the funds placed with them are for the most part contractual, so that the inflow of funds is relatively steady and predictable and the funds are placed generally for the long term. It is, however necessary to distinguish life from general insurance business, the latter being of a short-term nature with investments to match. Pension fund assets, once small in total, are

97

now approximately equal to those of insurance companies so that they have become a major force in capital markets.

The third group of financial institutions are special agencies that have been created to meet the needs of specific groups of borrowers – mostly industrial and commercial – not already adequately covered by other institutions. Such institutions exist in both the public and the private sectors. Some of the latter were set up with official support, but are financed by banks and other financial institutions, or by issuing securities on the market.

In this chapter the activities of the first two categories of institution are discussed, together with some of the key features of the main organized securities market – the Stock Exchange – followed by discussion of two particular forms of financial instrument: guaranteed loans for small businesses and the index-linked bond.

7.2 Clearing banks

British companies commonly have a gearing ratio of about 40 to 50% (where gearing is defined as the ratio of debt plus bank borrowings to shareholder interest in ordinary and preference shares plus revenue, capital and tax reserves, and minority shareholders interests). This figure is low by international standards, but this may be because equity markets are more important in the UK and the USA than elsewhere. It could be held to reflect undue caution but there is little hard evidence to substantiate this view. It is more likely that present-day levels of uncertainty tend to engender greater caution among industrialists and bankers alike. Although some term loans are now made, the overdraft is the traditional method of bank financing, a method designed to cover relatively risk-free activity, not risk capital for which equity (ordinary shares) is the appropriate channel.

Logically the rate of interest charged on a loan should consist of two parts: a rate for a risk-free loan plus a variable rate on top, dependent on the level of risk involved. There is little hard evidence available as to the precise way in which lending organizations relate the cost of lending to their assessment of the risks concerned. An examination of the accounts of American banks shows that their loss ratios (expressed as a percentage of the amount of money lost in a year) are around 0.5% per annum for commercial and industrial loans, and a little higher for personal loans. These figures vary slightly from year to year and from bank to bank, but the figures quoted appear to be representative. Only recently have data (summarized in Table 7.1) become available from British clearing banks. The average advance is taken as the average of the appropriate published end-year figures, and hence may not be precise daily average for the year.

Although overall the loss percentages are consistently around 0.25% each year, there is considerable variation between the four banks which persists across the four years. These ratios are the resultant of thousands of individual transactions, and are greatly affected if there are one or two large items of loss in any one year, which happened, for example, to the Midland Bank in 1981. The overall stability is, however, very marked and demonstrates a set of institutions that have clearly developed a means of controlling risk to an acceptably low level on a consistent basis. There are, of course, consequences in terms of lending foregone, lending which is presumably of lower quality, i.e. of higher risk. The figures are not available sub-divided between commercial and personal advances. Overall, the figures are comparable, but a shade lower, than for American banks.

An added piece of information concerning losses comes from the 30-year experience of Industrial and Commercial Finance Corporation (now an arm of Finance for Industry). The organization, which specializes in providing finance for particular risky types of activity for small businesses, has found that an average annual provision of 0.6% in their accounts has been sufficient to cover losses made.

If figures such as these are representative of the UK banking scene, it would seem to imply that banks have an average probability of total loss (or risk) of well under 1% on each individual advance on an annualized basis. This is presumably made up of a number of situations with very variable risks of loss such that the average annualized risk weighted by the size of the loss, works out at 0.0025. Furthermore, the interest rate charged would presumably be the rate appropriate to a risk-free investment (government or gilt-edged stock), plus around 0.25% on average for risk,

Table 7.1. *Loss ratios* (%) *in British clearing banks*

	1978	1979	1980	1981
Barclays	0.37	0.49	0.31	0.28
Lloyds	0.09	0.10	0.08	0.13
Midland	0.16	0.11	0.14	0.27
National Westminster	0.24	0.14	0.16	0.20
Overall	0.24	0.24	0.20	0.23
Total average advances (£ mill.)	47158	56895	66097	92091
Total write-offs (£ mill.)	115.2	136.3	135.3	211.5

plus an administration charge. The Industrial and Commercial Finance Corporation has confirmed in discussion that, once a proposal is accepted, the term offered are virtually the same and do not vary greatly with any perceived variations in risk among the accepted proposals.

Many margins are, it is true, higher than the 0.25% mentioned above and this is particularly the case with personal lending where the margin can rise as high as 12%. Banks have suggested, however, that a more normal range of risk margin is from ⅝ per cent (which would be regarded as rather on the low side) to about 4%, the latter being for small companies and persons. The margins are commonly linked to the category of borrower rather than to the particular project concerned. It would seem that the present high interest rates leave little scope for risk taking of an equity type which is really more suitable for many-risk ventures. (Dividends can only be paid from profits generated, so extremely high rates of profit are necessary to provide good dividends after payment of interest and capital on loans.)

Correspondence with Alan Gibb of the Durham University Business School suggests that, in the clearing bank sector, there is perceived to be little scope for taking higher risks compensated for by higher interest rate; the emphasis is on a low-risk profile which was confirmed by much of the evidence given to the Wilson Committee on financial institutions (1980). This may reflect the fixed nature of the return from a loan, unlike that on equity investments. Some lenders of loan capital are thus led to demand a share of the equity as part of the price for making a loan. A recent small business set-up was achieved with a £10000 loan from the founders, together with a £7500 loan at bank base rate plus 3% from a company that wanted to be associated, who in turn also demanded 41% of the nominal £100 equity. Banks were not prepared to lend without personal security as the company was in a service industry and would have few physical assets.

Many would-be borrowers are not willing to give up large slices of equity as a condition for a loan and do not proceed with their projects for this reason. Loan guarantee systems (see Section 7.8) could help with such a problem, but can still saddle an organization with debt and interest payments when it really needs a substantial equity injection.

7.3   Judgemental gates

The evidence suggests that the market does not assess risks and shade interest margins to correspond, but rather sets up some hurdle and only allows items assessed to be below that hurdle to receive funds.

To illustrate how such an approach operates, imagine a large set of projects (or proposals) being rated as to expected return by some analytical cum judgemental approach in advance, with the subsequent achieved rates of return being noted, assuming the funds to have been granted. The possible relationship between the assessed and actual returns is demonstrated in Figure 7.1. The vertical axis shows the achieved returns for the projects with the frequency distribution of returns laid on its side against that axis. Similarly the horizontal axis illustrates the frequency distribution of the prior judged rates of return that would be achieved for the same set of projects. The body of the diagram illustrates the inter-relationship.

Ideally the relationship between rating and outcome would be perfect falling along the line AB. A rating level could then be selected to guarantee that all projects over this rating would reach some corresponding actual return. (Or alternatively allow the terms of lending to be directly related to the anticipated return.) In practice, the line AB represents only the average rate of return achieved by all the projects rated at each level L, and there would be a distinct spread of actual returns about the line. This spread is indicated by the shading, the thicker shading representing the more common combinations of rating and outcome, the lighter shadings the less common combinations.

If C_0 represents the acceptable level of return that it is desired to achieve, then the judgemental criterion L_0 can be used as an appropriate cut-off point. The further the cut-off level L_0 is moved to the right, the greater

Figure 7.1. Relationship between judgement and return

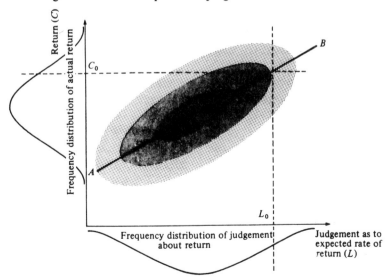

will be the chance that the achieved return exceeds C_0 and vice versa. On the other hand, the further L_0 is moved to the right, the fewer the projects allowed through the sieve and, as a consequence, the larger the number of projects turned down that would have exceeded the C_0 level if accepted.

The direct relationship between L and C could be improved through better forecasting techniques to dovetail interest rates more closely to risk and enhance overall achieved levels of return. This would be equivalent to concentrating the shading more closely around the line AB in Figure 7.1. If this could be done, it would be possible to choose, in the ultimate ideal situation, a cut-off level L_0 such that all investment projects whose achieved return would fall above C_0 can be isolated and accepted (or interest rates geared precisely to risk).

While the argument for the low-risk profile is primarily that the required interest rates would otherwise be too high to be acceptable to the borrower, the more likely reason is the difficulty lenders have in discriminating between a 1% risk situation and a 3% risk situation (say). The aim of the lender is to train himself first to recognize a risk situation, and then to recognize an acceptably low one; he does not feel able to discriminate between various shades of risks. Einham and Hogarth (1978) discuss how judgement can be re-inforcing: a waiter gives bad service and an inconvenient table to a young couple whom he thinks will tip poorly; when they do so it reinforces his view that young people tip poorly. The same can be true in the judgemental field of assessing risks and allocating resources.

7.4   Insurance and pension funds

These two types of fund are concerned with long-term investment. Pension schemes, moreover, commonly have benefits expressed in terms of

Table 7.2. *Distribution (%) of funds by market value, end 1980*

	Insurance companies (long-term funds)	Pension funds
British Government securities	27.2	21.4
Company securities		
loan and preference	3.8	2.0
ordinary shares	30.9	51.7
Property	22.9	17.6
Mortgages and loans	6.5	0.5
Other	8.7	6.8
Total	100.0	100.0

final salaries and a need for invested funds to achieve at least a rate of return (capital growth plus interest) equal to salary inflation. Table 7.2 gives the percentage distribution of the funds at the end of 1980 and shows broad similarities between the two types of institution. The three main categories of investment in each case are gilts (British Government securities), equities (ordinary shares) and property (either directly owned or through property company ownership). Generally speaking, the first category is taken up for high immediate income, the other two for growth in both dividends (or rent) and capital appreciation.

In the main, investment by these institutions is not primary in form, i.e. setting up and managing companies or financing individual projects, but rather through the secondary market by the purchase of existing stocks and shares, taking up rights issues etc. With the increased monies available for investment and the search for real growth, the proportion of total ordinary shares available in the market held by insurance companies and pension funds has risen rapidly (Table 7.3). This trend is known to be continuing and it is believed that the institutions now hold around half of all ordinary shares. As a consequence, many companies have the majority of their shares held by institutional investors. Furthermore there is a considerable concentration effect in that relatively few institutions hold the bulk of the assets. At the end of 1978 some 43 insurance companies had assets of over £200 million, accounting among them for 86% of all assets held by insurance companies. Similarly 56 pension funds had assets over £100 million at the same date, accounting among them for 69% of all assets held by such funds (for details see Wilson Committee (1980) Tables 3.45 and 3.49).

There are important consequences of this concentration of funds effect. The first is the increasing difficulty for funds to 'beat the market' because they themselves are the market. Secondly, many funds are managed by outside bodies such as merchant banks, stockbrokers, etc. This produces pressure to make regular valuations of returns and hence emphasizes the

Table 7.3. *Equity holdings (percentage of market value in issue)*

	1957	1963	1969	1975
Persons	66	54	47	37
Insurance/pension funds	12	16	21	33
Investment/unit trusts	6	11	12	14
Others	16	19	20	16
Total	100	100	100	100

(Based on Moyle (1971) and the 1975 HMSO survey)

notion of short-term, as opposed to long-term, maximization of returns. It may well be that long-term objectives and short-term results coalesce, but this seems unlikely to be more than an occasional coincidence. Assurance companies want to maintain competitive bonus rates on with-profits life assurance policies, and pension funds need to match wage inflation. The considerable increase in their holdings of investments in equities and property designed to achieve this growth has resulted in portfolio values becoming more volatile. This in turn creates difficulties in determining 'fair' bonus rates between the different generations of policy holders.

A more general problem, of a rather different kind, that arises is the role that financial institutions ought, as the legal owners, to play in managing and directing the affairs of the many major public companies that they now effectively own. In particular the balance to be maintained between growth and stability, between diversification and single product, between risk seeking and risk avoiding are all issues that the institutions will have to face as they become the ultimate owners.

7.5   Stock markets

The foregoing discussion highlights the position of the Stock Exchange in risk investment. All developed countries have securities markets, but the United Kingdom stock market is probably the most developed. The objectives of having such a regulated market include:

(*a*) facilitating saving and investment by providing a range of securities which borrowers may wish to issue and savers may wish to hold, thus creating a choice of ways of meeting the risk and other requirements of both borrower and saver;

(*b*) valuing securities so as to reflect consistently the returns expected from them, taking into account the risks which they involve for investors;

(*c*) applying pressure on management to use efficiently the resources already under their control.

Savers and borrowers have differing financial requirements. Some savers accumulate funds for the long term, others want their savings to be liquid. Most want their money to be safe, though some are prepared to take risks with part of it. Borrowers, on the other hand, usually want funds for a long period, and some risk of loss is normally unavoidable. The capital market aims to reconcile these differences and provide a range of instruments, which allows borrowers to tailor terms to the situation involved and investors to choose from a variety of risks and a variety of ways of hedging against them.

Debenture (fixed-term, fixed-interest) investments have become unpopular. The borrower wants high rates of interest to cover himself for actual or potential levels of inflation. The lender is reluctant to tie himself to high rates for a long period in case a delay means a fall in interest rates, which would give a competitor who waited a financial advantage. The cost of new equity capital for a company making an issue on the stock market combines the expected dividends in the immediate future with an allowance for prospective growth in dividends thereafter. In theory the combined cost is the same as that facing other companies after allowing for different degrees of riskiness. But companies rated by the market as having good growth prospects will face a lower cash flow burden in the form of dividend payments than other companies since a higher proportion of the return expected by the market will be in the form of capital gains and the dividend yield can be correspondingly lower. A poorly rated company may find the terms offered by the market expensive, and may not be prepared to raise funds in this way.

In general, price/earnings ratios appear to be poor predictors of subsequent earnings or dividend growth, and it is not clear that companies obtaining new funds from the market, for example through rights issues, are then able to achieve superior growth and results. Some critics use this feature as evidence of the stock market's inability to identify those companies which will employ scarce financial resources most effectively. Supporters of the market system contend that the price/earnings ratio could not in any case be expected to predict subsequent earnings or dividends, since risk and retentions also need to be taken into account. Successful companies are, indeed, often earning sufficient profits to enable additional investment to be financed internally, without calling on the stock market. Such fresh investment does not, however, stand the test of the market place and can reinforce low-yielding projects at the expense of the new higher-yielding investments.

Critics of stock markets have also argued that the new issue market does not supply firms with sufficient risk capital, and that the secondary market is over-active at the expense of the primary function of supplying new funds to industrial firms. The Stock Exchange emphasizes the need for an active secondary market if the primary market is to function effectively. Savers will only be prepared to place their funds at risk with firms if they know that they will be able to withdraw their money at a time of their choosing by selling their securities for a reasonable price on the secondary market. The secondary market confers liquidity on securities and keeps the return demanded by investors, and hence the cost of capital to firms, below what it would otherwise be. Furthermore, although new issues provide only a small part of companies' financial needs, the retention of profits, which is the major source of funds, is facilitated by the existence of a secondary market in that investors seeking to realize the gains corresponding to retained profits are able to sell their shares easily.

In recent years, stock market turnover in ordinary shares has been much higher than it was in the 1960s, while the new issue market has been less active. Sales of ordinary shares each year by the investing institutions as a percentage of the average value of their holdings rose from an annual average of 7% in the mid-1960s to 19% in the mid-1970s (see Figure 7.2). This paralleled a similar rise in the rate of turnover in ordinary shares on the stock market as a whole. The sales rates vary markedly between the different types of institution (from 13% for insurance companies on average in the period 1973–7 to 46% for unit trusts). Higher levels of turnover may be a reaction to the more unstable economic conditions of recent years making it desirable to adjust assessments of companies more frequently in the light of new information. In view of the long-term nature of many of the liabilities of financial institutions, it is questionable whether high levels of trading activity are compatible either with long-term investment performance, or an environment in which a healthy primary market can operate.

Figure 7.2. Sales activity in ordinary shares by investing institutions

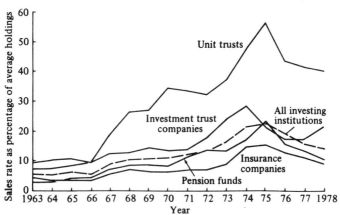

7.6   High-risk finance

Most high-risk investment is undertaken by established companies out of retained profits. Where retentions are insufficient, companies can go to the capital markets to augment their overall resources by a rights issue. Only in exceptional circumstances would such funds be earmarked for particular projects.

New companies are unable to raise risk finance through a Stock Exchange listing, but issuing houses can, however, raise capital for a new venture from their institutional and private clients on the basis of a Companies Act prospectus, and the Stock Exchange allows shares in such companies to be dealt with.

In addition there are specialist institutions whose main purpose is to provide venture or high-risk capital. Most, however, have maximum limits on the amount of capital they are prepared to provide in any single case. Since they are reluctant to invest in totally new company ventures, their services appeal mainly to existing small or medium-sized companies.

Assistance with the financing of high-risk investment is also available from the public sector. Interest relief grants, via the National Enterprise Board and the regional development agencies or, where the product or process involved is of a technological kind, from the National Research and Development Corporation are illustrative forms of assistance.

Broadly speaking, public sector involvement in this particular form of financing can be justified on three grounds. First, the private capital market may undervalue long-term innovations. This point can be exaggerated as there are many examples where such innovations have been developed through the private sector and the public sector's judgement of projects is not necessarily better.

Secondly, it is possible there are some risks which are too large to be borne by any one company, or even by a consortium of companies. This may typically be the case, for example, in large aerospace projects where the final market is uncertain and there are long delays before the project begins to pay back. A further example is the provision of performance bonds through the Export Corporation Guarantee Department.

Finally there may be some risks which the public interest requires to be taken but which the private sector is unlikely to undertake on its own. In principle the creation of new companies by the National Enterprise Board (NEB) in the micro-electronic and software fields falls into this category. Whether or not the NEB's judgement will be borne out by events in these particular cases has, of course, yet to be proved.

Although it is difficult to generalize about high-risk investment and its financing, some broad conclusions can be drawn. First, there are factors affecting all forms of investment. In periods of low profitability companies are less likely to have the balance sheet strength to wish to undertake such investment, or sufficient internally generated funds to finance it. Depressed equity prices make companies less willing to seek external finance, and make it more difficult for newer and unlisted companies to come to the market for the first time.

Second, most investment of whatever sort is undertaken by existing companies out of retentions, and new equity finance provided through the institutions is fairly marginal.

Third, the financial system seems to have particular difficulty in handling innovative projects developed by small firms, especially new firms.

Fourth, virtually all institutions specializing in providing high-risk finance, including those in the public sector, give repeated assurances that they are not in practice constrained by shortage of funds in supporting projects which they regard as viable at the prevailing cost of capital. Of course, as they candidly accept, there are cases where the institution's judgement of viability turns out to be wrong. For this reason a plurality of institutions operating in this part of the market is to be welcomed. Moreover, they could do more to reduce the risk attached to particular propositions put to them, for example by encouraging greater research into their viability. This might require reappraisal of the amount and scope of industrial and technical expertise which they employ, either in-house or from outside. Another possibility is the greater use of more specialized investment vehicles to spread the risks by diversifying their investments into a number of different projects within the same specialized area. The mining finance houses, a number of which were formed before and just after the First World War, are a classic example and the North Sea oil investment handling companies are in a similar mould. But the recent record of existing venture capital companies is not such as to suggest that any new institution is likely to find this to be a particularly profitable activity.

Fifth, the public sector already has in principle a range of financial avenues to help deal with particular types of exceptionally high-risk ventures if it chooses to use them. The Government could, however, do more to help firms wishing to undertake high-risk investment in other ways. The North Sea oil report for the Wilson Committee (see Chapter 6), for example, suggested that it was not finance which caused the major problems for firms anxious to break into the new markets; it was the problems of acquiring the relevant expertise, and of establishing sufficient credibility to gain their first major order.

7.7   Small-business finance

Small businesses provide a special example of the high-risk investment situation that has just been discussed. A regular supply of such businesses is generally accepted as a desirable goal for a healthy economy.

Many will die, but a reasonable proportion must flourish if the economy is to grow, or even maintain itself. In recent years, evidence has been deployed to show that, in the UK, the propensity for small firms to be founded and grow is below that of other developed countries such as USA, Germany or Japan.

In raising money to develop a small business an important factor has been the undoubted shift in attitudes towards risk taking that has occurred among the population at large, both employees and self-employed, in recent decades. The consequence is that while lenders, such as banks, commonly still insist on the traditional forms of security to small would-be entrepreneurs, the latter now seem less willing to give such security. Thus either funds are then sought from elsewhere, or the proposition is abandoned. This change in attitude has probably occurred because many self-employed individuals see a substantial measure of security in employment (pension schemes, redundancy payments, sick pay, etc.) while they are denied such benefits without adequate compensating expectations or rewards. Hence they feel it unreasonable to pledge private assets, such as their family house, which puts a possible penalty on their family that is not present for the employee. The possible loss of job and set-back to career is seen by the skilled entrepreneur as enough motivation in itself for one who may well be giving up a good career possibility in an established organization. Again, in an age of share schemes for employees it is essential that the legitimate desires, of both the entrepreneur and the financial backer, to hold substantial equity as a condition for a loan does not inhibit growth of a successful launch when further partners are required to assist in developing the business. A powerful motivational tool for a small company can easily be lost if equity is given away too readily at an early stage.

The UK Government has in recent years given specific forms of help to encourage small businesses, for example the business start-up scheme of 1981. This aimed to give special reliefs for equity investments made in new companies, but there are substantial restrictions as to who can obtain such relief for a particular company.

In a small or new business there are commonly insufficient retained profits to take advantage either of using them as a form of fresh equity, or as funds against which immediate depreciation can be obtained; hence there is a waiting period which could be alleviated to some extent by capital gains tax exemptions. Alternatively individuals could be allowed to invest tax free each year equity finance in small companies up to some limit, as is done under the 1978 *Loi Monory* in France. A third approach would be the development of tax-option corporations as in the United States whereby ten or fewer shareholders can elect to treat their company as a partnership, so that any losses incurred by the company are allocated pro rata to the shareholdings and can be offset against the earned income of the individual shareholders. A fourth approach is to relax the conditions for loan finance, which can be achieved by some form of provision of a system of loan guarantees.

7.8   Loan guarantees

The published experience of major lenders such as banks and Finance for Industry (FFI) shown earlier suggests that they seem to be working, possibly intuitively, on risk levels that lead to loss ratios of under 1%, a loss ratio reflected in the charge made for lending. If the judgemental criterion were relaxed (either by raising the acceptable risk level of the project itself, or by relaxing the security constraint, or by a combination of both) the interest rate charged would have to go up to accommodate the higher expected losses in the long run. If this surcharge were spread over all borrowers, as is the case in a number of schemes (for example, the Small Business Administration scheme in the USA) it raises the costs to all borrowers and implies a form of cross-subsidization. To restrict the surcharge to the extra borrowers a fine graduation of rates with assessed risk levels would be required. Because of the practical difficulties with such a system some form of government-backed loan guarantee has been mooted.

A government guarantee poses operational problems if the scheme is to provide a cost-effective addition to total lending, and not just replace the existing facilities. The vast majority of the lenders concerned are big enough to carry out their own internal insurance in relation to small lending, and the opportunity of sharing risks on an even larger scale with others is unlikely to induce any radical change of behaviour. Hence any scheme to encourage additionality would have to be underwritten in some way to be effective and a number of countries currently have schemes of this kind. Besides the USA scheme, for which the loss rate averages about 5% per annum, schemes also exist in the Netherlands and West Germany.

In the Netherlands entrepreneurs can borrow through the banks up to 80% of total funds required with a low level of security. The Government guarantee operates in a number of different ways according to the purpose of the loan. The charge is 3/16 of 1% per quarter (with some special arrangements for mortgages) and the losses over time have not exceeded the charges made. The responsibility for putting forward loans for guarantee is the bank's, not the borrower's.

For the West German scheme the maximum guarantee again covers 80%

of a loan, and the maximum loan is about £150000. Firms with turnovers exceeding about £1 million per annum are ineligible. The risks are shared between the bank, the guarantee association established in each state, and the Government which provides counter-guarantees to the association. An initial charge is made by the guarantee association of $\frac{3}{4}\%$ of the sum to be guaranteed and an annual charge at the same level on the amount outstanding. Indications are that the default level is about 1% per annum of guarantees given.

In both those countries there is a clear impression that additional worthwhile investment has been achieved, although no formal proof can be adduced.

In the UK it was not until April 1981 that the Government introduced a scheme, after extensive negotiations with the clearing banks. The essence of the scheme then launched is that the clearing banks (some seventeen banks and institutions have been included in the scheme to date) make the loan, but 80% is guaranteed by the Government for a fee of 3% to cover the possible losses. The banks charge whatever they consider appropriate for the loan, which has generally turned out to be in the range of $1\frac{1}{2}$ to $2\frac{1}{2}\%$ above the bank's base rate. There is thus no inbuilt Government subsidy as such in the scheme. The Government set aside a limit of £50 million for the first year guarantees but this was later increased to £150 million, with a further £150 million pledged for the second year (1982–3) of the scheme. The maximum loan that can be covered is £75000.

At the end of the first fifteen months of the scheme, some 4500 loans totalling £150 million had been made (an average of £33000 per loan) and, while this is small compared with the banks' routine lending activities, it has had a significant effect. About half has gone to new businesses, while the breakdown by types of business shows that about 60% went to manufacturing, the balance being equally split among retail trade and other service industries.

Four main ways of using the scheme are emerging. First, the loans are being used in place of equity. Secondly, the scheme is being used to enlarge the financial package, and thus give a business more chance to expand if it has already got off the ground. Thirdly, banks are relaxing to some extent their rules about commercial viability, managerial experience and product potential. Fourthly, small-business executives are trying to use it as a way of avoiding having to provide the personal guarantees required for other forms of financing.

The failure rate up to mid-1982 was about 7 to 10% in terms of both number of failures and amount lent. This was somewhat higher than the 3% guarantee fee built in the system and faced the Government with a problem when considering its support for 1983–4. It seems likely that the risk profile would be changed by making it slightly more difficult to get a loan: some personal security, a lowering of the 80% limit, or raising the premium. It seemed unlikely, however, that the scheme would be wound up because of the political consequences.

7.9   Index-linked bonds

Index linking of financial securities is not a new concept. It's main purpose has usually been to maintain capital market facilities of borrowers in the face of rapid inflation, particularly if the likely future rate of inflation is uncertain. There has been a mild form in the UK for some years with the National Savings Indexed Certificates and the SAYE (Save As You Earn) scheme. Other countries have, or have had, index linking in much wider forms, and have also used a wide range of indicators to provide the indexation. France has had a number of public sector issues linked to the price of various commodities or services. Examples are bonds linked to the price of 100 kilowatts of electricity, the cost of second-class railway travel, the price of coal, or even the 4.5% Giscard bond linked to the price of the 20 franc gold Napoleon (which has proved a winner to those who invested in it when initially issued). In Brazil, extensive corrections based on the wholesale price index are applied to tax debts, Treasury bonds, rents and mortgage contracts, balance-sheet figures, etc. In Israel nearly all bond issues, whether public or private, have been linked since about 1954 to either the cost-of-living index, or to the US dollar exchange rate. Such a straight linking has put tremendous pressure on the Israeli Government to keep the cost-of-living index down, for example by subsidies and artifically cheapened imports, and the weight of taxes has been placed on items excluded from the index.

Without any form of indexing, long-term fixed money stocks have become a gamble in a way that in the past was only applicable to equities; hence the reverse yield-gap. One consequence has been that such stocks with their high coupons are only issued by governments (industrial companies having effectively opted out) and are largely held by pension funds and life assurance offices (who have special tax positions vis-à-vis individuals). The existence of indexed bonds makes it feasible for pension schemes to index link pensions in payment, and for life assurance companies to offer index-linked policies, something that is effectively ruled out without them. The case for institutions to welcome them was eloquently made by Wilkie (1981).

While the lenders see the advantages of any such move, the borrowers are more cautious. Industrial finance directors fear that it might have an adverse effect on equity prices, with investors seeking to rearrange their portfolios to take advantage of the new opportunities. Furthermore, such borrowers are reluctant to accept the open-ended commitment involved in index-linked borrowing, even though it would have the advantage of easing cash flow problems in the early years of a project, when rather less money interest would be paid. The capital gains tax position for industrial and Government index-linked bonds would have to be equalized. Similarly house purchasers, through Building Societies, might be reluctant to accept index-linked borrowing, but be attracted by the low level of initial repayments. Above all, Government reaction in the UK has in the past been unenthusiastic, both towards the general availability of such bonds or for bonds linked to particular users, for example pension funds where the quid pro quo might be for the funds to buy a regular tranche of such bonds. Apart from the commonly advanced argument that such a move institutionalizes inflation, governments effectively feed on nominal values and fixed interest rates that are being eaten away by inflation. With the inflation of recent years, the total Government debt at market prices in real terms is actually diminishing, not rising. In 1966 Government debt was equivalent to about one year's gross domestic product (GDP). In 1979, despite the massive new issues of Government stocks in recent years, it was only about 60% of a year's GDP, as shown in Figure 7.3. If inflation were reduced to zero 'at a stroke' the total Government debt would rise by about

Figure 7.3. Public sector debt 1966–79

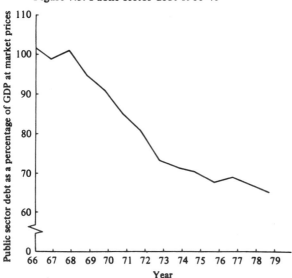

Year

8% per annum in real terms if borrowing continued at present levels. Thus, while the 'money illusion' still persists, governments may be tempted to see fixed money term securities as preferable to fixed real term securities. There are two other arguments in favour of indexed bonds that are not so commonly deployed. In the past the situation was that gilts were risk free in money terms, while equities had varying degrees of risk. But there have been awkward situations, such as the so-called gilts strike in 1974, when institutions, who sop up two-thirds of available gilts anyway, were accused of withholding funds to get better money terms because of the risks they perceived they were being asked to carry. If such a risk was removed, a more orderly form of market would emerge as long-term expectations in real terms do not suddenly change. Secondly, only a small part of the Government debt needs to be index linked and, from trial and error, terms could be pitched at an equivalent to unindexed debt. The risk preference of lenders could thus be ascertained and some investors would possibly pay a premium to avoid risk, with consequential benefit to the Government as lender.

In April 1981 the UK Government at last bowed to pressure and issued by tender £1 billion of 2% index-linked Treasury stock maturing in 1996. It was restricted to pension funds and the pension business of life assurance companies, who can both invest free of taxes.

The total amount tendered for was £1.6 billion, the 2800 tenders ranging from 80% to 200% of nominal value. The stock was allotted at £100, giving a real rate of interest of precisely 2%. The stock went rapidly to a discount with a price of 93 (at which the yield rose to 2.8%) but returned to nearly 100 shortly afterwards and has been as high as 106. The index used is the retail prices index (which has been used earlier for the so-called 'Granny Bonds' available initially only to those over retirement age). It could be argued that an index related to average earnings to accord closely with pension liabilities would be preferable. There are, however, difficulties in using a variety of indexes for different securities, although at one time it seemed possible that the British Government would issue oil bonds linked to an index of North Sea oil profits, without any money raised thereby being necessarily directly invested in the industry.

Subsequently the Government issued two further index-linked stocks, 2% 2006 and 2.5% 2011 before, in March 1982, opening index-linked stock to all holders and bringing out a further stock, 2% 1988, again by tender. The tender price was £97.5 per £100 nominal stock. The wider potential ownership should improve marketability and hold up the value of these stocks.

The emergence of such stocks makes the investment managers' task harder as they must now demonstrate that they can outperform them in real terms. For example, the equities all-share index showed a 2.1% per annum real rate of return over the two decades 1962–82. Index-linked gilts show that rate of return on a guaranteed basis. While fund managers have not rushed to purchase the stocks, they have been put on notice as to the minimum expected of them in the future!

8
Risk and portfolio investment

8.1   Introduction

In recent years a great deal of theoretical and empirical work has been published on the movements of equity share prices. This reflects the considerable interest currently being shown in the formation and performance of investment portfolios, particularly with regard to their equity (share) content. Controlling a portfolio is essentially a matter of making buy-and-sell decisions and, since portfolio managers must be interested in future performance, information about future prospects is needed. Newspapers and stockbrokers commonly give only limited help with enigmatic statements such as '... the market for electrical shares could be up 25% within the year, or even more if inflation moderates. On the other hand it could...'

An analyst faced with this portfolio management problem would doubtless start by analysing the past variability of shares. Of course, there is no guarantee that the future mirrors the past, but it is reasonable to assume that a portfolio composed of shares with histories of high variability will also have a less predictable future performance than a portfolio of shares whose past performance has been more stable. The basic concept in portfolio management theory is that some shares are consistently more volatile or variable than other shares. The more variable the company's shares, the riskier is that share.

8.2   Share variability

The monthly fluctuations in price over four years for a share that is generally regarded by analysts as having high risk (Paterson Zochonis) and one that is similarly regarded as having low risk (British American Tobacco) are shown in Figure 8.1. The values have been adjusted to a common starting price of 100, with all dividends re-invested. The visual

116

impression of price changes is one of high volatility for the former share and low volatility for the latter share, although in both instances these variations appear to be superimposed on a more general longer-term movement.

To calculate a measure for risk either for a particular share or for a class of investment (for example, equities, also known as common stock), or for a collection of investments held by an institution or individual, the variability of the return over a series of consecutive periods of time can be examined. A good surrogate for this variability is the statistical measure of standard deviation. Table 8.1 shows this measure for ten United States common stocks over the five-year period 1974–8. The calculations were made by Merrill Lynch on monthly rates of return (some 60 returns over the five-year period) and the monthly variance (variance is the square of the standard deviation) converted to an annual variance by multiplying by 12. The standard deviations given are then expressed as percentages per year. This method of conversion assumes that successive monthly returns are statistically independent. Kendall (1953) has examined the behaviour of

Figure 8.1. High-volatility and low-volatility shares

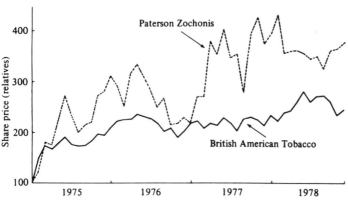

Table 8.1. *Standard deviations of common stock returns 1974–8*

Company	Standard deviation	Company	Standard deviation
AT & T	13.7	Consat	32.3
IBM	22.7	Digital Equipment	35.9
Eastman Kodak	28.8	Polaroid	49.7
General Motors	22.4	Chrysler	43.6
US Steel	29.1	Kaiser Steel	43.5

weekly changes in nineteen indices of British industrial share prices and in spot prices for cotton (New York) and wheat (Chicago). After extensive analysis of serial correlations he suggests: 'The series looks like a wandering one, almost as if once a week the Demon of Chance drew a random number from a symmetrical population of fixed dispersion and added it to the current price to determine the next week's price.' His research has been replicated by other workers suggesting that the statistical independence argument is well founded.

The shares in the left hand column are 'blue chips' relating to large well-established companies; those in the right hand column are for smaller firms in the same industries. The standard deviations seem quite large, and most of the shares are substantially more variable than would be the case if a portfolio made up of the stock market as a whole were examined. This may seem surprising at first sight in that the variability of the market might be expected to equal the average variability of the component equities. The reason lies, however, in the concept of diversification.

8.3   Portfolio diversification

A first step in examining the diversification effect in portfolios is to examine the characteristics of hypothetical portfolios formed with varying numbers of shares. For this purpose three simplifying assumptions are made. First, all holdings in the portfolio are assumed to be of equal (monetary) size. Second, all holdings are assumed to be equally risky in the sense described in the previous section. Third, the risks of each pair of holdings in the portfolio are assumed to be mutually independent.

An examination of price changes in recent years shows that, on average, about 30% of the price movement of a share has been contingent on what has been happening to the market as a whole. Of course, any two shares selected from the same industry group of shares would have had considerably more in common than just this 30%. However, since the object of the hypothetical portfolio is to measure the maximum effect that diversification can reasonably be expected to have, it will be assumed that such duplication is never necessary in a portfolio, and that the shares in the portfolio have only the market influence in common.

The maximum theoretical benefits from diversification are secured with a portfolio composed of an infinitely large number of holdings. If the only relationship between any two holdings in a portfolio lies in the fact that 30% of each share's prospects is contingent on the behaviour of the market, then mathematical calculations on the assumptions given above show that no amount of diversification can reduce the risk, or standard deviation of possible returns, below 74% of that of a one-share portfolio.

Not only is the potential total benefit from diversification limited, as shown in column 2 of Table 8.2, but a large part of this potential can be realized with a portfolio of relatively few shares. This is demonstrated in column 3 where the reduction is expressed as a percentage of the total potential reduction with an infinite portfolio. A portfolio of ten shares provides 88.5% of the possible advantages of infinite diversification; one of twenty shares provides 94.2% of these advantages; etc.

Column 4 expresses these results in a different form by giving the percentage reduction in risk contributed by the addition of the last holding. Thus, the effect of going from a nine-share to a ten-share portfolio is a fall in risk of only 0.4%. The diversification policies of some European funds with their large range of holdings look somewhat suspect in the light of the figures shown towards the bottom of this column. These theoretical results have been mirrored by practical experiments conducted on the behaviour of share markets. Wagner and Lau (1971) constructed portfolios of differing size from samples of US shares and then calculated the standard deviations of returns from each end of these portfolios.

The risk that can potentially be eliminated by diversification is called *unique risk*. This risk stems from the fact that many of the perils that surround an individual company are peculiar to that company and perhaps

Table 8.2. *A theoretical portfolio diversification*

No. of holdings	Risk as percentage of one-share portfolio	Reduction in risk as percentage of potential reduction	Change in risk of last holding (%)
2	88.0	46.3	−12.0
3	83.6	63.2	−5.0
4	81.3	72.0	−2.7
5	79.9	77.4	−1.7
6	78.9	81.0	−1.2
7	78.3	83.7	−0.9
8	77.7	85.7	−0.7
9	77.3	87.2	−0.5
10	77.0	88.5	−0.4
12	76.5	90.4	−0.3
14	76.2	91.7	−0.2
16	75.9	92.7	−0.2
18	75.7	93.5	−0.1
20	75.5	94.2	−0.1
30	75.0	96.1	−0.05
50	74.6	97.7	−0.02
100	74.3	98.8	−0.004
500	74.07	99.8	−0.0002
1000	74.04	99.9	−0.00004
2000	74.02	99.94	−0.00001

its immediate competitors. The other element of risk that cannot be eliminated, however much diversification takes place, is generally known as *market risk*. This risk stems from the economy-wide perils which threaten all businesses, explaining why shares tend to move together and investors are exposed to market uncertainties no matter how many equities they may hold.

In Figure 8.2 the risk has been sub-divided into these two parts: unique risk and market risk. For a reasonably well-diversified portfolio, only market risk matters. Therefore the predominant source of uncertainty for a diversified investor is that the market will rise or fall, carrying the investor's portfolio with it.

8.4   Portfolio risk

When there are only two shares in a portfolio, the variance of the expected portfolio return is given by the formula

$$x_1{}^2\sigma_1{}^2 + x_2{}^2\sigma_2{}^2 + 2x_1x_2\sigma_1\sigma_2\rho_{12} \tag{8.1}$$

where x_1 and x_2 are the proportions of the portfolio in shares 1 and 2 respectively, σ_1 and σ_2 are the standard deviations of the rate of return for each share, and ρ_{12} is the coefficient of correlation between the returns for share 1 and those for share 2. This formula can be generalized for a portfolio of n shares in the form

$$\sum_{i=1}^{n} \sum_{j=1}^{n} x_i x_j \sigma_i \sigma_j \rho_{ij} \tag{8.2}$$

where $\rho_{ii} = 1$.

As more shares are added to the portfolio the covariances become more important since the number of terms in expression (8.2) rises with the

Figure 8.2. Diversification versus risk

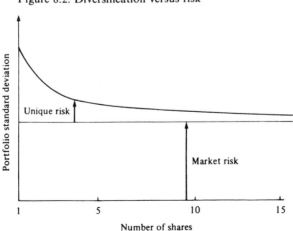

Number of shares

square of n, although the terms not involving ρ_{ij} only rise linearly. Thus the variability of a highly diversified portfolio reflects mainly the covariances. If the covariance (the term used to describe the expression $\sigma_i\sigma_j\rho_{ij}$) average were zero, it would be possible to eliminate all the risk by holding sufficient shares. Unfortunately shares move together, not independently. Thus most of the shares that the investor can actually buy are tied together in a web of positive covariances which set the limits to diversification. It is the average covariance that constitutes the bedrock of risk remaining after diversification has done its work.

Investors are concerned with the effect each new share that they consider holding would have on the risk of their total portfolio. The risk of a well-diversified portfolio depends in turn upon the market risk of the securities included in the portfolio. To understand the contribution of an individual security to the risk of a well-diversified portfolio it is not adequate to consider merely the risk of each particular security held in isolation; it is necessary to know its market movements. The sensitivity of a security's return to market movements is generally referred to as its beta (β) factor. The average beta of all securities in the market is, by definition, 1.0.

The standard deviation of the return on a well-diversified portfolio, whose overall beta value is 1.5, is 1.5 times that of the total market portfolio; while if it has an overall beta of only 0.8 its standard deviation of return is 0.8 times that of the market portfolio. This can be important in terms of bull (rising) markets, or bear (falling) markets as demonstrated in Figure 8.3 where the relative performances of two portfolios, one high beta and one low beta, are charted over the course of 1975 and 1976

Figure 8.3. Returns from high-beta and low-beta portfolios

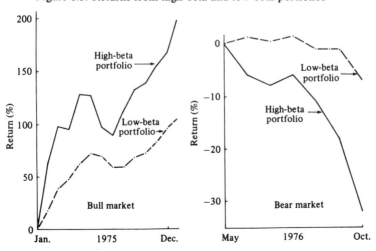

respectively when the market moved in opposite directions. The portfolios were constructed by taking the 10% of shares with either the highest or lowest beta values on the UK stock market as measured over the previous five years. The different performances of the two types of portfolio are evident: the high-beta portfolio rises and falls more rapidly with market changes than does the low-beta portfolio.

If a portfolio consists of n different securities the proportionate contribution of the jth security to the overall risk of the portfolio is given by the expression

$$x_j \sigma_{jm}/\sigma_m^2 \qquad (8.3)$$

where σ_{jm} is the correlation of the jth security with the market portfolio, σ_m^2 is the variance of the market, and x_j is the proportion by value of the portfolio in share j.

While diversification makes sense for individual investors, it is not automatically true that it is the best course of action for a commercial firm to follow. If investors were unable to hold a large number of securities they might reasonably want firms to diversify for them. But investors are well able to diversify by their choice of shares to hold. In many ways they can do so more easily than a firm, and can also switch their financial investments more readily than is possible for a firm to switch its capital investments. Thus if investors can diversify on their own account, there is no reason why they should pay extra to purchase the shares of firms that diversify within themselves. Hence, in countries like the UK with its large, competitive and comprehensive capital market, diversification within a firm neither adds nor subtracts from a firm's value; the value remains the sum of the constituent parts. The reasons for diversification are thus not related to an investment point of view of the company, but are commonly due to other reasons such as continuity of employment or the long term future of the company itself.

8.5   Portfolio theory

The fundamental work on portfolio theory emanates from Markowitz (1952) and Sharpe (1964). When shares are combined, not necessarily in equal proportions, not only is a weighted expected return obtained, but also a weighted risk or beta factor.

Consider first a portfolio consisting of only two shares as follows:

Share	1	2
Expected return (%)	15	20
Standard deviation	20	30
Correlation (ρ_{12})		0.3

The expected return from a mixture (x_1 of equity 1 and x_2 of equity 2) is given by

$$15x_1 + 20x_2 \quad \text{with} \quad x_1 + x_2 = 1$$

while the standard deviation of the return will be given by equation (8.1). The results are shown in Table 8.3 where it should be remembered that x_2 is equal to $1 - x_1$. The surprising thing about the results is that, by starting from a portfolio of equity 1 alone, it is possible both to increase expected return and to diminish the risk – but only marginally. Nevertheless, it is possible to make quite large improvements in expected return for a relatively low increase in risk. The combination that best suits a particular investor will depend upon his attitude towards risk.

In practice the investor is not confined to investing in only two securities, and Figure 8.4 shows what happens when there is a large choice of securities. Each cross represents the combination of risk and return offered by a different individual security. By mixing these securities in different proportions reductions in risk can be achieved with an even wider selection of risk/expected return combinations. The range of attainable

Table 8.3. *Expected returns and standard deviations of mixed portfolios*

x_1	Expected return (%)	Standard deviation (%)
0	20	30.0
0.2	19	25.5
0.4	18	24.0
0.6	17	19.3
0.8	16	18.7
1.0	15	20.0

Figure 8.4. Risks from mixtures of equities

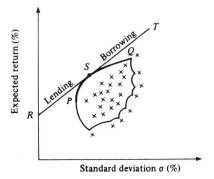

combinations might look something like the broken-egg-shaped enclosed area in Figure 8.4. Since the usual aim is to increase expected return and reduce standard deviation, interest will be confined to portfolios that lie along the heavy black line PQ as these minimize risk (standard deviation) for any given level of expected return. Markowitz called portfolios that fall on this line *efficient portfolios*.

The choice between portfolio P (low risk, low expected return) or Q (high risk, high expected return) or somewhere in between, depends upon the investor's attitude towards risk. The optimal portfolio deploys a fixed amount of capital to give the highest possible expected return for a fixed standard deviation, (or possibly for a fixed ratio of expected return to standard deviation). In principle the optimal portfolio can be found by trial and error, but it can also be structured as a quadratic programming problem (see, for example, Wagner, 1969) and standard computer pro-grammes then used to find the optimal solution.

The portfolio determined in the preceding section could be fruitfully augmented if it is possible to borrow or lend at some risk-free rate of interest (for example, through Government stock or Treasury bills). Under this scenario it is possible to produce a series of portfolios that lie along the line RST, where R corresponds to the risk-free rate of interest obtainable and the line RST is the tangent to the arc PQ, touching it at the point S. If money is lent (invested) at the risk-free rate, the portfolios obtained are in the portion RS (i.e. lower returns than at S but lower risk) while, in the portion beyond S, money is borrowed and invested in the portfolio to give higher return and higher risk, but the risk is lower than could have otherwise been obtained from any share portfolio with that particular expected return.

This interesting possibility shows that the investor's task is essentially twofold: first, to choose the best portfolio of shares S and, second, to blend it with risk-free investment so as to give the required balance of expected return and risk.

8.6   Capital assets pricing model

Investors in shares require a higher expected return from an investment in the market portfolio than from Treasury bills or other forms of gilt-edged securities. The difference between the two returns is referred to as the *market risk premium*. Over the past 50 years in the USA the average market premium has been 8.8% per year, and the UK situation has been little different. Figure 8.5 plots the risk and return from Treasury bills and shares to give two benchmarks for the expected risk premium, where r_f is the risk-free rate of return and r_m the market portfolio rate of return. The principle of the capital asset pricing model (CAPM) is that, in a competitive market, the expected risk premium varies in direct proportion to beta. Thus all investments should lie along the sloping line in Figure 8.5 and

> Expected risk premium on equity j = beta × expected risk premium on market

or

$$r_j - r_f = \beta_j(r_m - r_f) \tag{8.4}$$

The expected risk premium $r - r_f$ of a portfolio that has a proportion k in the market equity portfolio and a proportion $(1-k)$ in risk-free Treasury bills will be

$$k(r_m - r_f) + (1 - k) \times 0$$

and hence

$$r - r_f = k(r_m - r_f)$$

But, since the beta of the portfolio must be equal to k, the proportion in the market equity portfolio, it is also true that

$$r - r_j = \beta(r_m - r_f) \tag{8.5}$$

Then the required risk premium on any investment is $\beta(r_m - r_f)$, where β is applicable to the equity under consideration. In well-functioning stock markets nobody would hold a share that offers an expected risk premium less than $\beta(r_m - r_f)$. Now the beta for all equities is 1.0. Since equities on

Figure 8.5. Relationships between expected return and beta

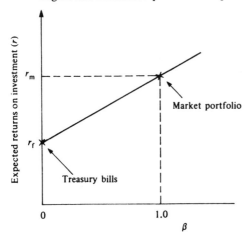

average offer an expected risk premium of $(r_m - r_f)$ and none should offer a return lower than $\beta(r_m - r_f)$, there cannot be any that offer a higher return than $\beta(r_m - r_f)$ or else the market figure would be higher than 1.0.

Any economic model is, to a greater or lesser extent, a simplified statement of reality. The CAPM captures three main principles within it. First, investors require extra return for extra risk. This is why equities have on average in the past given a higher return than Treasury bills. Second, investors are critically concerned with risks that they cannot diversify away. Third, the CAPM assumes that the expected returns on any security can be expressed in terms of two benchmark securities, although this is only true if investors are content to describe an equity's prospects by the two numbers: expected return and the standard deviation of return.

In putting together the model it has effectively been assumed that

(a) each investor acts on the basis of predictions about the future performance of eligible securities,

(b) each investor selects an efficient portfolio,

(c) each investor can borrow or lend at a defined rate of interest (same for borrowing or lending),

(d) investors have the same set of predictions,

(e) transaction costs and taxation are negligible.

8.7   Some empirical verification

The CAPM is concerned with expected returns, whereas only actual returns can be observed. Fama and Macbeth (1973) studied the relation between expected and actual returns on the New York Stock Exchange by grouping all equities into 20 portfolios. They then plotted the estimated beta of each portfolio in one ten-year period against the portfolio's average return over a subsequent five-year period. This was repeated for six different periods. If the principle of CAPM is correct, investors would have expected these portfolios to have performed no better or worse than a comparable package of Treasury bills and the market portfolio. Hence the portfolios should lie along the line in Figure 8.5 joining the risk-free rate of return (with a beta of zero) to the market rate of return (with a beta of 1.0). The actual rates of return do plot approximately, but not exactly, along such a line for each of the six periods. This result is encouraging but it would be helpful if the reasons for the discrepancies could be pin-pointed.

The second area where some verification is required relates to the stability of the betas, on which an extensive study was made by Sharpe and Cooper (1972). Shares were divided into ten classes according to the estimated beta in a base five-year period. Each class contained one-tenth of the equities in the sample. The equities with the lowest beta went into class 1, the next lowest in class 2 and so on. They then looked at the frequency with which equities jumped from one class to another in subsequent periods of five years: the more jumps, the less the stability. The results showed that equities with very high or very low betas tended to stay that way; but about 30% of equities changed by more than one class in a subsequent five-year period.

One reason why these estimates of beta are only imperfect guides to the future may be that equities genuinely change their market risk. But it could be an illusory effect in that the betas are only statistical estimates based on limited past data. Thus changes may not be real but a function of imperfect initial estimation, so that the stability of true betas is probably better than implied by Sharpe and Cooper's results.

Because of interest by the investment community in market risk, a number of organizations offer estimates of betas for quoted shares on a regular basis. The London Business School, for example, has a Risk Measurement Service which makes such beta estimates available to subscribers on a regular basis.

8.8 International investment

International diversification is a simple extension of the principle involved in domestic diversification. Most of the benefits of diversification can be captured within a domestic market by as few as ten shares. If a foreign stock market does not move perfectly in line with the UK stock market, then the domestic risk can be further reduced by international diversification.

The extent of the international risk reduction achieveable depends on the degree of correlation between the returns in the various markets. The correlations will be less than 1.0, since the various market portfolios represent claims on different underlying real economies with industrial structures that are subject to varying national, political and economic effects. However, these correlations are likely to be relatively large since there are numerous economic and political events that have general international ramifications. Moreover, a significant proportion of every national equity market portfolio includes claims on the foreign activities of multinational firms based in that country.

It is possible to get an approximate idea of the scope for international diversification by looking at the correlation coefficients for movements in

various national markets with that of the UK. Figures for the period 1972–9
are as follows:

Australia	0.35	France	0.37	Netherlands	0.03
Belgium	0.38	Germany	0.20	S. Africa	−0.09
Canada	0.25	Italy	0.27	Switzerland	0.36
Denmark	0.12	Japan	0.11	USA	0.35

The risk reduction potential implied by these correlations is substantial.
Experiments described by Dimson, Hodges and Marsh (1980) examined
the simple strategy of splitting available funds equally among a number
of countries. With one country the minimum risk factor achievable was
29%, with five countries it was 14.5%, with ten countries it was just over
13%. Hence including overseas shares in a portfolio enables risk to be
substantially lowered, although the figure of 13% appears to be the limit
for a 'world portfolio'.

8.9   Commentary

The study of portfolio risk made here raises a number of issues.
Portfolios that rise faster than the market will generally be found to hold
high beta shares and hence, if a fall occurs, will plunge much more sharply
than the market. This has implications for those seeking to make short-term
judgements on portfolio performance. For example, monitoring systems
for pension funds commonly put strong emphasis on short-term performance, whereas they ought to consider the return achieved against the risk
assumed, and to be clear about the long-term risk attitudes.

Secondly, the analysis throws doubt upon the commonly assumed
identity of objectives between employees and shareholders. Most governments have schemes to encourage employees to own shares in their own
companies. But the employees of a firm cannot generally diversify their
risks in the way that can be done by the general body of shareholders. The
latter may not be unduly concerned if the company takes on unique high
risks, but the employees will be rather more concerned. Hence employees
may well want the firm to diversify the risks in ways which run counter
to the shareholder's perceived interests.

A number of writers do not accept the validity of the portfolio model
put forward in this chapter. For example, Clarkson (1981) argues that risk
assessments based on past prices alone are unrealistic, and the lack of
evidence that investors currently select portfolios on the basis of the
expected returns and their standard deviations, invalidates the approach.
However, such writers invariably put forward alternative procedures,
sometimes of considerable complexity, that inherently contain a greater

degree of subjectivity than the approach outlined here. CAPM endeavours to reduce the area of subjectivity required and to increase the effectiveness of portfolio management. Investment management is a highly competitive activity and any new approach will only flourish in the long term if its results can be shown to be superior. While the methods of the CAPM are much used, tested and accepted in the USA, they are currently only used to a limited extent in the UK.

9
Gambling and speculation

9.1 Gambling scenarios

George Bernard Shaw once remarked of gambling that many lose so that few can win. Basically gambling is a system whereby money is re-cycled among the gamblers, usually with a banker or bookmaker or owner taking a 'cut' of the re-cycled turnover. Normally the cut is virtually certain, and it is the gamblers as a whole who suffer a corresponding loss. Three examples show the basic characteristics of gambling schemes.

The first relates to the one-armed bandit or fruit (slot) machine. A typical basic fruit machine (nowadays a massive array of more complicated forms are available) has three dials each with 20 symbols, the symbols being of six types (commonly different fruits). There are thus $20 \times 20 \times 20$ or 8000 different positions in which the dials may come to rest. The various fruits appear with differing frequencies on the dials, and prizes are awarded for some, but by no means all, the different combinations that can appear.

Table 9.1a. *Arrangement of fruits on dials of a typical fruit machine*

	Number on		
	Dial 1	Dial 2	Dial 3
Cherries	7	7	0
Oranges	3	6	7
Lemons	3	0	4
Plums	5	1	5
Bells	1	3	3
Bars	1	3	1
	20	20	20

Tables 9.1*a* and *b* give a typical set of dials, the winning combinations, and prizes awarded in units of 10 pence, the coin required for each entry. Thus Plum, Plum, Plum receives £1.40 for a £0.1 stake. The 'payoff' for the various winning combinations is built into the machine, and the average number of occurrences of each winning combination per 8000 trials can be straightforwardly calculated from the basic rules of probability. Table 9.1*b* shows that on average £588.80 will be returned for each £800 inserted (i.e. 8000 units of £0.1), a return of about 74%. The banker, or machine owner in this instance, keeps the other 26%. Of course, there may be runs where the machine pays out more than the average, or runs where it pays out less but, taken over a long period, the average cut to the owner is precisely predictable.

The second example is that of the staple casino game, roulette. (Fielding (1977) gives a full historical discussion of the development of the game.) It is gambling in that it involves placing something of value (i.e. money) at risk in relation to an uncertain outcome. To the extent that the outcomes are determined at random subject to the laws of probability, it is a game of pure chance. Random in this sense implies that no information about past plays and their outcomes is of any use in predicting future outcomes. For illustration we concentrate upon just two of the many types of bet that can be made in the usual 37 compartment game, the slots being numbered

Table 9.1*b*. *Prize-winning combinations on a typical fruit machine*

Paying permutation			Payoff	Average number of occurrences per 8000 trials	Average total paid out per 8000 trials
Bar (Jackpot)	Bar	Bar	62	3	186
Bell	Bell	Bell	18	9	162
Bell	Bell	Bar	18	3	54
Plum	Plum	Plum	14	25	350
Plum	Plum	Bar	14	5	70
Orange	Orange	Orange	10	126	1260
Orange	Orange	Bar	10	18	180
Cherry	Cherry	Lemon	5	196	980
Cherry	Cherry	Bell	5	147	735
Cherry	Cherry	X[a]	3	637	1911
Average number of winning plays in 8000 trials				1169	5888
Average number of non-winning plays in 8000 trials				6831	

[a] X can be anything except a lemon or bell.

from 0 to 36. Players may not use zero in their betting; half the remaining numbers are coloured red and the other half black. If I stake 1 unit on an individual number, and that number turns up on the play concerned, I am paid out with odds of 35 to 1. Alternatively if I back red or black and the colour I backed turns up, the odds paid to me are 2 to 1. In either case, if I lose, my stake is forfeit. If the number zero (coloured green) turns up I lose my stake if I have backed a specified number, but I lose only half my stake if I have backed a colour.

The banker's 'take' can be calculated as follows:

For number bets the true probability of success is 1/37. Hence the player's expected gain for a stake of 1 unit is

$$\frac{1}{37} \times 35 + \frac{36}{37} \times (-1) = -\frac{1}{37} \text{ or } -2.7\%$$

(i.e. the banker's expected gain is $+2.7\%$ of the total amount staked)

For the other type of bet the player's expected gain is

$$\frac{18}{37} \times 1 + \frac{18}{37} \times (-1) + \frac{1}{37} \times \left(-\frac{1}{2}\right) \text{ or } -1.35\%$$

(i.e. the banker's expected gain is $+1.35\%$ of the total amount staked).

Three aspects should be emphasized. First these percentages are *expected* gains or losses and fluctuations can occur both ways, although with a true roulette wheel the percentages should in the end be correct. Secondly, most players play again and again and hence the banker's expected gain is not 2.7% (or 1.35%) based upon the player's playing wealth when he enters the casino, but is the appropriate percentage multiplied by his wealth and multiplied again by the average number of times he stakes his money. The latter is currently referred to as the 'drop' and has been estimated in many casinos (see the Report of the Royal Commission on Gambling (1978)) as about seven times the stake money exchanged for chips at the casino at the beginning of play. Thus the expected return to the casino would be either 19% or 9.5% of the money exchanged for chips each session according to the backing system adopted by the player. This is a truer measure of the return on turnover than the odds per play.

Thirdly, most casinos have a maximum and a minimum stake level. The former safeguards the casino from a single huge win occurring, the latter – particularly as it commonly includes a higher minimum on low-margin bets such as the colours – discourages small players from concentrating on these low-margin bets and cluttering up the tables. The pursuit of foolproof winning systems is discussed later in Section 9.2.

A third illustration of gambling is that of Premium Bonds, introduced in the UK by Mr Harold Macmillan as Chancellor of the Exchequer in

1958. Each £10 worth of bonds held entitles the holder to participate in a draw for prizes each month. The prize money is effectively the interest earned per month on the bond, so that whether you win a prize or not, your original bond (stake money) is returned to you on demand. Hence this is a modified form of gambling; you leave capital on deposit with the Government and gamble with the interest on the capital. The revealing feature is that the interest payable on premium bonds (i.e. the prize fund) is at a lower rate than the Government normally has to pay on borrowed money. In other words, the investor's expected net gain is lower through premium bonds than it would be through other forms of lending (even after allowing for taxation implications). This reveals another factor in gambling, namely the psychological fascination or attraction to it, even when there is no way in which the player (punter or investor) can control the odds concerned. Moreover it seems clear that the way in which the prize fund is divided (even though the total is fixed) affects the popularity of the bonds. A few years ago a change to splitting the prize money into a few big prizes, with a myriad of small prizes, increased the popularity of the bonds compared with the previous situation when there were rather more middle-level prizes but no really big prizes.

9.2   Gambling systems

The bogey of an infallible system for winning at gambling was laid to rest in the nineteenth century. Nevertheless this has not prevented a continuing search. Fyodor Dostoevsky observed the gamblers at Homborg in 1867 'with ruled papers in their hands, whereupon they set down the coups, calculated the chances, reckoned, staked – and lost exactly as we more simple mortals who played without any reckoning at all'. Many offered systems for sale at Monte Carlo in the late nineteenth century but mostly these were spurned: 'If Lord Rosslyn is so sure of making money at Monte Carlo, why isn't he down there busy making it?' asked a contributor at that time to the Paris edition of the *New York Herald*. (Today we make the same comments of those who seek to advise us, for a fee, on Stock Exchange investments.)

Almost all the systems in use both then and now are based on some form of doubling up on an even chance. Thus the simple *Martingale* supposes a bet of 1 unit on an even chance, doubling the bet every time you lose until you win. When this occurs your net gain is 1 unit so that you are in the same position as if you had won on the first trial. The problem is that, with a run of losing bets, your required stake mounts up rapidly. Suppose there is a run of 10 consecutive losses, your stake at the eleventh play is 1024 units with your total loss to date 1023 units. Thus your capital to get so far is 2047 units and – if you win – you will be just one unit to the good! Moreover if your stake now exceeds the casino maximum your house of cards (to mix metaphors) will collapse upon you. It collapses even more quickly if your stake unit is higher, as the length of losing run that you can withstand is reduced. Thackeray, writing in 1850, warns against the system: 'You have not played as yet? Do not do so: above all avoid a martingale if you do.'

There are many other variations; the great martingale when the stakes go up rather more rapidly; the *boule de neige* which is a martingale in reverse doubling up after each win; Lord Rosslyn's system which is a complicated form of progression; and the Labouchère (devised by the Victorian journalist and politician) which works on the principle of dividing your stake into three unequal parts, so that although the bank may win more often than you do, the net result will be in your favour. All these systems – and many more – can be shown from the laws of probability to be misconstructed, but the fascination remains and many gamblers pin their faith on the roulette wheel (or other gambling games) not obeying the laws. Many have studied the actual results: the distinguished statistician Karl Pearson in the summer of 1892 observed 16019 spins of the roulette wheel at Monte Carlo with red numbers occurring 8053 times; a deviation from expectation of only 0.25%. Admittedly he didn't find such good agreement in the lengths of runs of red numbers observed, but then the expected numbers were relatively lower and good agreement is less likely. Perhaps he should have spent more than a fortnight at the casino!

A winning system aims to leave one ahead. Yet we have already seen that this is going to flout probability laws. Return for a moment to the one-armed bandit illustration. There is a probability of 0.15 that a player is a winner after one trial. A win on the first trial gives a player enough money to finance at least two more trials. The probability of being ahead after two trials is equal to the probability of having a win on either the first trial or the second trial or both, and this is one minus the probability of losing on both trials, which is equal to $1 - (0.8539)^2$, or 0.27. The probability of being ahead after three trials is made up of a large number of different cases, but it is again easier to look at the converse: the probability of being down after three trials. For this to be so, there can be losses on all three trials, or alternatively a win of the minimum prize (£0.2) once, and only once, in the three trials. These probabilities are $(0.8539)^3$ and $3 (0.8539)^2 (0.1)$ respectively, so that the probability of being ahead is

$$1 - 3(0.8539)^2(0.1) - (0.8539)^3 = 0.16$$

The chances of being ahead now begin to fall quite steadily, being approximately 0.1 after 100 trials, 0.05 after 200 trials, and 0.025 after 300 trials. Hence being ahead after two trials is no real guide to what will happen in the long run.

These figures can be misleading to the would-be players in another sense. A player is a winner after 300 trials if he is as much as £0.1 ahead; whereas the majority of players would, after 300 trials, be sadly in the red to the tune of about £7.50. This is typical with gambling. An apparently reasonable chance to be a little ahead, and an enticing although very minute chance to make a killing, are overwhelmed by the average expectation of going well into the red.

Whether it is true or not that a bad system is better than none, it is undeniable that, according to your objectives, some methods of staking at games like roulette are better than others. Since the bank has a probability advantage over you at every play, the more plays you enter the greater your chance of a win. Your chance of winning is also related to the amount by which you wish to increase your original stake. If you play only to double it, and stake only once, you stand an almost even chance of doing so. If, on the other hand, you plaster the board by splitting up your stake into a number of smaller bets placed at the same time, you increase the bank's chances proportionately and therefore decrease your own chance of winning.

9.3 Skill and probabilities

The preceding sections dealt with situations in which it was assumed the laws of probability applied, with the probabilities concerned pre-determined and the same for all players. A further stage contends that the probabilities may themselves be capable of refinement, different individuals having unequal opportunities of making such refinements. Three illustrations are discussed, the first two being taken from sport.

Football pools are completed regularly by millions. A common approach is to ask participants to make eight match choices for each entry, points being scored according to the results (3 for a scoring draw, 2 for a no-score draw, $1\frac{1}{2}$ for an away win, 1 for a home win). Those participants who obtain 24 points receive a first dividend and sometimes there are other dividends for lower numbers of points. The pools firm deducts its expenses and tax, so that only about half the money comes back in prizes. If the pool is a pure lottery, the expectation is clearly negative, but people enter for two reasons. First, they may hope for a huge win (£1 million is not unknown) and use it as a dream activity. Secondly, they may hope to make a steady income from it in the belief that the results are not just random, but to some extent predictable. Many syndicates are formed to enter the pools for this latter purpose. They analyse past results, form, state of the pitch, weather, sickness of players, etc. to make predictions for a large block of entries. Such syndicates, not uncommonly, win prizes of some substance but very rarely, if ever, do they win a unique first dividend. The reason is clear: the uniqueness of a first dividend means that something very improbable indeed has turned up. This is unlikely to be from the entry of a syndicate that has been studying the position in a scientific manner; it is more likely to be from somebody who has used the birthdays of his children, or the hymn numbers from last Sunday's church service. But this does not invalidate the point that study of relevant data could make the expectation positive instead of negative, while reliance on chance will leave it negative. The question is whether the effort and outlay involved in the scientific study is worth the likely improvement in expected gain that may be achieved.

The second illustration relates to horse racing where it can be argued that there is some skill involved in choosing which horse to back. On a totalizator system, the odds for a win are a purely arithmetic function of the money placed on each horse (less a deduction for expenses and the profit of the totalizator). Through a bookmaker, the odds will be changing all the time until the race is held, as the volume of money going on each horse varies with the changing views of the backers. Thus a horse which a couple of days before the race could be backed at 100 to 1 to win, may shorten to 20 to 1 at lunch time on the day of the race. Equally, the converse may hold. The work by Hoerl and Fallin (1974) based on two racecourses in the USA described in Chapter 3 suggested that some knowledge element was going into the betting system, since the relative amounts of money backed on the various horses at the tote followed closely the proportion of times the horses came in first, second, third, etc. Thus knowledge was being used to improve the situation over an 'equal ignorance' approach whereby all horses were held to be equally likely to win. A further question arises as to whether this knowledge is equally shared, or whether it is available to some backers and not others. Alternatively it can be argued that the information available may be the same for all, but the way it is processed, and the conclusions drawn, differ. Thus a gambling element exists in so far as the information available is incomplete. Given the substantial 'cut' by the bookmaker or totalizator, there will be a considerable probabilistic variation in the likely outcome position for a backer after a six-race meeting (say), since the number of separate bets made by an individual is relatively small. Thus the 'gambling' element is a combination of three factors: availability (or unavailability) of information; poor information processing; and a small number of races.

A slightly different situation arises with the game of bridge where the information, although unequal between the players, is strictly controlled according to the rules of the game. Moreover it is generally accepted that there is a substantial element of skill in playing the game. This does not mean that a skilful player will always win, since the luck of the deal, i.e. the particular cards held by his partner and himself, will affect the probability of winning. Thus, with four trumps in your hand and with three in dummy on the table, the probability that the remaining six are split equally (three and three) between the opposing partners is only 0.36, although it is the most likely split. To play such a hand assuming that this must always be the split is likely to lead to more disappointments than successes. However, for any given set of cards the skilful player's chance of winning will be higher than the less skilful, so that over a number of plays, the skilful player will win more often than the less skilful player and it is this factor that makes the difference.

It is perhaps ironical that gambling is often defined as staking money on uncertain outcomes under such conditions that in 'the long run' the gambler will lose. This discussion has demonstrated that the longer the gambling goes on the more certain is the result, i.e. that the gambler will lose. The greater relative uncertainty about the outcome lies in the short term where the probability of being ahead will be greater.

9.4 Insider trading

An area of information availability of much public concern in recent years has been that of insider dealing on the stock market, Put shortly, insider dealing (or trading) is the dealing in shares with an unfair imbalance of information. The insider is one who has secret information and can use it to his financial advantage. This is a controversial issue and the notion that privileged persons (insiders) have, as result of their position, access to information that can be exploited in stock market transactions, has a wide and negative emotional appeal. Yet in all transactions there is some degree of inequity as to information. For example, when you buy a house the current owner tends to downplay any defects in the interests of his bargaining position. Legislation such as the Trades Description Act attempts to reduce the exploitation of superior information by commercial organizations, but there are clear limitations to the effectiveness of such legislation and vast areas where information discrepancies will never be eradicated.

In the case of share dealings, some have argued that insider trading is not deleterious in that long-term investors are unharmed by its effects and only gamblers are affected. Insider trading, it is argued, smooths out the fluctuations in prices and makes for more gradual rises and falls than those which would occur when the relevant information is publicly disclosed in the absence of insider trading. If it is true that long-term investors do benefit, is it worth the cost of trying to suppress insider trading?

This is not likely to be a majority view, but it is more difficult to do much about the practice (see Ashe, 1976). First, to make it a criminal offence requires a definition that is both acceptable and workable: no mean feat. Secondly, the cost of monitoring such an offence may be met by using money diverted from more worthy causes. An alternative is to make it a civil rather than criminal action, but this is fraught with difficulties as to who sues who, and where any damages fall. A third, and perhaps more promising approach, is for the law to promote better commercial morality. Thus, tightening of professional ethics where necessary could be encouraged and legislation could require all employees' share dealings in their own company or in a company with which there is a business relationship to be scrutinized. Such a move could well endanger the wider share ownership and share bonus profit-sharing schemes that are being encouraged through taxation relief on the grounds of their possible motivational effects. Indeed the 'culprits' may not only, or even usually, be employees. Thus it has to be asked whether these possible moves are taking a sledgehammer to crack a nut, or whether wider share ownership itself would not reduce the problem.

9.5   Gambling and insurance

If casino activity is gambling as far as the players are concerned, it is not so for the casino operator who sees it as a business with a positive expectation of gain. He does not see himself as a gambler and reckons that, provided he has sufficient capital and controls his running expenses properly, he will achieve a realistic return on his capital employed. As discussed earlier, another contingent transaction where money is paid over (premium) and the payee gets no goods or services immediately, but a monetary return later if an uncertain event occurs, is insurance. The uncertain event takes a different form in this case: your house burning down, your dying within some specified time, your car being involved in an accident, etc., but these differences in form are not of importance. The viability of insurance operators indeed depends upon there being considerable similarity with the process underlying gambling. Whether or not the individual believes that the incidence of accidents, deaths, disease or other misfortunes are determined by someone playing a giant roulette wheel, it is essential, as discussed earlier, that the process be significantly indeterminate and unpredictable if commercial insurance is to exist. In both cases the customer engages in an activity with negative expected value and the operator enjoys the positive equivalent, out of which expenses are paid and a profit obtained for the shareholders who put up the capital.

It is commonly argued that the distinction between the two types of contract is that the insurance contract is *risk-averting*, the gambling contract is *risk-seeking*, even though to a financial conglomerate the two forms of transaction are identical. An alternative distinction is that gambling involves risking the loss of a smaller amount of money (the stake) in order to have the chance of gaining a larger one, whereas insurance involves accepting the certain loss of a smaller amount (the premium) in order to avoid the chance of a greater loss. To illustrate the difference consider Mr A who goes along to Prubroke Ltd, and enters into two transactions with them

  (a) £20 on Fancy Lily for the Derby at 100 to 1 against, and
  (b) £20 to insure a cottage valued at £2020 against burning down this year.

In each case, in exchange for a specific sum of money, £20, Prubroke agrees to pay Mr A another greater sum of money (£2020) if a specified event occurs. To Prubroke Ltd the two transactions may seem identical in principle and any distinction must lie elsewhere. Perhaps one distinction is that if Mr A entered into neither transaction he would neither be better nor worse off financially than under (a), but could be £2000 worse off than under (b). On this basis a transaction of type (a) is referred to as a gamble, while type (b) is referred to as insurance. Moreover, gambling is a value-laden term in society, while insurance is a much less emotive term. In the UK, gambling contracts are unenforceable at law (under the Gaming Act of 1845) while insurance contracts are completely enforceable. Given this distinction, a lot of legal energy has been dissipated in clarifying the precise nature of a gambling contract as opposed to an insurance contract. The crucial distinction is the presumption of an 'insurable interest' in the uncertain event that is the subject of an insurance contract.

This definition dates from the 1892 law case of *Carlill* v. *the Carbolic Smoke Ball Co.* Judge Hawkins defined in that case a gambling contract as one by which two parties hold opposite views as to the issue of a future uncertain event, and mutually agree that one shall hand over to the other, dependent upon the determination of the event, a defined sum of money, neither party having any other interest in that contract other than the stake he will so win or lose. An insurance contract, on the other hand, is one in which one party has a 'real' interest in the uncertain event concerned beside the interest generated by the contract. This real interest is typically the property of the party taking out the insurance.

The word 'real' is normally equated with 'financial' and accordingly non-material events are de-valued. Thus a broken heart is difficult to insure against, but a hi-fi can be insured against breakage. The dividing line is a narrow one. It is possible to insure against there being no rain in Scotland (and hence no fish in the rivers) but one doesn't necessarily have to be planning to go fishing in that week (see Barr, 1976). The 'real' interest in such an insurance seems very remote and hence it is a borderline situation. These are bound to arise when there is really a continuum of interest which has, perforce, to be divided into two distinct categories for legal purposes. The insurance industry argues that the non-insurable interests are those where moral hazards enter, for example a false claim for a broken heart would be difficult to detect.

9.6   Gambling, investment and speculation

Investment involves the placing of funds in such a way as to expect some positive return for so doing. The expected return may vary and in general the higher the risk associated with the investment the higher is the expected return. This is true both within a firm (Chapter 6) or when the investment is made through the purchase of property, or of stocks and shares on the Stock Exchange (Chapter 8). A share market operates only because there exist differences in view as to what will happen in the future, and varying preferences regarding risk and desired return. Uncertainty about the future profitability of a company and the future prices of its shares will not in itself generate transactions. Whether it is difference in beliefs (probabilities) or in values (utilities) that is the main generator of share values has been the subject of much inconclusive debate. Nevertheless the stock market provides the opportunity for buyers and sellers – who may well have the same information – to trade, in that A buys because the implicit combination of risk and return is in line with his preferences, while B sells because it is out of line with his. Maynard Keynes once castigated the stock market as a casino, but this would only be true if there were no relevant information available concerning particular stocks and shares or, alternatively some people had more relevant information available to them than others. It is, of course, precisely because of the latter that insider trading is controlled and there are strict Stock Exchange rules concerning the timing of various announcements made by a company. Nevertheless it is not entirely self evident that all shareholders, or potential shareholders, are treated equally in this matter of information.

Investment thus differs from gambling in that the expectation of gain is positive, the size depending on the associated risk, while gambling has a negative expectation with the lower returns associated with the higher risks. This leaves a middle area covered by a set of transactions commonly referred to as *speculations*. These are usually transactions whose expectations are around zero, but exhibit considerable variability or volatility, particularly if there is a high level of risk. They differ from gambling in as much as they are seen by many to have a useful economic function. Two examples will illustrate the principles.

The first relates to commodity *futures* for items such as tea, cocoa, gold, lead, copper, rubber, grain etc. The attraction of such a market to the investor is that futures offer a cheap and highly efficient way of getting into a commodity (for example, gold) without all the headaches of delivery, insurance, storage, and re-assay upon the sale that go with direct ownership of the physical metal. Whether you buy (going long) or sell (going short) depends upon which way you think the price will move. The contract lasts for a fixed period, possibly buying forward up to 15 months, during which you can take your profit, or cut your loss and start all over again. The gain (or loss) comes primarily from the gearing, in that only 10% of the agreed price is paid immediately although you will have to top this up if the price goes persistently against you. So a small change in price produces a tenfold change in the value of the commodity future and it is possible to double your money, or the converse, very easily. The system thus provides a form of margin trading that gears up the risk by a factor 10, a 1% change in price leading to a 10% change in your profit or loss. The argument for such a system is that these facilities give the volume of trading activity necessary for producers and consumers of commodities to hedge and provide a reasonably smooth progression of prices, i.e. the speculators smooth the actual prices paid in the shops. In spite of the high financial risks involved, and the disfavour in which the whole system is held in many political circles, it attracts a substantial amount of money. It is not for the cautious or nervous investor as there are large risks; it is for the speculator who can stand the heat in the kitchen. A financial futures exchange based on stock market prices was opened in London in late 1982; they also exist in North America, Tokyo, Hong Kong and Australia.

The second example is that of traded *options*. This is a form of contract which gives the holder the right to buy shares at named prices during a specified period of time. Because the contracts are standardized (impersonal with no names of vendor or purchaser), they can be bought and sold by investors during the lifetime of the option, without any transactions in the shares themselves.

Profits from option trading can be spectacular in relation to the money which has to be put down. Someone paying £0.05 for an option on a share standing at £1.00 can double his stake if the shares rise by only 10%. If the shares go down, he might lose all of his investment, but the amount of potential loss to the buyer (£0.05) is fixed and known from the beginning. As has often been said, the similarity with a flutter on the Derby is obvious.

The option market brings together the buyer, who is hoping to make a profit if share prices change sufficiently (either up or down), and the writer of the option. The writer may be an institution, a jobber or anyone else who holds the shares that are the subject of the option contract. In exchange for giving the buyer the right to purchase the shares at the specified price any time during the coming three months, the writer receives the option payment. He thereby increases his cash flow and reduces (by £0.05) his potential loss if there is a fall in the price of the share in the market (though he also loses some of its gain potential). The options market therefore re-distributes the risk inherent in holding shares. Whether options trading affects the price of the share to which the option relates is the subject of great controversy, although there is some indication that the speculative element in the share's trading is largely transferred to the options market. If this is so, options trading has a stabilizing effect on share prices even though the overall amount of speculation may be greater.

A final example of speculation, of a rather different kind, is that of so-called angels in the theatrical world. These backers put up the money required to launch a theatre production. Any money received above the initial and subsequent running costs of the show is paid out to the angels in proportion to their share of the total backing money. In many, indeed

Figure 9.1. Investment, speculation and gambling

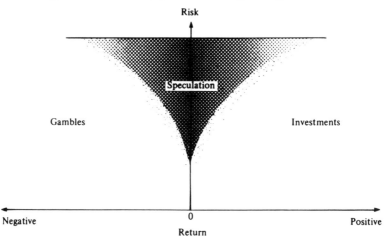

in most, cases the angels lose their money. In a few – very few – cases they make a huge profit. In a number of cases they make a modest return. The risks differ for different types of production, as does the total money required for launching the production.

Figure 9.1 attempts to distinguish the three activities of investment, gambling and speculation diagrammatically in terms of the levels of risk run and the expected returns. There is no clear cut distinction that can be made between the three activities, but the general principles just outlined are encapsulated in the approximate boundaries drawn.

9.7   Investment versus speculation

There is another way that is sometimes used to distinguish between investment and speculation. For the former, even though one owns only a piece of paper, it is normally linked directly to a company or organization that is working to provide profits to service that investment. Thus an insurance company uses any capital raised on the market to provide its basic reserve against risk fluctuation; a manufacturing company may either have debentures against assets, or equity (ordinary shares) against new developments; a consultancy firm uses its capital to provide the necessary background base with which to start the firm and carry it until the point of profitability is reached. In each instance the money raised can affect directly the success or failure of the enterprise concerned.

However, a number of so-called investments effectively have no such direct backing and are in reality gambles against some index which the money invested can in turn do nothing to influence. A first illustration relates to the so-called Coral Index whereby an investor either buys or sells units of the Financial Times Index of London share prices (or the New York Dow Jones Industrial Index) and can close his bet by the opposite transaction any time within a month. If the index moves up before he closes, he makes a profit, and if it falls he makes a loss. The Coral organization have a buying and selling price each day, allowing them to make their own turn on the deal. (A letter describing the original system operated by Coral is appended to this chapter). Thus the individual can take a view in one transaction as to the general movement of the market, without incurring the expense of dealing in a large number of shares. Ironically, if this kind of betting grew, it could affect the real market in shares by removing the speculative element from Stock Exchange investment as such. On the other hand such an activity by an investor already holding a portfolio of shares could be seen as an insurance policy if he is betting the wrong way. This parallels the Conservative businessman who bets heavily on a Labour victory at Ladbroke's (who now own Coral) to get some compensation for possible harm to his business in the event of a Labour victory at a General Election.

A second form of such investment relates to items such as possible North Sea oil bonds mentioned earlier in connection with index-linked securities. Although the dividends and capital values of the bonds would be linked in some way with the prices of oil or profits being obtained in North Sea oilfields, the money raised would go to the Treasury. The number of bonds that could be issued is indefinite, and the amounts of money raised would have no direct connection with the industry: for example, it need not in itself affect the rate of new exploration activities or well sinkings. It is only a mirage effect whereby the Government attracts funds from the public by offering an apparent share in a successful industry. In this sense it is not investment in the true sense, but financial placement. It certainly is not, as was originally suggested in many quarters, a way of achieving 'privatization' of the industry, and was ultimately abandoned in favour of a straightforward sale of common stock in November 1982.

Of course, governments use other means of attracting funds, in ways that would not realistically be open to non-state-supported organizations. The most obvious of these are index-linked savings certificates for which the term is five years and the initial value is paid back by adjustment in line with the change in the retail price index (RPI) over the same period, plus a small bonus. The UK Government (as at late 1982) also offers individuals a savings certificate that provides a 9.5% return over a fixed term of five years. In both instances the returns are free of all taxes and hence can be directly compared. Clearly if the RPI rises by less than 9.5% annually compound over the five-year period, then the savings certificates would be a better buy; if the RPI rises by more than 9.5% the index-linked bonds would be better. The investor's behaviour is a function of two factors: first, the probabilities relating to inflation rates and, second, the utility function, or risk preferences, of the individual. Some individuals might be primarily interested in maintaining purchasing power: they would look to indexed bonds; others might be out to make a real profit and would invest in savings certificates if they felt the inflation rate was going to be below 9.5%. If they felt otherwise they would not invest in these securities at all, but seek other forms of security to fit their profile of risk and expected return. These two securities demonstrate, however, a very important distinction, namely a guaranteed return in money terms, or a guaranteed return (albeit virtually zero) in real terms. The term 'risk free' has traditionally been applied to the first form of security, although it could be argued that the term ought more realistically be applied to the latter form of security.

The boundary between gambling, speculation or investment can be seen to be narrow, although they all involve elements of risk. Moreover, to be successful in any of them a knowledge of the risks involved is essential. For gambling, the expected gain is negative and the only advantage is whether the utility of a high prize with low probability outweighs the loss of stake money. A firm will not normally gamble, since in gambling it cannot control the risks, but it may speculate (for example, a confectionery firm, in cocoa futures) or invest in a new product, arguing that in these situations it can control the outcomes in the sense that it is a better predictor of outcomes than others in the market. Speculation and investment differ mainly in the levels of risk involved, that in speculation being larger with less unanimity in assessment terms than for investment.

It is ironical that a company's annual accounts do not have to disclose much information covering risk activities under way. For example, contingency exploration costs committed but not yet incurred, and contingent liabilities in the pension fund, are omitted. Hence the accounts, far from giving a true and fair view of a company, may actually distort the picture by excluding items related to risks already decided upon but not yet paid for.

CORAL INDEX LTD.

(A SUBSIDIARY COMPANY OF J. CORAL HOLDINGS LIMITED)

BERKELEY SQUARE HOUSE. LONDON, W1X 5PE

DIRECTORS
N CORAL B A . C HALES
D SPENCER F C A   H YOUNG F C A   TELEPHONE 01-493 5261

TELEGRAPHIC ADDRESS
CORALDEX LONDON W1X 5PE

Dear Sir,

This Company provides a service to the public whereby their views on the rise or fall of the Financial Times Industrial Ordinary Share Index over a period can be supported by a wager.

From experience, it is very rare indeed to find that everyone's thinking is alike, and invariably we find that one Broker may be bullish of the market and has expressed very cogent reasons for his thinking, whereas another Broker proceeds to give equally good reasons why the market should go down. In other words, two Brokers, whose opinions may be respected, have completely different views as to the future of the market. We are sure there are very many such Brokers and in fact, people like yourself who would, if they could, back their particular opinion in tangible form.

Were you to sell I.C.I., Courtaulds, Dunlop or other shares it could well be that the very shares you sold are the ones to go up, and yet the market in general goes down. Similarly the reverse could happen if you bought. Add to this the fact that expenses of so doing are high, and that money has to be laid out on the full operation and risks taken on the bear operation, such operations are risky even if one is a shrewd operator.

In our view there is quite a simple answer to all this and what is more, an answer which will provide a most interesting method of backing your opinion.

This Company was formed to allow people to buy or sell the Financial Times Industrial Ordinary Share Index according to their fancy with units of £1 per point and a maximum of £250 per point (not less than 5 Units of £1 each will be accepted). Two prices are quoted, i.e., a buying and selling price, based on the F.T. Industrial Ordinary Share Index and moves either way according to supply and demand. Dealing hours are from 10 a.m. to 1 p.m. and 2 p.m. to 5.30 p.m. daily.

The Client may close his position at any time at our quoted price within a maximum period of thirty days comprising two fortnightly accounts, with two prior days, dealing for New Time. These fortnightly accounts commence on a Wednesday and close on a Tuesday. On closure, the account is made up on the Tuesday at the end of the period and payment either way is made within seven days thereafter. The Client has to close his position finally whatever happens, at the end of the period at the precise F.T. Index ruling at 3.00 p.m. on that particular day.

It might be useful to give an example of what might happen to a Client:

Say he buys 10 units at 290 and that about two weeks later he sees the Index is 302. He would then contact this office, enquire the price and be quoted, say 299½/304½. He may well sell at 299½, and thus have made the difference between 290 and 299½, equalling 9½ points, thus showing him a profit of £95. However, if the market turned dull, and in the hope that the market would go better, he kept his position open until the last day, he might find that the price he obtained at the end of the period was only, say, 280. He would thus lose 10 points, for each of 10 units, equal £100. Similarly, if he had sold 10 units, the opposite would apply.

This method of backing one's opinion in tangible form has been enthusiastically received, and we are confident that you will be equally interested.

Our Closing price is published daily in the Financial Times on the Money Market page.

We enclose a copy of the Rules and an Application Form. Members of recognised Stock Exchanges, Commodity Markets, Partners or Directors of Merchant Banks and Exempted Dealers are free to deal immediately.

EXTERNAL ACCOUNTS. Under the U.K. Exchange Control regulations, a margin of £25 per unit in External Currency ($60 per unit) is required. On closure of the transaction, the margin is returnable together with any profit or less any loss, on the ensuing Settling Day in the same currency as it was provided.

Yours faithfully,

CORAL INDEX LIMITED

[signature]

Chairman

Registered Office: Mark Lane House, New Road, Dagenham, Essex RM9 6LB

Incorporated in England: 824535

10
Physical risk and its perception

10.1 Introduction

Physical risks to life or health are accepted as part of everyday life since achieving virtually anything involves some element of physical risk, even if it is just travelling to work. It is however, the perception of the risk concerned to which the individual primarily responds. If perceptions are faulty, efforts at personal, public and environmental protection are liable to be misdirected. For some risks, extensive statistical data is available to guide public perceptions, but in other areas the data are either very scanty or somewhat complex in form so that acceptable risk assessments on an agreed basis become difficult.

Physical risks range from trivial injuries to forms of permanent disability and possibly death. In this chapter, for physical risk we shall concentrate primarily upon accidental or occupational deaths, but these are only a surrogate for physical risks in general. Chapter 11 discusses some other

Table 10.1. *Accidental deaths in UK industry (1976)*

Industry	No. of deaths (1)	Deaths per million employees per year (2)	FAFR (3)	Annual risk of death (prob- abilities) (4)
Quarrying	16	333	19.0	0.00033
Underground coal mining	58	196	12.0	0.00020
Agriculture	41	141	10.0	0.00014
Chemical industries	30	70	5.1	0.00007
Food, drink and tobacco	22	31	2.3	0.00003
Clothing and footwear	1	2	0.15	0.000002

aspects of physical risks, arising mainly from medical and surgical treatments.

Table 10.1 summarizes data concerning occupational deaths due to accidents in a number of UK industries. Column 1 gives the number of deaths occurring in each industry in 1976. (For all industries combined there were 750 occupational deaths in that year). These figures are very relevant in one sense – it is where the deaths occur – but misleading in another, since they give only a superficial indication as to which industries are the more dangerous. The later columns attempt to express the degree of danger in three alternative ways. Column 2 scales the figures in column 1 by the average number of workers employed in the industry during 1976 and expresses it on a per million basis to avoid a large number of decimal places. This column immediately suggests that the coal mining industry is about a hundred times more dangerous than the clothing and footwear industry. Column 3 expresses the same figures in the form of a Fatal Accident Frequency Rate (FAFR) where

FAFR = Average number of fatal accidents in a working lifetime (100 000 working hours) among a group of 1000 men.

British industry as a whole has an FAFR of a little under 4 but, as shown by column 3, there are wide variations between industries. The relative values obtained for the different industries are the same as in column 2: it is only the way in which the measure is expressed (i.e. per 1000 working lives) that has changed. For clothing and footwear the number of deaths is extremely small and the FAFR has to be treated with caution, although it seems clear that the rate is significantly lower than that of the other five industries. Finally, column 4 expresses the experience in the form of an annual probability of death. Again the relative probabilities between industries remain unchanged, compared with columns 2 and 3, and it is only the scaling factor that has been modified.

One prominent writer recently suggested that a human risk of 1 in 10 000 (probability 0.0001) or less is not normally worth serious consideration. This, however, is an over-simplification because it completely ignores the time dimension in the risk assessment. An annual probability of death of 1 in 10 000 does not sound particularly large, but it is rather greater when looked at over a 40-year career. A monthly probability of death of 1 in 10 000 would look even worse over a career span. Hence it is probably more useful to think in terms of the FAFR, bearing in mind the norm of 4 for industry as a whole. Such a risk index is effectively saying that, for a group of 1000 men entering the industry at age 18 or thereabouts, the FAFR number will die from an industrial accident before retirement age if the current mix of activities and levels of safety remain unchanged.

10.2 Degree of exposure

A second factor of importance in assessing physical risk is not just the time of exposure, but the degree or intensity of exposure. The examples just discussed dealt with people who each worked for about 2000 hours a year in the industry concerned, and were presumably broadly comparable as regards average intensity of exposure to risk. Consider alternatively the risk of death on the roads where, in the United Kingdom, some 6500 are killed annually. To express this as an annual risk rate of 1 in 7500 by merely adjusting for the size of the population is of limited meaning since those exposed to the risk of road deaths are not in this instance all equal. The person who drives 50000 kilometres a year on business is in a rather different position from the widow who is taken out for a Sunday afternoon drive once a month by her son. The homogeneity of the risk exposure between one person and another that was more or less present in the industrial situation is now absent. Again for a parachutist, the risk is related not so much to the years over which he (or she) has been parachuting, but more to the number of jumps made. (The situation with relation to aircraft accidents is even more stark: per million of population is clearly meaningless; but should it be expressed per 1000 trips made, or per million aircraft miles travelled, or per million passenger miles travelled, or what?) Such situations are well recognized by motor insurers, although the methods that they use to deal with them are commonly relatively crude as discussed earlier in Chapter 3. Such distinctions become important, however, when considering the possible benefits of financial measures taken to reduce risk.

Table 10.2 gives annual death rates for a number of *voluntary* activities

Table 10.2. *Annual death risks for sporting activities*

| Activity | Risk of death per year per active person in the sport concerned | |
	Probability	Odds
Motor cycling	2000×10^{-5}	1 in 50
Car racing	120×10^{-5}	1 in 850
Car driving	17×10^{-5}	1 in 6000
Rock climbing	14×10^{-5}	1 in 7000
Football	4×10^{-5}	1 in 25000

in the sporting sphere based upon average levels of involvement per person per year. The figures are approximate and, because of paucity of data, not entirely consistent in their methods of compilation. Nevertheless, they give an indication of the orders of magnitude of the risks incurred and can be seen in some instances to be relatively large when compared with the *involuntary* industrial risks summarized in column 4 of Table 10.1.

10.3   Incidence and consequence

The occurrence of incidents may be independent, i.e. the happening of one incident does not influence the chance of another incident. But the consequences of an incident as regards individuals may not be so independent, i.e. the death of one person in an accident may imply the involvement of others. This distinction becomes important when events such as aeroplane crashes or nuclear reactor disasters are considered. Both these events have very low *incident* risks and low overall human risks. For example, the annual death risk from escape of radioactive substances for somebody living within a 35-mile (56 km) radius of a reactor has been put at one in a million per year. Even though a large number of aeroplanes make trips, and a large number of nuclear reactors exist with a population at risk that may be large, the expected number of deaths per annum is very small. Yet it can still be true that, when an incident *does* occur, the consequences are very great.

For illustration consider an airline for whom the risk of an incident to one of its planes involving a fatality is estimated at 1 in 500000: the average load of a plane is 100 persons, and 30000 flights per year are made by the airline. Assume, a trifle implausibly, that when such an incident occurs everybody on board is killed. The average number of deaths to be expected per year would be six. In such a situation there would in most years be no deaths but, when an incident does occur, the death roll is 100. Suppose next that bigger planes come into service which have an average loading of 300 persons, the same incident rate as before, but make only 10000 flights a year carrying the same total number of passengers as before. The 'expected' deaths per annum remains six, but the average number of incidents per year is reduced by a factor of three, making the maximum single incident death roll now 300 in place of the previous 100. It is this latter difference that may well account for the apparent insensitivity of the public to the steady drip-drip of road casualties, compared with their attitude towards aircraft accidents or nuclear hazards.

For transport it is common to express risks in terms of passenger miles travelled as a means of comparing alternative modes of travel. The same principle can be followed in other fields such as energy, where currently there is a debate on the relative merits of coal, oil and nuclear fission as primary sources of energy. The British coal industry has an annual output of a little over 100 million tonnes of coal. Over the period 1967–77 the coal industry incurred 1.7 industrial deaths per million tonnes produced. There have been virtually no known deaths from accidents in the nuclear industry in the same period, so the equivalent figure is apparently close to zero. However, while the safety record of nuclear energy has to date been good, there is no real statistical evidence of a long-term nature on which to base an appropriate assessment of the incident risk. It is apparently of a small order of magnitude, but might be of some significance if an incident, should it occur, is of a chain type involving more than one person. Nevertheless, the concept of expressing the risk in terms of output required, i.e. units of energy, rather than per worker employed etc., is a major step forward in making a meaningful comparison of alternative means of reaching the same goal. In doing this all the risks are included: the raw materials to construct the power station, their conversion into steel, transporting the materials, getting the coal or gas or oil to the power station, etc. The figures in Table 10.3, calculated in this way, come from Lord Rothschild's Dimbleby Lecture (1978) which was broadcast on BBC television, and demonstrate that windmills provide the most dangerous form of power generation!

Table 10.3. *Estimated deaths for constant energy output* (10 GW/year)

Source	Deaths per 10 GW per year
Natural gas	1–4
Uranium	$2\frac{1}{2}$–15
Coal	50–1600
Oil	20–1400
Solar space heating	90–100
Wind	230–700

10.4   Perceived risk

A number of interesting studies have been made on individual's perceptions of various risks, and the discrepancies between those perceptions and experts' assessments, in an attempt to explain individual's extreme aversion to some hazards and their apparent indifference to others. For example, a community may well object strongly to having a liquid gas terminal located in their neighbourhood, even though this is judged safe, but continue to live along a geological earthquake fault line or below a dam in an area that experts assess as risky.

Table 10.4 drawn from Slovic, Fischhoff and Lichtenstein (1981) and Upton (1982) gives the results of studies in which three different large groups of people were asked to rank 30 hazardous activities, substances or technologies in column 1 according to 'present risk of deaths from each across US society as a whole'. The groups were drawn from Oregon; a women's group (column 3), a student group (column 4) and a business group (column 5). The table gives the mean rank orders of the hazardous

Table 10.4. *Ranking of risks*

Sources of risk (1)	Actuarial estimated deaths (2)	Rank orderings		
		League of women voters (3)	College students (4)	Business club members (5)
1. Smoking	150000	4	3	4
2. Alcoholic beverage	100000	6	7	5
3. Motor vehicles	50000	2	5	3
4. Handguns	17000	3	2	1
5. Electric power	14000	18	19	19
6. Motorcycles	3000	5	6	2
7. Swimming	3000	19	30	17
8. Surgery	2800	10	11	9
9. X rays	2300	22	17	24
10. Railroads	1950	24	23	20
11. Central aviation	1300	7	15	11
12. Large construction	1000	12	14	13
13. Bicycles	1000	16	24	14
14. Hunting	800	13	18	10
15. Home appliances	200	29	27	27
16. Fire fighting	195	11	10	6
17. Police work	160	8	8	7
18. Contraceptives	150	20	9	22
19. Commercial aviation	130	17	16	18
20. Nuclear power	100	1	1	8
21. Mountain climbing	30	15	22	12
22. Power mowers	24	27	28	25
23. Scholastic football	23	23	26	21
24. Skiing	18	21	25	16
25. Vaccinations	10	30	29	29
26. Food colouring	—	26	20	30
27. Food preservatives	—	25	12	28
28. Pesticides	—	9	4	15
29. Prescription antibiotics	—	28	21	26
30. Spray cans	—	14	13	23

activities within each of the three groups separately. There was a reasonable measure of agreement between the three groups in their ranking with a few marked differences, for example swimming, aviation, contraceptives, mountaineering and food preparations.

To see how far the individuals were equating risks with the number of deaths concerned, column 2 gives the annual contribution to the number of deaths in the US determined by actuarial estimates. The whole table has indeed been laid out according to these latter estimates, although the various risks were presented to individuals in random order. Some marked discrepancies between the ranking in column 2 and the three later columns emerge. Individuals viewed electric power, surgery, swimming and X-rays as relatively less risky, while they viewed nuclear power, police work and mountaineering to be relatively more risky. Since these differences seemed to be consistent across the groups it suggests that the individuals incorporate other considerations besides fatalities into their concept of risk.

A further clue to the apparent inconsistencies was the especially high rank given to nuclear power generation. A possible explanation here is that individuals considered nuclear power to be a high-risk technology because of its believed *potential* for disaster. The same respondents were accordingly asked to indicate for each hazard, 'how many times more deaths would occur if next year were particularly disastrous rather than average'. For most hazards these multipliers were quite small, indicating the people saw little potential for disaster. The striking exception was nuclear power. More than 25% of respondents expected 100000 or more fatalities in such a situation. Disaster potential thus seems to go some way to explain the striking discrepancy between the perceived risk and the annual fatality estimates for nuclear power. Yet it provides only a partial explanation for most of the hazard discrepancies, and further work by Slovic and his fellow workers suggests that it is the combination of beliefs or lack of control of risks, combined with risks that are unknown, unobservable, new or delayed in their manifestations that cause the problems.

We would expect a lay person's assessment of risks to improve with the further availability of relevant data. If the data base is common to all and complete, then we should expect reasonably compatible assessments. This could, in reverse, indicate a concomitant cause of the observed discrepancies.

Combs and Slovic (1979) reported some interesting work in which they took some 40 causes of death in the USA, subjects being asked to estimate the annual numbers of deaths (rather than ranking the causes). A correlation between the actual deaths and the estimates was there, but it was relatively low. However, the authors then examined the newspaper coverage of these same 40 causes of death over the year for two well-known newspapers, one on the East, and the other on the West, coast of the USA. Both newspapers had remarkably similar patterns of death coverage, and both had similar biases in their coverage of life-threatening events. For example, diabetes was the 9th most frequent cause of death in the USA, it was 16th in the subjects' list, and virtually bottom in newspaper coverage. Deaths from tornadoes were 31st in actual deaths but 24th in subject's estimation and 8th in newspaper coverage. The correlation between judged frequency of death and the number of deaths reported in the newspapers was about 0.70. Subjects in general underestimated common causes of death and overestimated the rarer causes. The newspapers tended to cover the latter rather than the former. Although it is tempting to conclude from these correlations that media coverage biases perceptions of risk, it could also be the case that people's opinions about what is news-worthy in turn influence the media. The journalism literature is replete with instances in which influence has occurred in each direction.

10.5   Travel fatalities

One of the most obvious – because it is so relatively common – hazards of normal life is that of travel accidents. The numbers of the deaths over a decade in Great Britain are shown in Table 10.5. Road deaths are clearly more numerous compared with deaths by other forms of transport, and, perhaps surprisingly, do not seem to have reduced significantly in recent years. However, in absolute terms, the figures by themselves are not enough: they need anchoring in some way. A first approach is to use 'hours of exposure'. Figure 10.1, based on a paper by Chauncey Starr (1979), shows how the chance of a fatality from a motor accident per hour of exposure has declined since the turn of the century. It seems to have levelled out at around 1 in 10^{-6} per exposure hour which, perhaps not quite coincidentally, is in line with the overall fatality rate from natural disease. (These figures are all based on US data.) This suggests the existence of a

Table 10.5. *Road, rail and air deaths in Great Britain 1968–78*

	1968	1969	1970	1971	1972	1973	1974	1975	1976	1977	1978
Road	6810	7365	7499	7699	7763	7406	6876	6366	6570	6614	6831
Rail[a]	334	352	381	373	328	306	360	416	382	401	449
Air[b]	53	—	—	63	118	—	—	—	63	—	—

Source: Department of Transport.
[a] 'Rail excludes railway staff on railway premises.
[b] 'Air' is for scheduled passenger services of UK airlines.

possible risk threshold such that, as the threshold is approached, further safety measures tend to be counteracted by individuals' actions (for example, faster driving) which satisfy other needs, always provided that the risk is kept below a level which he (or she) regards as the acceptable risk norm.

A second anchoring approach is to look at the deaths linked to the distance travelled. On this basis UK deaths in 1977 per 10^8 passenger kilometres ranged from 0.1 for public service vehicles, to 0.7 for car occupants, to 6.8 for pedal cyclists and 15.9 for motor cyclists. (The figures come from work carried out by the Transport and Road Research Laboratory.) Rail travel on the other hand has a very low death rate on this basis, being 0.1 per 10^8 passenger kilometres.

Another factor of interest from Table 10.5 is that while rail and air travel are basically public services, road travel is not. It could be that public services are expected to be safer than the transport that an individual provides and controls for himself, i.e. involuntary risk levels are expected to be lower than corresponding voluntary risk levels. The attitudes displayed towards safety measures support this view.

Seat belts are compulsory in aircraft and one way in which many lives could be saved on the roads is thought to be through the compulsory wearing of seat belts, a measure that has come up for debate in Parliament on countless occasions. Such a move arouses base emotions: 'This is a

Figure 10.1. Risk trends for motor vehicles

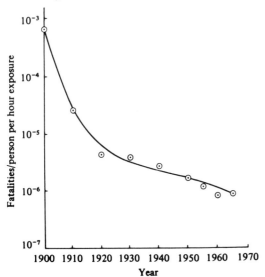

wicked, evil, horrific Bill that offends the very ark of the covenant of a free society' says one MP before rushing to catch an aeroplane for Brussels and fastening his seat belt! Calculations based on experience elsewhere (such as Canada and Australia) suggest that 600 lives and 8000 serious road casualties could be saved annually. To allow free choice conveniently ignores the indirect human costs involved in such accidents; the hospital costs, the possible disability pensions, widow's pensions etc. all of which fall on society as a whole. For the odd eccentric to risk his neck ballooning is one thing; for tens of thousands of serious casualties needing scarce resources for their alleviation is another. Parliament has at last grasped the nettle, and has taken action in early 1983 to make the wearing of seat belts compulsory but it has been a long furrow to plough.

10.6   Risk in physical systems.

To determine the probability of failure of a physical system such as a motor car or a chemical plant or a complicated journey, quantitative reliability techniques can be used. These require a model to be constructed of the way the system works as a whole, with the role of the various component parts in which failure can occur correctly defined. Reliability is then the probability that the performance of the system will meet the standard required, under stated conditions.

Section A.5 of Appendix A describes a simple model for the failure of a car's braking system and analyses this probabilistically on the basis of first a series structure, and secondly a parallel structure. In the former each component in the series must work for the overall system to operate while in the latter the system effectively has more than one life, in that as long as one component in each section of the parallel sets of components works, the system as a whole will operate.

A question arising from this analysis is the level of improvement that can be achieved by having what might be regarded as redundant parallel items. Figure 10.2 indicates a simple system composed of three items, A, B and C, each of which must work if the system as a whole is to operate satisfactorily. Failure might cause a serious accident with the possibility

Figure 10.2. Possible system configurations

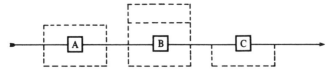

of injuries or deaths. The dotted lines indicate the possibilities of having one or more parallel components for the three items. The failure rates for the three types of component are q_1, q_2 and q_3 respectively. Assume that there are n_1 components of type A, n_2 of type B, and n_3 of type C and that the system works provided at least one of each of the components A, B and C works. The probability (reliability) that the whole system works is

$$P_s = (1 - q_1^{n_1})(1 - q_2^{n_2})(1 - q_3^{n_3}) \tag{10.1}$$

on the basis that success or failure of each individual component is independent of the others. Table 10.6 gives some specimen values for P_s for three sets of probabilities, and various configurations of components. For case (i) raising the numbers of components increases reliability, rapidly at first and then more slowly. In cases (ii) and (iii) component A has a higher relative failure rate, and the reliabilities then rise faster if component A is duplicated in preference to B or C.

More complicated system formulations, commonly known as *fault trees*, can be constructed to examine the reliability of aircraft systems, or of the operations of an oil refinery or a nuclear reactor, etc. Such trees can be used to assist in designing fail-safe systems and also to estimate failure rates for complex systems when historical data for the system as a whole are unavailable, but rates for individual components are known.

A comparison can also be made with parallel complete systems, for example two ABC systems in parallel; as opposed to two A components in parallel, joined in series to two B components in parallel, and further

Table 10.6. *System reliability rates*

| Case | Failure probabilities | | | Numbers of components | | | Reliability of system |
	q_1	q_2	q_3	n_1	n_2	n_3	(P_s)
(i)	0.1	0.1	0.1	1	1	1	0.729
				2	2	2	0.981
				3	3	3	0.997
(ii)	0.1	0.05	0.05	1	1	1	0.812
				1	2	1	0.853
				2	1	1	0.893
				2	2	2	0.985
(iii)	0.2	0.05	0.05	1	1	1	0.722
				1	2	1	0.758
				2	1	1	0.866
				3	1	1	0.895
				3	2	2	0.987

joined in series to two C components in parallel. The reliability of the latter is 0.981 from Table 10.6, and for the former is

$$1 - (1 - 0.729) \times (1 - 0.729) = 0.927$$

so that the fully parallel arrangement is the more reliable.

10.7   Catastrophes

Catastrophes appear to carry more importance in people's minds than would be expected from general considerations of attitudes towards other forms of deaths or injuries. Table 10.7, abridged from Starr (1979), gives some US data relating to catastrophes that hit the headlines and make the news, although the frequencies per event in the last column (based on differing runs of years) show that such catastrophes are very rare events in most instances. However, even if the level of incident risk is low, the consequences when the risk occurs can be very large, which has implications for any insurance cover sought. Insurers commonly divide the risks into two types: natural hazards (storm, hurricanes, floods, earthquakes, etc.) and man-made hazards (riot, aviation disasters, chemical explosions, nuclear risks, etc.). The insurance assessment is then split into two parts: first, the probability of the risk concerned occurring (an earthquake in San Francisco, say) is assessed; secondly, the possible range of intensity or scale of damage is assessed (see Lockett, 1980). Neither of these is a simple task, particularly that of the level of intensity. For earthquakes the Mercalli Scale may be an appropriate and agreed scale of intensity. For other natural hazards similar notional scales of severity affecting an area or site could be visualized, but are not commonly available.

Table 10.7. *Single-event major catastrophes*

| Type of event | Time period | Magnitude (deaths/event) | | Frequency (events/year) |
		Maximum	Average	
Major air crashes	1965–1969	155	78	6.0
Earthquakes	1920–1970	180 000	25 000	0.50
Explosions	1950–1968	100	26	2.0
Major fires	1960–1968	322	35	0.67
Floods, tidal waves	1887–1969	900 000	28 000	0.54
Hurricanes	1888–1969	11 000	1 105	0.41
Major railway crashes	1950–1966	79	30	1.0
Major marine accidents	1965–1969	300	61	6.0

For risk probabilities use is commonly made of available historical data on natural disasters which have occurred in the particular region concerned. However, there is rarely a sufficiently complete, detailed and credible record of past events available for good assessments to be made. In Japan, earthquake records from 1498 are used in the risk rating process. A period of 480 years may seem very long but, for a single location, few large earthquakes will have occurred even in such an active area as Japan. Hence, it is unwise to attach complete confidence to point estimates of extremely low-level risks of this kind, even when based on research over such a long period. Moreover there will always remain some scintilla of doubt as to whether the level of activity indicated by the period available can be considered representative of levels of activity. Similar problems affect the data available for hazards in other parts of the world. Sometimes, the records that exist relating to catastrophic events in history are incomplete and probably biased, and cannot be considered reliable as a basis for calculations. For many areas, particularly outside Europe and Asia, there was nobody available to record events with any degree of completeness, if at all, until the last century. Greater world-wide comprehensive data have become available for nearly all areas in recent decades as sophisticated measuring devices, communications systems, and satellite monitoring devices have been introduced.

A great deal of research into the causes of natural catastrophes, the prediction of the time of future occurrences, and possible measures to alleviate their effects is being carried out around the world. For example, the increased use of geological surveys, detailed measurements of minute movements of the earth's surface, the measurement of underground pressures and temperatures within rock structures etc., have given a greater understanding of the mechanisms of earthquakes and volcanic eruptions. Similar investigations of winds and cloud formation, and the development of storms are also being carried out. Short-term predictions of some potential catastrophes, such as an impending hurricane, can indeed be confidently made on occasions for some areas. Unfortunately, this is not possible in all areas of the world, or for many types of hazard, although any sort of warning is valuable in reducing potential loss of life. The same applies to property: movable articles can be removed from the area at risk or placed in relatively protected positions and, in some instances, other measures taken to protect fixed property. Further research into the development of improved methods of design and construction of buildings, greater supervision to ensure that existing building codes and other regulations are properly observed, and the introduction of new codes and legislation over wider areas can also help to reduce property losses.

Insurers need to be aware of these developments which could affect their future methods of operations. If long-term accurate predictions of catastrophes can eventually be made, elaborate disaster plans could presumably be put into operation to protect lives and movable property. While land-use restrictions and building codes can reduce damage to fixed property, they cannot eliminate the losses completely. At present the difference between the developed and the lesser developed countries in these respects is immense.

Other research is directed not so much at the prediction of occurrence of a hazard, but at the elimination or reduction in severity of its effect. For example, major earthquakes can be averted by the triggering of small tremors to release slowly any pressures which build up in the rock formation, and hurricanes can be prevented by chemical dispersal of developing atmospheric formations. If successful, these measures would be of great benefit. Depending on the costs involved in carrying them out, such projects could prove of particular benefit to the poorer countries of the world. In these areas the inhabitants have no opportunity to move out of the way of natural (or man-made) hazards, cannot afford to purchase insurance cover, nor be given any cover by their governments, partly because of the burden of past disasters. If such projects reduce wastage of resources resulting from natural hazards in developed regions of the world, the financial benefits will follow.

If communities collectively pay for measures to reduce the severity of impact, for example through tighter building controls, they will expect to see at least a corresponding reduction in the insurance premiums payable. The same would go for measures to avoid earthquakes or hurricanes. Yet the insurance company would need a substantial period of lowered claims before it would feel able to reduce its premium rates.

10.8   Cost/benefit ratio for risk reduction

For many forms of physical risk, adequate data sources are available for their broad assessment. As shown earlier there is sometimes a considerable difference between the factual assessment and the public perception of the hazard because it is distorted by overemphasis on the consequences and underemphasis on the chance – often very low – of occurrence. Even more subtle, however, is the personal evaluation of the risk as measured against the benefit which emerges by the way in which money is or is not spent on risk reduction. The costs involved for a given absolute level of risk reduction can vary enormously, a topic explored further in Chapter 12. Moreover the differences commonly go unrecognized because the public is so much more concerned with multiple accidents (or the apparent possibility of multiple accidents) that resources are not necessarily put where the maximum immediate expected gain can be achieved. The attitude towards car accidents shows this. A thousand killed or injured on UK roads per day generates no public outrage and is accepted rather in the way that typhus was accepted as an incurable disease a century and a half ago. Yet an accident which involved several people is likely to provoke demands for legislation etc. and cause expenditure that is considerably greater, on a per-life-saved basis, than would be incurred in other spheres. The following example illustrates the trade-off that has to be made whenever changes are mooted.

A chemical intermediate was being carried 500 kilometres by road from one plant to another for further processing. The intermediate was in the form of an aqueous solution and so was harmless, but money was effectively being spent to transport water. It was therefore proposed to transport an alternative intermediate which was water-free, but corrosive, in high-quality vehicles by well-trained drivers. The quantity of material to be transported would be reduced by over 80% at a considerable cost saving. Calculations using average figures for the incidence of road accidents, allied to the number of people killed in ordinary road accidents on the one hand and in accidents involving chemicals on the other, showed that reducing the volume of material to be transported by 80% would save on average one life every 12 years. This calculation allowed for an accident involving a tanker of corrosive chemicals being slightly more likely to result in a fatality than an accident involving a tanker of harmless material. However the question raised was whether the putative risk to the public from the transport of a hazardous chemical was so low that it could be accepted, against the higher but more certain level of risk with a bulkier and more costly material.

Another form of trade-off is between different ways of spending defined amounts of money to achieve some given level of safety improvements. Thus the British chemical industry has a FAFR of about 4. Imperial Chemical Industries if it identifies any single activity that contributes more than 0.4 (i.e. 10% of the industry average), tries to lower it to 0.4 or below as a matter of priority, leaving lesser risks on one side in the mean-time. Experience suggests that the costs of such a strategy, though often substantial, are not unbearable, despite the fact that competitors do not necessarily incur this expenditure. Some of the extra costs can be recouped by the greater plant reliability which safety measures often bring; the rest is a self-imposed tax which has to be balanced by greater efficiency. An alternative strategy would be to allocate funds in a priority ranking governed by the relative costs of reducing the FAFR by 1 unit taking the less costly first, and so on.

Industrial risks are seen as being of an involuntary nature and there is strong pressure to reduce the risk level to what is considered to be an acceptably low level. In making any such reduction the costs must be borne in mind. If we spend large sums of money on safety measures for a commodity we effectively take it from something else. It may be true that the same money spent elsewhere could make a better improvement in safety, but there is no social mechanism by which such transfers of cash can easily be made. This is particularly so when money for one kind of improvement comes from a private company, while for another kind of improvement it comes from the Government via taxes. Ultimately, neither the Government nor companies pay, but the public. If train travel is made safer or all public buildings made more fire-proof, then we spend more in taxes; if the chemical plant is made safer we pay more for our nylon shirts. In either case we have less money to spend on other things. The more we spend on safety the less we have to spend on other things such as fighting poverty or disease, or to spend on those other goods and services which make life seem to us worthwhile. Whatever money is made available for safety should be spent in such a way that it produces the maximum benefit to society. There is nothing humanitarian in spending lavishly to reduce a hazard because it hit the headlines last week, and ignoring other risks merely because they did not hit the headlines.

11
Morbidity and medicine

11.1 Introduction

This chapter looks at a number of ways in which various aspects of risks to life (or limb) can be assessed and treatment decisions made. The discussion is divided into three parts. Sections 11.2 and 11.3 deal with the concept of total risk. Section 11.4 deals with the assessment of medical risks, illustrated in Section 11.5 by the smoking controversy. Sections 11.6 and 11.7 then deal with the problems facing the doctor in a therapeutic situation, linking assessments of probability with those of utility, and suggesting expectation of life as a useful measure of utility for decision purposes. Chapter 12 returns to the discussion of outcome values, and attempts to link the kinds of risks discussed in this and other chapters to the costs of risk avoidance or minimization measures in the public policy domain.

11.2 The total risk concept

The total cost (or loss) to society of many endeavours is not always solely the main items apparently ascribed to the endeavour. Thus the social cost of constructing a large building is not just the direct building costs and the cost of the one fatal accident that occurred on site, but also the costs corresponding to the physical risks involved in producing the various raw materials needed, making the steel and bricks, transporting the products, etc. in terms of deaths, sickness and disabilities. Although many of these deaths and injuries are 'statistical' in the sense that they cannot be identified as being directly linked to the project concerned, it seems reasonable to include and not discard such deaths (and accidents) on an average statistical basis. It could, of course be argued that, if the building had not taken place, alternative economic activity would have occurred that itself involved other, possibly different, hazards. However, for comparative purposes it is appropriate to incorporate all such risks in evaluating the activity concerned. The concept of total risk can be illustrated by looking at alternative systems that could be used to produce a given amount of usable energy, following the methods described by Inhaber (1981).

The overall risk is divided into three parts. The first relates to the direct production of (say) coal. For example, suppose mining a million tonnes of coal requires X man-hours. If the number of deaths per man-hour of work is Y, then the number of deaths per million tonnes of coal is XY. Similarly if the man-days lost through either sickness or illness per hour worked is Z, then the man-days lost per million tonnes of coal is XZ. If one death is assumed to be equivalent to 6000 man-days lost, the total man-days lost per million tonnes of coal is $X(6000Y+Z)$.

The second part of the risk relates to the distribution of the coal and its manner of use, and also to the maintenance of the coal mine itself. The various trades, electrical work, plumbing, roofing, etc. will each have to be separately determined in terms of the time required per million tonnes of coal production. The risk per time unit (as opposed to tonnage unit) can be obtained from industrial statistics.

The third part relates to the construction of the coal mine. The raw materials and construction labour will all have their appropriate risk factors which must be added together and amortized over the projected life of the mine to produce a risk contribution per million tonnes. The three sets of data can now be combined to give a total energy risk estimate.

Difficulties arise when calculating the total public risk for some forms of energy generation, such as hydro-electricity or nuclear power, because of the need to include rare events such as dam failures or reactor radioactivity releases. For these, there are basically two approaches: historical and theoretical. The historical method takes what has happened over time as the basis for computations. Since there have been no directly applicable theoretical calculations for the frequency of hydro-electric dam failures, the number of people killed by these accidents in the past is divided by the total amount of hydro-electricity ever produced to yield the public risk from this source. This is rather crude as the data over a long period may be rather heterogeneous, but it will certainly provide an order of magnitude for the risk.

On the other hand, there have been at least two very extensive theoretical studies of the public risk from nuclear power. Values based on these studies are available from a number of literature sources and, in general, 'maximization' of nuclear risk, i.e. taking the highest values from these sources, is commonly used to avoid potential charges of pro-nuclear bias.

In this instance historical values of risk are considerably lower than the theoretical values, even when the 1979 accident at Three Mile Island is taken into account. Of course, there is no guarantee that this situation will remain unchanged in the future.

11.3   Comparisons of energy risks

Maximization of nuclear risks does not mean that the worst case imaginable should always be used for risk estimation. One can easily conceive of 'worst cases' for any energy system, in which the fraction denoted as risk per unit of energy is very large. Examples come to mind such as the Vajont disaster for Italian hydro-electricity in 1963, the largest such disaster in history; the ocean thermal gradient systems off Africa in the 1950s, which produced very little energy; or Pennsylvania nuclear power production risks for 1979, the year of the Three Mile Island disaster. In all these situations extrapolation of the observed risks for general risk estimation would be misleading since catastrophes, almost by definition, are rare occurrences.

While most data in risk studies are fairly straightforward, a distinction ought to be made between present-day experimental data and comparable data anticipated for the future. The distinction can be important in the case of certain non-conventional systems, since their advocates have frequently suggested that the efficiencies of these systems could greatly improve in the future. For example, photovoltaic systems have at present an efficiency (ratio of energy output to incoming solar energy) of 5–10%; it is forecast that this could rise to 20% in the future. This would produce more energy per unit of materials and labour used in the construction of such systems, reducing in turn the risk per unit energy output. Current data are commonly used to construct most forms of risk analyses, regardless of beliefs about the future, since the latter rarely agrees with expectations.

Figure 11.1, based on Inhaber and other sources, gives the total man-days lost per megawatt-year net output for eight different energy sources. The vertical scale of total man-days lost is on a logarithmic basis to aid comparisons of disparate sources. The relative rankings show conventional fuels such as coal and oil as high risk, for which air pollution plays a part, along with the direct risks of coal mining. The second group is of non-conventional systems such as solar systems which employ dilute energy from sunlight. Since the energy is dilute, large numbers of solar panels are required per unit of energy and these in turn require considerable amounts of steel, glass, copper etc. all of which generate risks. The final low-risk group contains natural gas and nuclear energy. Overall the graph shows that many energy systems commonly assumed to be low risk, or even risk free, can contain substantial risks when the entire energy cycle is considered.

Siddall (1980) raises questions as to how much society can or should spend to reduce risk, and whether we are reducing risk in one place by increasing it somewhere else. As an example, the risk to the public from nuclear reactors is non-zero, although probably small. In principle, this risk could be reduced even further by building more concrete containment systems than the one per reactor used in the West, or even building reactors underground. On the other hand, extra occupational risks would be introduced by the new types of construction. It is by no means clear that total societal risk regarding fuel generation would be reduced by such a change since the cost of saving further lives in nuclear power generation is high, if the theoretical and experimental data on safety are to be believed. Transferring some of the money now spent (or planned to be spent) on nuclear safety to other life-saving activities may actually reduce the overall fuel generation risks to society. At present there are few who would make this argument in public.

Figure 11.1. Man-days lost per unit energy output

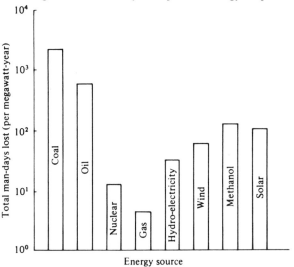

Energy source

11.4   Medical risks

In carrying out most medical procedures the benefit is likely to exceed the risk by a sufficient margin to make detailed quantification of the risk seem unnecessary. In other instances, however, it is important to estimate the likely level or risk involved and to put it against the expected benefit in order to determine whether, or when, the use of the proposed procedure is justified. Such risks can commonly be estimated, at least in terms of some limited criterion such as the probability of death or improvement in the quality of life attributable to the procedure. When so quantified, the risk/benefit ratio proves to range widely for different conventional methods of diagnosis and treatment.

Such variations are illustrated by Girdwood (1974) in an examination of the number of deaths during a ten-year period that could be regarded as being due to different medicaments. He compared these figures with number of prescriptions issued annually by general practitioners, estimating the number of deaths per million prescriptions that might be due to the use of different drugs (excluding known instances of overdosage). Of over 200 types of drug or preparation for which prescription rates were obtainable, 20 had mortality rates of one or more deaths per million prescriptions. In one of these the estimated rate was about 150, while the rates for the remainder ranged from one to eighteen deaths per million prescriptions.

Sometimes the same treatment will have differing levels of risk according to the individuals concerned. Thus the frequency with which death may result from the prophylactic vaccination of healthy people varies with a number of factors, such as the type of vaccination used and the age at which it is performed. Overall a low fatality risk in the order of 1 in 10^6 is indicated by the average number of 3.3 deaths per year between 1967 and 1976 in England and Wales attributed to the effects of vaccinations. During this period an average of 3.7×10^6 vaccinations were carried out each year, against the eight types of infectious disease for which vaccinations were predominantly made (see Social Trends, 1979).

Risk estimates, both of death and of any other serious side effects, for different types of vaccination, are important. They enable risk benefit assessments to be made as to whether at any given time the risk of vaccination exceed the benefits obtained in the prevention of the disease. A decision not to vaccinate, however, requires as good an estimate of the benefit as of the risk. Hence assessments are needed of the frequency of mortality or other effects of the disease without vaccination, as against its frequency and effects despite vaccination. The occasional fatal effects of smallpox vaccination illustrate the risk/benefit imbalance in any continued vaccination campaign, following the elimination of this disease. The actions of the World Health Organisation over smallpox is one of the most cost-effective major risk reduction operations ever staged. The total cost of smallpox eradication is estimated by WHO to have been about US $300 million and to be saving an estimated 2 million lives per year. Whatever cash value might be assigned to a human life, it must certainly exceed the sum of $20 implied by 12% annual interest on the capital sum expended.

In 1982 there was considerable debate in the UK concerning the efficacy of whooping cough vaccine. In 1951 there were 169 000 cases of whooping cough, with 453 deaths. Vaccination was introduced in the 1950s with a determined national campaign in 1958. In 1959 there were 33 000 cases, with 25 deaths. By 1970 there were 16 500 cases, with 15 deaths. The public then became scared by the alleged dangers of brain damage from the vaccination, put at 1 in 300 000 injections. The immunization rate fell and an epidemic occurred in 1979 with 100 000 cases and 30 deaths. In 1982 only about half the number of young children were vaccinated, and an epidemic was building up which promised to be worse than that of 1979. Given annual births of around 650 000, there appears to be a direct trade-off to be made between the risk of epidemics with a substantial number of deaths and the risk of two or three brain-damaged children per annum from the vaccination which virtually eliminates deaths from the disease.

Medical risks change over time as a consequence of research and better training. This is illustrated by deaths attributable to the anaesthetic used in major surgical operations which are linked to the length of operation, the state of health of the patient and other factors. The Office of Health Economics (1976) quotes estimated values for the overall average rates of death attributed to the anaesthetics used, the rates falling progressively

Figure 11.2. Deaths attributed to anaesthetics

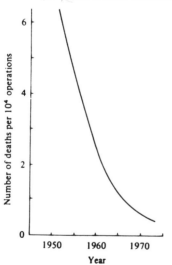

from about 6×10^{-4} in 1951, to 4×10^{-5} in 1973 (Figure 11.2), indicating a halving of the rate about every six years during the 22-year period covered.

The risk of maternal death at childbirth has fallen rather more slowly from a similar starting point of about 5×10^{-4} per maternity in 1953, to 1×10^{-4} in the mid-1970s (OPCS, 1979 and Figure 11.3) while the maternal risk per legal abortion in England and Wales is estimated to have fallen from rather over 1×10^{-3} in 1967 to 4×10^{-5} in 1973 and subsequently.

Figure 11.3. Maternal deaths

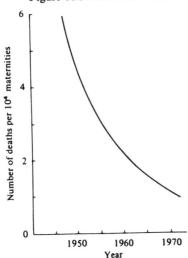

11.5   The smoking controversy

Although not strictly a medical procedure, the question of dose response concerning carcinogen in humans has been a subject of much study (and some controversy) for many years and the methods used to estimate the risks incurred through smoking are of intrinsic and historical interest. The most comprehensive and best-known study was that carried out by Doll and Bradford Hill (1956). This was based on the smoking habits and mortality of some 60000 UK doctors over a five-year period. The information recorded was simply the smoking habits and continued existence of each doctor at yearly intervals and, if he or she had died in the preceding year, the cause of death. The latter data were then subjected to an actuarial form of examination in two phases to estimate the 'excess risk of death due to smoking'.

Tables 11.1 and 11.2 (based on Doll and Bradford Hill's paper) give the salient results from the enquiry for men. Table 11.1 gives the number of 'doctor-years' of exposure in each age group for each type of smoker. For example, suppose in the first year there were 250 doctors aged 50 who were non-smokers. They would contribute 250 man-years of exposure to the third entry in the second column. The process would be repeated for each age from 45–54, and then for each of the five years in the study, to reach the total number of man-years of exposure (4136) in that entry of the table. The 35000 male doctors concerned contributed overall some 150000 man-years of exposure during the survey. The smokers in the survey are given first as a combined total and secondly, in the right hand side of the table, sub-divided according to three different levels of smoking. The definitions used to define the smoking categories are given under the table.

All deaths occurring among doctors were meticulously followed up to establish both date and cause of death. The number of deaths under the age of 35 were very small and this age group was ultimately omitted from the later analyses. The remaining six age groups were re-arranged into four slightly wider groups. The deaths due to cancer of the lung were now allocated to the various cells of the table and expressed as a rate per 1000 man-years of exposure, as given in the right hand side of Table 11.2. There is a marked gradient in the rates at each age by level of smoking, although at the highest age this excess seems to drop slightly. This result may be due to the inevitable rise of other forms of mortality at older ages which would tend to swamp any excess mortality due to smoking.

Such a study to assess risk is of prospective form by which the smoking

Table 11.1. *Man-years of exposure by male non-smokers and smokers*

Age in years	Non-smokers[a]	All smokers	Men smoking a daily average of		
			1–14 g[b]	15–24 g	25 g or more
Under 35	10143	25346	12548	10002	2796
35–44	7130	34081	13625	13380	7076
45–54	4136	28020	9477	10371	8172
55–64	1907	18002	6333	6514	5155
65–74	1078	11384	5201	3893	2290
75–84	720	5711	3334	1701	676
85 and over	136	892	616	230	46
All ages	25250	123436	51134	46091	26211

[a] A non-smoker is defined as a person who has never consistently smoked as much as 1 g of tobacco a day for as long as one year
[b] 1 cigarette is equivalent to 1 g of tobacco

habits of a large group have been recorded over a period of time and the deaths subsequently observed. The alternative type of retrospective study has serious drawbacks. If you ask those with severe cancer of the lung as to their past smoking habits you lack a control group for comparison and cannot estimate the excess effect due to smoking unless you also examine all other forms of death occurring at each group to ascertain their smoking habits. The latter would be extremely difficult to carry out and hence the retrospective approach would be very difficult, if not well nigh impossible, to carry through effectively.

The evidence from Doll and Bradford Hill is, of course, only statistical and not proof of cause and effect in a scientific sense, a point that has been frequently emphasized by a number of vocal opponents of the apparent conclusions of the study. Interpretation of the risk estimates made by such approaches obviously need care, but the following example illustrates a situation when it is decided to ignore the statistical evidence in a similar situation with no scientific causal evidence, either positive or negative.

The problem concerned the mortality from cancer of a group of workmen engaged in the refining of nickel in South Wales. There were about 1000 workmen and pensioners concerned. During the ten years between 1929 and 1938, 16 of them had died from cancer of the lung, and a further 11 had died from cancer of the nasal sinuses. At the then current age-specific death rates for England and Wales, one death from cancer of the lung might have been expected (to compare with the 16) and a fraction of a death from cancer of the nose (to compare with the 11). For all other parts of the body, cancer had appeared on the death certificate 11 times, and it would have been expected to do so 10 or 11 times. There had been

Table 11.2. *Annual mortality rates from lung cancer*

Age in years	No. of deaths	Death rate among men smoking a daily average of			
		Non-smokers	1–14 g	15–24 g	25 g or more
35–54	10	0.00	0.09	0.17	0.26
55–64	24	0.00	0.32	0.52	3.10
65–74	31	0.00	1.35	3.34	4.81
75 and over .	19	0.70	2.78	2.07	4.16
All ages	84	0.07	0.47	0.86	1.66

Death rates are expressed per 1000 man-years of exposure.

67 deaths from all other causes of mortality over the ten-year period, and 72 would have been expected from the appropriate national death rates. Finally, a division of the workmen concerned according to their jobs, showed that the excess mortality from cancer of the lung and nose had occurred wholly among the workers employed in the chemical process used in refining nickel.

Some time later the story of the group of workmen was re-examined and brought a stage further. In the nine years 1948 to 1956 inclusive, there were 48 deaths from cancer of the lung and 13 deaths from cancer of the nose. The numbers expected at normal national rates of mortality were 10 and 0.1 respectively (if the reader will allow the concept of 0.1 of a dead man!).

In 1923, long before any special hazards had been recognized, certain changes took place in the refinery. No case of cancer of the nose had been observed in any man who first entered the works after that year, and for this group of men there has been no excess of cancer of the lung. In other words, the excess of both forms of cancer was a unique feature of men who entered the refinery in, roughly, the first 23 years of the present century. No causal agent of these neoplasms has been identified. Up to now no animal experimentation has given any clue or any support to this wholly statistical evidence.

> Yet, [remarked one commentator], I wonder if any one of us would hesitate to accept the evidence as proof of a grave industrial hazard? We have the striking contrast between normality in general mortality and in general cancer incidence, and the gross abnormality in cancer of just two forms. We have the limitation of that gross abnormality confined entirely, or almost entirely, to certain workers, namely those occupied with the chemical process. We have the apparent disappearances of the abnormality in workers who entered the changed environment after 1923. Yet, let me repeat, all this is statistical evidence of events in a population of whose genetics we are ignorant and whose general environment we have not been able to examine exhaustively. Further, we know of course, that cancer of the lung and cancer of the nose both occur in persons who do not refine nickel. Yet, if you have an interest in maintaining your expectation of life, I urge you not to tell the refinery workers of South Wales (or more usually their widows) that there can be no case for paying them industrial compensation as the evidence is only statistical.

11.6   A clinical decision

Another illustration of the way in which risk plays its part in the allocation of scarce resources is to look at the manner in which therapeutic decisions are made. For this allocation to be made it is desirable to estimate not only the probabilities of success with various treatments, but also the 'value' to be placed on the end results. The latter will normally have to be in the form of a scale of benefit, not necessarily in monetary terms, but more likely in the form described earlier as 'utility' (see Chapter 5). The procedure is illustrated by the following situation.

A man aged 55, has complained of indigestion for eight months for the first time in his life. He is examined and an X-ray taken. The radiologist finds a gastric ulcer and gives the probability of a benign ulcer (S_1) as 0.90 (p_1), with the probability of a malignant ulcer (S_2) as 0.10 (p_2). The first treatment option is T_1, a medical treatment, that could be expected to heal the ulcer if it is really benign. If, however, the ulcer is really malignant then a second option T_2, a surgical gastrectomy, should be done. If the medical treatment T_1 is given and the ulcer is really malignant, it will fail to heal and time will have been lost by using the wrong treatment. If, however, the ulcer is really benign and gastrectomy is carried out, then the patient will have undergone an unnecessary operation.

The values, or utilities, placed upon the four combinations of S and T are shown symbolically in Table 11.3. A comparison can now be made of

Table 11.3. *Payoff matrix for ulcer patient*

		States of health	
		S_1	S_2
Treatment	T_1	u_{11}	u_{12}
decision	T_2	u_{21}	u_{22}
		p_1	p_2
		Probabilities	

the expected utility value for treatment T_1, namely $p_1u_{11}+p_2u_{12}$, with that for treatment T_2, namely $p_1u_{21}+p_2u_{22}$, and the treatment with the higher utility chosen. It is, however, also possible to ask for an endoscopic examination (T_3) when the ulcer can be seen directly and biopsy specimens taken for microscopic examination. This latter diagnostic method (called gastroscopy) gives a close approximation to perfect information and would enable the 'correct' treatment among T_1 or T_2 to be carried out. The appropriate utility value if this method is employed is then the maximum utility in each column of Table 11.3 and, since u_{11} will normally exceed u_{21}, while u_{22} will normally exceed u_{12}, the maximum expected utility will be $p_1u_{11}+p_2u_{22}$. Thus the overall choice position is now:

Treatment	Cost	Expected utility
T_1	C_1	$p_1u_{11}+p_2u_{12}$
T_2	C_2	$p_1u_{21}+p_2u_{22}$
T_3	C_3	$p_1u_{11}+p_2u_{22}$

Estimates have to be made of (*a*) the probabilities, for which sufficiently accurate estimates are likely to be available from experienced clinicians or published work, (*b*) the costs of medical and surgical treatment or gastroscopy and, most difficult of all, (*c*) the outcome values or utilities. To make the overall choice the costs have to be placed on a common scale with the patient's utilities and this may well be a highly contentious procedure. One scaling method that can be used is to look at the gain in utility per unit cost for each treatment.

11.7   Life expectancy criterion

In general, the state of health encountered in medicine is multi-dimensional and one of the possible dimensions along which its utility might be measured is duration of life. This cannot be estimated with certainty for any particular individual, but it is possible to discuss changes in the 'expectation' of life, i.e. the duration of life that an individual with his particular state of health may expect 'on the average'. While it is a simplifying assumption to suppose that the value of utility of life can be directly measured by 'expectation' and that the quality of life as such can be disregarded, it is not too gross a simplification. Using such an assumption, it is then possible to obtain estimates of the values to be placed on possible outcomes using the method of wagers outlined in Chapter 5.

To illustrate this, a plausible background situation has to be devised; one that involves some physical condition which carries a severe threat to life so that its expectation is shortened. The condition, moreover, has to be capable of a complete cure by an operation which also carries with it a substantial mortality risk. One possible scenario involves a vascular lesion and a situation in which a patient aged 55 is found to be suffering from an aneurysm of the posterior communicating artery at the base of the brain following a subarachnoic haemorrhage. Without treatment, life expectation is assessed at only three years. The operation mortality is assumed to be 10% and, if the operation were successful, the patient would enjoy his normal expectation of life from the Registrar General's tables of about eighteen years. The decision maker is then asked: what is the minimum chance of success from the operation needed for the patient to be advised to undergo it? If the utility of normal life expectation is 1 and that of immediate death is 0, the decision maker's value or utility of a life expectation of three years can be calculated from his answer. It is then possible to devise further plausible situations in which life expectation is improved and to repeat the questions with other levels of mortality. In this way, estimates of value or utility could be obtained from a number of subjects corresponding to a range of life expectations.

In a particular case when this was done (see Card, 1980), the graph of the utility function obtained was concave (Figure 11.4). This means that the future years of life are implicitly discounted, with greater value being attached to the proximate years. A number of functions can be used to describe this concave curve, an exponential or logarithmic function (as shown in the figure) being perhaps the simplest.

If we revert to the earlier problem of section 11.6 the life expectation in the patient suffering from a possibly cancerous ulcer has to be estimated. For this purpose reliable statistics of the prognosis following surgical treatment are available. Of all patients with stomach cancer, about 5 to 10% survive five years, but ulcer cancer has a somewhat more favourable prognosis and might be judged as having a five-year survival rate of 15%. The 'expectation' of this condition is then calculated at about 1.8 years and, from the graph of an appropriate utility function such as Figure 11.4, the corresponding utility is read off. This figure is now entered into the matrix of utilities in Table 11.3 in place of u_{22}. If the cancer is first treated medically for two months so that time is lost, the utility is less. It might be judged that it would be reduced to a 10% survival at five years. This, after reconversion into a utility value, allows a new figure to be entered in place of u_{21}. The utility of u_{11} can be taken as 1 since the patient with a healed ulcer can be regarded as normal for all practical purposes. If an unnecessary operation is done to a patient with a benign ulcer, his expectation will be slightly diminished and the utility is calculated for, say, a 10% reduction in 'expectation'. This figure can be entered in place of u_{12}.

With the matrix of utilities completed, it is now possible to calculate the

Figure 11.4. Utility of life expectation

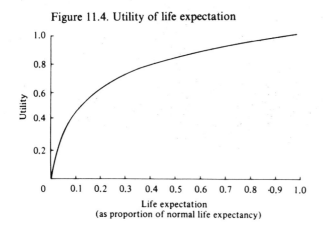

Life expectation
(as proportion of normal life expectancy)

best treatment between T_1 and T_2 which, given the various assumptions made here and earlier, proves to be the medical treatment. But the utility gain in using gastroscopy (T_3) is known so that, with the introduction of costs, a view can be formed as to whether gastroscopy is justified. The efficiency of each treatment is now re-calculated by measuring the gain in expected utility per unit cost. This can be done both for the medical treatment, the optimal initial treatment, and also for treatment using gastroscopy which provides perfect information. When this was done in the particular situation described here it was found that gastroscopy was not justified.

One further step can be taken. Suppose that after six weeks of medical treatment the ulcer fails to heal. If all ulcers were given medical treatment the 10% which are malignant would not heal, together with a small proportion of the truly benign ulcers, so that the probability of an ulcer which fails to heal being malignant rises steeply and would approach 0.5. It is now possible to re-analyse the decision options after adjusting the matrix of utilities to include the increased probability of malignancy. When this is done the most favourable treatment becomes surgical (T_2) and the additional cost of gastroscopy is justified. Given the various assumptions used here, the derived decision rule is: initially treat all ulcers medically; if any ulcer fails to heal after six weeks carry out gastroscopy and treat accordingly. This is, indeed, the advice that many clinicians would give. The various options and outcomes are illustrated in the decision tree of Figure 11.5 with the optimum strategy shown by the thick black line.

This analysis has been made on the assumption that gastroscopy is error

Figure 11.5. The ulcer patient decision tree

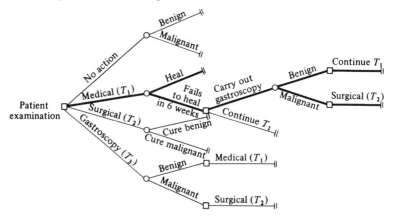

free. Strictly this is untrue, but the implied error is slight and, moreover, the error rate could be measured and incorporated in the calculations. While clinical analyses of this form are clearly not yet commonplace, the example indicates the strides that have been made in recent years in formalizing the use of all relevant information into the diagnostic process.

12
Risk in public policy

12.1 Introduction

Public policy is an all-embracing term. In this chapter, three strands are distinguished for discussion. The first relates to social policies, such as the wearing (or non-wearing) of seat belts; the second to commercial-type decisions that come within the public domain (for example, the development of *Concorde*, the possibility of a Channel Tunnel, or the planned size of British Steel); the third to decisions in the political area concerning matters such as the scale of disaster preparations, or the balance of public expenditure between education and health services. These sub-divisions are not watertight, but provide a framework for discussion.

Two general points tend to colour most decisions in the public policy domain. The first is the view of politicians that their primary task is to be re-elected. This leads to an overriding emphasis on the short-term effects of decisions, with correspondingly lower emphasis on longer-term consequences. This would not matter if the areas in which public policy operated were confined to those of little consequence and easy reversibility but with the increasing involvement of governments – particularly in the UK – with commercial-type operations and large-scale capital development program-mes, this shortened time horizon has some very unfortunate side effects. Moreover, such a policy framework conditions those concerned with decisions outside the public domain to think not so much in terms of 'what can be done best within this Government policy' but 'what can be done that will as far as possible be robust under a change of Government policy'.

The second point relates to Government accounting conventions. Traditionally each year is considered separately and, moreover, capital and revenue expenditures are not firmly distinguished – especially with regard to the composition of the Public Sector Borrowing Requirement (PSBR) –

nor is expenditure directly set against any compensating forms of revenue that may be raised. This approach can mean that, while revenue expenditure will often have priority (salaries of civil servants, pensions for the elderly, etc. have to be paid) any squeezes come primarily on capital projects. Ironically many such projects that might have been welcomed by the Government and industry alike if they were in the private sector, are ruled out merely because they have perforce to be in the public sector. Such an anomalous approach to expenditure can, from time to time, have a deleterious effect.

An example of this confusion arose in summer 1981 over a proposal to build a North Sea pipeline at a cost of £2 billion to rescue gas currently flared from the drilling operations. The project was initially to be financed by private endeavours, but failed to get off the ground because all the gas had to be sold to one customer only: British Gas. Thus a single risk factor, the price at which the gas could be sold, was considered too uncertain for private investors to judge the project properly on the basis of expected returns. It was subsequently argued by a Member of Parliament that, if public capital was to bear the risk, it would be logical to maximize simultaneously total profit and total supplies, as opposed to maximizing profits and minimizing risk which he considered incorrectly to be the private sector aim. If we assume profits are struck after paying interest and amortizing capital, it is not generally feasible to achieve both the MP's objectives simultaneously. There would normally have to be a trade-off between the two, since supply maximization commonly leads to lower total profits than could otherwise be achieved. Transferring the project into the public domain does not eliminate the need to define the acceptable balance between conflicting objectives. Such a trade-off is, indeed, all the more important in this instance since the risk element dictates that the profits can only be expected profits, not certain profits.

12.2 Social policies

For many social policies a key issue is the value to be placed upon a human life, since the cost of reducing a risk has to be placed alongside the value put on the lives saved or the injuries avoided. For example, any analysis of the benefits of safety schemes on the roads requires such a valuation. In 1976 the UK put the value of a life saved at about £40000 (which would in 1982 presumably be about £80000); in Canada the figure used was £66000 and in Australia £78000. These differences are large enough to make it possible for the choice of figure used to affect the decisions made on the basis of standard decision analysis procedures. Card and Mooney (1977) have suggested three possible approaches for estimating the monetary value of a human life for public policy purposes, although no standard and agreed method exists.

The classical economist's approach, dating from the seventeenth century, looks at the value of a human life in terms of its future productive output which in turn is measured by the worker's earnings. The total expected earnings, discounted to its present worth, then gives a measure of the value of that life to society. Such a measure by itself would mean that, on a person's retirement from work at 65, the value of the life is then put at nil. Most societies do not behave like this, however, but instead provide a retirement pension, and various goods such as subsidized transport, free access to museums, etc., which implies that society continues to value retired people. For more accuracy, therefore, some addition must be made to the initial calculated figure. Nevertheless, this approach has been used in the UK by the Department of Transport to guide the development of road safety policies.

The advantage of such an approach is that it provides a minimal figure, since the value of life could hardly be less than the figure obtained in this way, and such figures can – at least approximately – be calculated on an agreed basis. The approach can be criticized for ignoring existing decision-making processes in areas such as the Health Service which, perhaps unconsciously, put a different implicit value on human life, and also for not considering the views of individuals.

A second approach, therefore, examines the decisions made within the Health Service and calculates the value of life implicit in these decisions. Such values are, however, rarely made explicit and commonly lead to a wide range of different values for the same human life. Suppose a man of 30 has chronic renal failure and is treated by renal dialysis at home. In the UK this is expensive and the cost over the years, discounted to present values, will certainly run into tens of thousands of pounds. Alternatively, suppose the same man is a drug addict. Almost certainly society will only spend on his recovery a small fraction of what it would have spent on assisting him if he had renal failure. Such decision making would thus be described as incoherent. However, only if all health measures were analysed to yield implicit values, and the public kept informed and encouraged to give their views, could a consensus opinion by the community be reasonably expected to emerge for the valuation of human lives.

The third approach ascertains from individual members of society the value(s) they individually consider should be used. To achieve this, the implicit valuation of life is made by enquiring how much the individual would pay to reduce the risk of death by a certain amount. The method is open to the criticism that people find great difficulty in estimating small chances of great gains or great losses, and their estimates can usually be shown to be incoherent. This approach has, therefore, not yet been developed satisfactorily.

A further and rather separate approach is to examine the monetary awards made by the courts in cases where loss of life is involved. The number of such cases is unfortunately (for this purpose!) relatively low, and the circumstances of each individual case vary so widely, that no general overall picture emerges. As far as it is possible to discern a trend, the damages given by the courts for the 'average man' broadly follow the figures suggested by the first approach.

Whichever approach is adopted depends on the value judgements of the individual. The third approach has clearly not yet been established. The second approach will ultimately reflect the feelings and valuations of the public who are paying for the Health Service, but the current valuations it yields range too widely to be of much value. The first method at least provides a readily obtainable minimal figure which agrees broadly with the approach of the courts. When dealing with states of health rather than life or death – an important area that is at present almost totally unexplored – it is probably better to be content with an approximation. Over time, methods of estimation should improve and the notion of relative values, combined with a few absolute values, can be used to smooth the progression values over age and degrees of severity of disabilities.

12.3   Accidental deaths

Technically the value put on a human life should be adapted to the age of the individual concerned; being in general highest for young adults and dropping to zero or even negative for elderly people. If pursued literally as a means of formulating public policy it would imply mowing down the old age pensioners on pedestrian crossings! This is clearly absurd from a social point of view, although the use of an *average* figure for a life does have some relevance to the formulation of public policy. The whole argument can, however, be turned on its head and alternative safety measures ranked according to the apparent cost per life saved; those where this cost is lowest being accepted as a first priority, and so on. In West Germany a study was made in 1972 of the costs and possible effects of various road safety measures on expressways. The lighting of all such roads was expected to save some 90 lives per year; the fitting of four lap-and-shoulder belts per car (with 70% usage) 2000 lives per year. (For details see Stork, 1973.) The costs of implementing these two measures, expressed on a per-life-saved basis, were estimated at £2.80 million and £0.16 million, respectively, in 1975 terms. Similar valuations were put on a whole range of possibilities, a ranking established and a choice made between alternatives on a cost-per-life-saved basis. Two difficulties with such analyses concern the very differing popularity ratings of the measures and, what is probably of more importance, the effect of the cost of implementation involved possibly falling on different groups.

An example of the inconsistencies resulting from not looking at proposals on the basis of cost per expected life saved is illustrated by the 1974 United Kingdom legislation on Health and Safety at Work. This has led, inter alia, to a tightening of fire precautions in public buildings to an extent that the full costs, falling on the owners, cannot even yet be estimated with precision. (It is interesting that the Act itself ducks the question of what is an acceptable level of risk by talking about a place of work that is 'so far as it is reasonably practicable, safe' etc.). Table 12.1 gives the deaths from fires in the UK in the three years around the time the legislation was enacted, broken down by location. The Act applied primarily only to the category 'other buildings'. Suppose the total cost of implementing this legislation is £1 billion (This is a low estimate; the true figure is certain to be considerably higher.) Amortizing this sum over 50 years at 15% per year gives a cost of about £160 million per year. Assume further that, with these added precautions, the annual death rate is halved, or in round numbers, 50 deaths per year are saved. The cost per life saved is thus about £3.2 million per life. While in no way denigrating the desire to save life, this may well be a very expensive way of spending money to save life compared with, say, selected improvements in road safety of the type discussed earlier. It seems that no detailed discussion occurred in Parliament, when the 1974 Act was passed, of the costs that would be incurred, or the consequences in terms of the number of lives saved. No formal comparisons were made with alternative safety measures, and the public may possibly even have felt that the hoped-for improvements were to be a 'free good' and not something that would eventually have

Table 12.1. *Deaths caused by fires*

Source of fire	Year		
	1974	1975	1976
Houses	549	480	458
Flats, maisonettes, etc.	238	240	232
Other buildings	136	83	84
Road vehicles	45	50	60
Other locations	78	67	61

to be financed out of rates and taxes, or by extra hotel charges, shop and restaurant prices, etc. We apparently expect fire precautions in a public building to be several times more stringent (and thus safer) than we accept in our own homes. This paradox may be the fault of a departmental system of Government, but it is probably equally the fault of a system that does not look at costs and benefits as a total system.

12.4 The smoking story

The previous chapter discussed the excess mortality apparently incurred by smokers; the excess showing up basically through increased incidence of cancer of the lung. There are a number of options for reducing the risk. One way would be to ban smoking altogether, another to raise substantially the rate of tax on tobacco products. The effects of such changes could be measured along a number of dimensions of which the following are the most immediate:

(*a*) effect on revenue to Treasury,

(*b*) loss of employment in the industry (manufacture, distribution, selling),

(*c*) saving of costs of hospital care for those who would be hospitalized due to smoking,

(*d*) increase of productive capacity by those who would otherwise be incapacitated or die early, balanced by increased pension costs for them.

(*e*) loss of enjoyment by those who smoke, set against gain in contentment through longer life.

Some of these items are capable of reasonably precise estimation. For item (*a*) a point of interest is the variation in revenue received in relation to the possible rates of duty that might be imposed. It cannot be strictly linear since, beyond a certain point, consumption will decline as rates of duty are raised. Indeed, if rates were heavy enough revenue would fall to zero. Item (*b*) is in one sense illusory in that purchasing power not used on tobacco, would be spent elsewhere – more travel, more housing, more consumer goods – and should thereby generate equivalent employment in other fields. Under (*c*) the financial saving should be the difference between hospital costs incurred and those that would have been incurred over a lifetime if the individual had been a non-smoker. This is a difficult calculation and is not just the cost of treating cancer patients. Item (*d*) is more substantial and could be estimated by applying the average annual added value per person to the number of persons dying from cancer of the lung each year for the number of years remaining to their retirement age, and deducting the estimated extra national pension costs. There is also a private cost here in that insurance companies and pension funds are affected, but this would be more in the nature of a transfer payment between individuals, and would not affect the national balance sheet. Item (e) is virtually incapable of quantification in money terms. Nevertheless it is a factor which colours political considerations as to the levels of tobacco duty that can reasonably be imposed.

Overall one recognizes that the problem is handled primarily as a political issue between items (a) and (e): the revenue earned in (a) versus the popularity at the ballot box as measured by (e). There have, in recent years, been efforts to swing public opinion on the health hazard basis but, judging from consumption figures, these have had little overall effect, although they have had considerable effect on individuals. The consolidated balance sheet approach is difficult, but it must remain an important objective if the smoking risk issue is to be put in a rational overall context.

12.5   Total safety

The conventional wisdom in many quarters on social risk has often been to aim for zero risk, i.e. perfect safety. However, the pendulum has not swung over completely to zero risk yet, as media reports of major accidents testify, and there is growing acceptance that the safety level to be aimed at in any particular area of risk is something short of absolute safety. The goal to be sought is a level of safety that, while short of total safety, provides enough safety, or an *acceptable level* or risk. Safety is a normal 'good' like any other (chairs, butter, ice cream, tractors, etc.) in the sense that more can be had of it at the cost of foregoing other things, in the shape of goods or time for relaxation. It is unlike many other 'goods', however, because the marginal cost of producing an extra unit of safety increases as the level of safety improves. The costs of safety in activities that can lead to accidents is made up of what *accidents* cost (which is broadly related linearly to the number of accidents) and what *preventing further accidents costs* (which broadly rises ever more sharply as the number of accidents reduces). Adding the two cost curves together as shown in Figure 12.1 gives a total safety cost curve with a minimum at the 'optimal' safety point. To the left of this point, accident costs fall more slowly than prevention costs rise so that the marginal value to society is negative. To the right, accident costs rise faster than prevention costs fall so that the marginal value is positive. The optimal situation occurs where the change from positive to negative takes place, that is at the point where marginal accident rates and prevention costs balance precisely.

There is room for debate about the shape of the curves. For example, it could be argued in a particular case that there may be increasing returns to prevention expenditure over a very wide range. This would imply that the accident cost curve falls more rapidly than the prevention cost curve rises (moving from right to left) for much longer than is depicted in Figure 12.1. As long as diminishing returns set in at some point however – i.e. the prevention costs curve eventually rises more steeply than the accident one falls – the original analysis holds. However, the method by which 'accident costs' are measured is important for it is this curve, which supposedly includes not only the reduction in life expectancy but also the reduction in life quality that accompanies the disability and suffering resulting from an accident, that plays a major role in determining the optimum point. Even if these 'non-monetary' costs are felt to be undervalued and accordingly given much greater weight, an analogous situation applies with the accident cost curve being shifted upwards. The optimal level of safety then becomes a much safer one. But it requires increased prevention expenditure – i.e. less consumption of other goods – to achieve this. The question is how much people are willing to pay for further reductions in accident level, especially when the prevention costs curve is rising more rapidly than the accident cost curve is falling.

Figure 12.1. Accident and prevention costs versus number of accidents

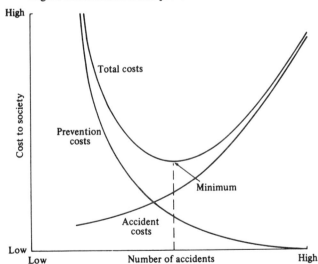

12.6 The cost of safety

Two ways have been used to find how much people (individually or collectively) are willing to pay for a defined improvement in safety and, by pushing this to the point where their answer is 'nothing', fixing the level of risk acceptable to them. An individual can be asked how he behaves in relation to safety, or alternatively he can be asked to express his attitudes. The approaches are designated the '*revealed preference*' approach (what preference regarding risk does one's behaviour reveal) and the '*expressed preference*' approach (what preferences concerning risk does one express when asked).

On the basis of observed (revealed) behaviour there is a level of risk below which a particular danger is effectively ignored, broadly set by the death rate from natural hazards (lightning strikes, snake or insect bites, meteors, earthquakes, etc.). This rate has been put by many analysts somewhere around one death per million people per year. On the other hand, the risk of death from disease hasn't diminished much this century despite the progress of medicine, remaining at around 10 000 in a million (or 1%) per year. Only a pathological minority seem prepared to run more than 1 in 100 chance of dying in a year, however high the benefits. Between these lower and upper boundaries of one in 10^6 and 10^2 per year, Starr (1976) claims that people reveal a willingness to vary the level of risk run in relation to the benefits involved. With a number of qualifications individuals' behaviour demonstrates that they are prepared to accept a level of risk (probability of death per year) many times greater in activities where participation is voluntary – private aviation, smoking, leisure sports – than when the individual is either not in control, or his exposure to the risk is involuntary (public aviation, pollution, floods, earthquakes, etc.). So, while requiring a one in a million chance of death (per year) or less on public transport, the individual accepts something like a one in 10 000 chance, or even higher, in private transport.

But risk acceptance also varies with the perceived benefits of the activity. At each level of risk there is a minimum level of benefit which will make such a risk acceptable, subject to the established fixed outer boundaries. In the case of involuntary activities, Figure 12.2 encapsulates Starr's hypothesis, an S-shaped curve portraying the risk/benefit threshold (both scales are on a logarithmic basis). The methodology and numbers have been criticized by a number of writers, but it seems to accord with direct observation. For example, a group of American anaesthetists who formulated a national programme on risk evaluation in anaesthetics were surprised to find that, over some 30 years of intensive research into the development of a new family of safer anaesthetics, the accident rate in surgery had not gone down. A physician pointed out that the surgeon, instead of keeping the patient on the table for 30 minutes for a simple operation, now kept him there for a complicated operation lasting six hours. The availability of better anaesthetics had widened the range of operating feasibility, but the overall accident rate had not significantly diminished.

A form of feedback system appears to be at work. The 'black spot' approach to accident prevention assumes that, if a particular spot (for example, a road junction) where many accidents occur can be identified, and steps taken to remove the cause a reduction in the overall accident rate will result. Drivers may, however, drive not so much to reduce overall risk, but to keep it below some acceptable level. If they don't get the 'feedback' in one form of accident – or, more frequently, 'near misses' – at the black spot then they will respond by increasing their risk level elsewhere in the road system, possibly by faster driving on roads in general. The individual black spot may well be abolished, but the whole system becomes 'greyer' as a result. A number of widely distributed small-scale accidents provokes less public concern than a substantial series of accidents concentrated at a particular spot. The concentration possibly suggests a simple cause and hence – at least at first sight – a simple solution. Starr's arguments question the assumptions underlying this attitude.

This discussion is relevant to the nuclear debate, which has already been touched upon briefly. There is substantial public resistance in many countries to the use of nuclear generation for power supplies because of the possibility of accidents. Much of the debate seems to rest not so much on the size of the risk which from all counts appears to be relatively small, but on the argument that it is unjustifiable to compare risks that individuals might accept voluntarily (such as gliding) with those imposed

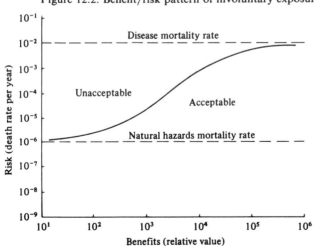

Figure 12.2. Benefit/risk pattern of involuntary exposure

on them in a way that they could not avoid (for example, by siting a nuclear power plant in their locality). A second strand of argument is linked to the view that an accident occurring in a nuclear power plant could affect a large group of people, rather than a lone individual. It seems that involuntary exposures, essentially controlled by Government appointed agencies, are apt by social demand to be about a thousand times safer (i.e. risk level one-thousandth part) than similar voluntary exposures where the choice is made by individuals.

A further question concerns the effort (and cost) involved in making improvements to the risk level. For example, suppose it costs 100 money units for nuclear energy to reduce the occupational health risk per unit output by one man-day of illness, but for coal it only costs 20 money units. With a fixed sum of money available for safety improvements, coal improvements would save five times as many man-days of lost activity as risk reductions in nuclear plants. Although the numbers are only illustrative, they reflect the correct relative orders of magnitude and indicate the need to be clear as to the objectives. Different people will be saved from injury or death if the money is spent on coal or oil rather than on nuclear power operations but, looking at it on a purely statistical basis, a higher overall social gain would be achieved for a fixed monetary expenditure. Expressed preferences of individuals are, indeed, not always consistent when viewed in this way.

There may be other motivations involved in arguing why not to follow the above form of analysis. A switch to nuclear power away from coal or oil may cost jobs, perhaps in a particular location where alternative opportunities are scarce. This is where a temporary social subsidy may be deemed desirable, although if it is done on a permanent basis it lowers industry's world competitiveness. A further concern would be the possible link of nuclear power generation with nuclear weapons. The link would still be there on a world basis, irrespective of whether or not such processes are used for power generation.

12.7   The *Concorde* saga

Although the *Concorde* plan to develop a supersonic commercial passenger aircraft began in the 1950s and led to a substantial report (which was never published) in 1959, the first positive phase opened in November 1962 with the British and French governments signing a joint agreement to develop and produce in collaboration a civil supersonic aircraft. The agreement contained no provision for unilateral withdrawal by either of the parties, and the project thus survived a British Government crisis shortly afterwards in late 1964. A second phase opened in mid-1968 when expenditure began on the first production aircraft, and the initial flight of a prototype aircraft took place in early 1969. Phases 1 and 2 involved substantial costs, but negligible receipts. Phase 3 began in January 1976 with the first scheduled flights of *Concorde*. In this phase the sale returns, though increasing over time, remained after deduction of the emerging operating costs (principally fuel and labour) insufficient to cover the amortized R & D and construction costs. Only in phase 4 when construction is complete, and full operational use is being made of all the aircraft, could the project expect to begin to earn a cash surplus and recover the costs incurred earlier.

There is considerable doubt as to whether phase 4 will ever be reached and it seems to be accepted that, on any conventional costing basis, *Concorde* has been and continues to be a money loser. The development costs (estimated in March 1976 to total cumulatively £2.1 billion at 1975 prices) have not been recovered, while later operating losses effectively continue to raise the figure rather than diminish it. As late as May 1982 it was reported that the *Concorde* project would continue to lose a further £2 million per annum on current account, but cancellation would cost a once and for all £34 million, mostly caused by the severance of various spares contracts.

Of course there are other external and intangible factors connected with the *Concorde* project, and Thompson (1976) examined eleven such factors in some depth. Five he rejected as having no net value either positive or negative. Three others, namely spinoff, temporary employment and technical achievement he valued positively at £47 million (1975 prices) while three others, namely balance of payments, engine noise and flyover rights he values negatively at £61 million, giving an overall negative balance of £14 million. These amounts in total are minuscule in relation to the cumulated losses on the project as a whole.

In structuring a programme for such a development three strands can be discerned. The first concerns the chances of technical success and associated development costs. These two elements are entwined, with higher development costs being commonly associated with higher chances of success. The second strand is the projected cost and success of commercial production once technical success is assured; the third strand is the projected cost of operational use and sales made, with the associated revenues. All three involve judgements of risks and the need to make simple point estimates for, say, future revenues. It is surprising, nevertheless, to find such divided views in retrospect as to whether a project such as *Concorde* has indeed been a success and this confusion seems connected with the administrative processes involved throughout the history of the project.

One reason why such difficulties occur is that governments work hard to form a single institutional view. The consequence is that the risks are obscured and results presented as a single figure (often to a highly spurious degree of accuracy) on which the total concept succeeds or fails to win the necessary political support. Little or no specific mention is made of risk factors. This penchant for obscuring the risk factors seems to be very prevalent and part of the British governmental machine. A quotation from the Report of the Committee of Enquiry on the Structure of the Electricity Supply Industry (1976) of England and Wales is relevant:

> In many of its dealings with other bodies, and particularly with Government, the industry finds it difficult to speak with a single voice. The Department of Energy told us that the Government seeks to obtain one considered and consistent view from the industry on a large number of topics many of which may be inter-related. Examples are energy policy, the effects of price controls and incomes policies, financial planning, tariff policy, and the well-being of the industry's suppliers. The lack of positive powers at the centre of the industry means that, although the Secretary of State naturally looks for advice to the Chairman of the Electricity Council, which has a duty to advise him, the Chairman often cannot speak with authority on behalf of the whole industry; at most he may be able to state a range of views or give those of council members.

The concern for the single voice and the single number embraces a danger that this number attains mystical importance and yet, ironically, is then owned by no one individual. If the varying views of the different experts were known, perhaps both as individuals and after attempts at reconciliation of the differing views had occurred, the complexities of making a final positive decision to go ahead with some course of action and the risks involved in taking that action would be better appreciated.

At the time of writing, there are active proposals for private investment in a tunnel beneath the English Channel. All the private promoters, however, are seeking what amounts to a Government guarantee about the level of rail traffic through the tunnel. This is asking for revenue guarantees and hence is equivalent to removing one major source of risk. If this guarantee has to be given, it increases the case for the Government itself to provide the investment and thus participate fully in any upside potential of such a project.

In some fields the performance of experts is measured fairly carefully; for example geologists working on oil exploration, batsmen competing for a place in a Test side, doctors who specialize in particular types of surgery, lawyers who specialize in certain types of case. In many major public projects the electorate seems to be content to allow risk assessments to be cloaked in collectivism and to be little concerned with past performance records.

12.8 The decision to prosecute

The Director of Public Prosecutions (DPP) (or other authorities) makes decisions about whether or not legal proceedings should be taken against specified individuals in relation to alleged offences. Among a list of criteria the DPP gave in an interview (reported in *The Sunday Times* of 13 January 1980) his overriding rule was: 'Would there be at least a 50% chance of a conviction by a jury?' (The DPP effectively only deals with more serious crime where a jury is obligatory.) Figures show that, in 1979, the conviction rate at Crown Courts was 81%. However, this figure was made up of 60% of all defendants pleading guilty, 21% being convicted by the jury and 19% being acquitted by the jury. Hence, of those cases that are put to the jury, 52.5% are convicted.

There must be some relation between the 50% rule, the rate of conviction, and the number of convictions. Figure 12.3 shows a possible illustrative relation between the frequency (f) of a given probability estimate of conviction made by the DPP against that probability (p) of conviction. If the cut-off point for prosecution is taken as p_0, i.e. when the estimate made by the DPP is above p_0 proceedings are started, otherwise not, the proportion of those sent for trial who are convicted can be shown by the use of the calculus to be

$$\frac{2}{3}\frac{1-p_0^3}{1-p_0^2} \qquad (12.1)$$

while the number of trials per 1000 cases put to the DPP would be

$$1000(1-p_0^2) \qquad (12.2)$$

giving the number of convictions per 1000 cases put to the DPP as the

Figure 12.3. Conviction probability frequency curve

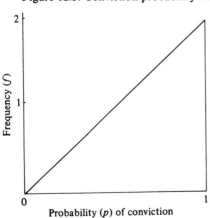

Probability (p) of conviction

product of (12.1) and (12.2) or

$$\frac{2000}{3}(1-p_0^3) \tag{12.3}$$

Table 12.2 gives numerical values for these expressions for a range of values of p_0. A direct trade-off is seen between the convictions and the conviction rate. Where should public policy put the boundary? There seems no particular reason why p_0 should be fixed at the 0.5 mark. A lower figure for p_0 raises the number of trials, but increases the number of convictions (and also the number of acquittals). The administrative costs involved also go up. Raising the level of P_0 has the reverse effect. This analysis looks at things from the point of view of the DPP, but there is also a public point of view in the sense that lowering the threshold of p_0 would presumably increase the possibility of false convictions. Hence, while it is conventional to use the figure of 0.5, rather than 0.4 or 0.6, say, this seems to be an uneasy compromise position.

Table 12.2. *Trials and conviction rates*

Cut-off point p_0	Trials per 1000 cases put to DPP (12.2)	Conviction rate for trials held (12.1)	No. of convictions per 1000 cases (12.3)
0.2	960	0.689	661
0.3	910	0.713	649
0.4	840	0.743	624
0.5	750	0.778	584
0.6	640	0.817	523
0.7	510	0.859	438
0.8	360	0.904	325

12.9 The political angle

Politics enters virtually all decisions made in the public domain. Rewarding one's supporters, sweetening possible antagonists, putting money into dockyards or a new road bridge just before a crucial local parliamentary by-election, have all become part of the way of life. One suspects the electorate is completely cynical about such actions and it is largely money down the drain in a political sense, but it goes on nevertheless. A multitude of other decisions in government are essentially political but not in the frothy and somewhat frivolous category mentioned above. Two examples are quoted here.

The first is a war-time example described by Jones (1965), a former Chief Scientist to the Government. In July 1944 the Germans launched the V1, or Doodlebug, attack on London with unmanned rocket-type aircraft that exploded on impact with the ground. The controls of the aircraft were not perfect and the bombs landed across London in a cigar-shaped pattern running roughly north-west to south-east. (The launching platforms were in the Netherlands and the aircraft flew basically in a straight line towards the centre of London.) The Germans were anxious to establish the mean point of impact so that the fuel input of the planes, which governed the distance travelled before the engine cut out and they fell to ground as a bomb, could be adjusted appropriately. It was believed that the Germans were obtaining information through reports of bomb damage in English newspapers which were freely available to German agents in Dublin. The scientists suggested that, if the press in South London could be persuaded to omit any mention of bombs falling in their area, while those bombs falling in North London continued to be reported, the Germans would deduce that the mean point of impact was beyond the centre of London and lower the planned mileage of the planes accordingly. A greater proportion of bombs than hitherto would then fall short of London in the Kent countryside, and hence lower total damage to property and lessen civilian casualties. The scheme was put to the Cabinet and met with violent hostility since it appeared to some members of the Cabinet that the Government was thereby interfering with individual liberty: i.e., although total casualties would be fewer, different people would be killed or injured from those that the Germans would injure if left alone. The plan was therefore rejected. However, by some strange irony, the rejection did not get through to the appropriate quarters so that the plan was actually implemented and a significant saving in damage and lives was made, even though more bombs did fall in the relatively rural areas of Kent.

A second example concerns the furore that arose in the summer of 1976 when, after a long dry spring and summer, water shortages emerged in many parts of the UK and complaints from consumers became rife. One water spokesman, in a television interview, stated that the planning of the water supply system (which involves crucial decisions as to the number, sizes and locations of reservoirs) was based on an assumption that a severe water shortage could only be tolerated about once in 50 years. If this figure were to be tightened, for example to one in 100 years, then substantial extra capital and revenue would be involved. The spokesman wondered whether consumers would be willing to pay these costs. Despite this explanation, criticism of the water authorities continued, although no fundamental change in basic policy has since been made explicit.

Few governments have any declared overall policy to guide decisions being taken on risks by their departments or agencies. Disparities are rife but the regulation of hazards is rarely, if ever, discussed in the Cabinet or in Parliament; political parties show little concern, intervening only to safeguard specific interests. Safety regulations and general risk policy are subject to none of the traditional checks or constraints.

In the absence of any coherent policy on the regulation of risks, government departments are turning increasingly to the acceptable risk philosophy, favoured and promulgated by the civil servants, and the 'independent' expert advisory committees that substitute for more open and democratic forums. At first sight this seems a reasonable approach. Only a few risks are severe enough to attract the need to make absolute prohibitions. In most cases, social and economic factors limit the 'ban-it' strategy. Thus risks that appear mild when weighed against the tangible benefits that the risky product or activity brings, or those so widespread that it is hard to delineate and protect the threatened group, or those that are expensive to control, are all ameliorated and not prohibited.

To take one example, regulations to protect coal miners against the debilitating dust disease pneumoconiosis appeared in 1975. An industry-wide study by M. Jacobsen and colleagues over a ten-year period had provided a relation between mean dust concentration and an index of damage to miners' lungs, while the regulations stipulated 'permitted amounts' of respirable dust ranging from 6 to 12 mg/m^3. Neither the regulations, nor the Jacobsen team's work, showed how these figures were determined. Jacobsen's paper indicates, however, that if an 8 mg/m^3 standard were observed, the risk of developing pneumoconiosis after 35 years in a pit would be 3.4%. Thus, under the regulations, the risk is not being removed entirely, but reduced to an 'acceptable' level; a level which it is not unreasonable to assume has been greatly influenced by the economic health of the coal industry. Determining the relation between exposure and the risk of developing some measurable damage is obviously a scientific process. But the final judgement of the end point – by how much the risk should be reduced and at what cost – is not.

If, as many contend, it is possible to determine the level of risk that is acceptable by society in general, such a level could be made the criterion by which any risk is scientifically declared 'acceptable'. However, in practice, it is difficult to quantify risks in the way this approach demands, and more crucially, it is impossible to compare risks of different types undertaken for different reasons in varying social circumstances.

The image of accuracy in measuring risks conjured up by the 'acceptable risk' approach is a mirage. A further fallacy is that there is a single quantitative level of risk that is 'acceptable'. Acceptable to whom? From whose viewpoint is the risk to be judged: its creators, its victims, experts, representative organizations, the community at large, the Government? Each viewpoint defines its own, sometimes widely different, level of acceptability.

A committee of enquiry set up to recommend measures to control the possibility of death or disease from, say, anthrax is bound (as it did) to recommend stringent and costly controls. Anthrax has caused only about six deaths over the past two decades. The forum, however, in which it is decided whether money is best spent this way or on some other form of risk reduction in an unrelated field (and possibly under a different Government department) remains unclear and its absence must lead to inconsistent decisions being made concerning risk-reduction measures.

There seems to be no discernible method by which government knowingly allocates scarce resources between, say, safety in the nuclear industry and on the roads. Proponents of the acceptable risk philosophy claim that such decisions can be guided by a comparison of relative risk reductions per unit costs in the various areas. But the comparisons normally made are inexact and discriminate against those 'areas of hazard' where risks are more difficult to quantify. More fundamentally, the numerical severity of a risk is only one dimension of it, and is an insufficient parameter on which to base a comparison. Just because the risk of working in a particular industry is no greater than, say, of being struck by lightning, is no reason for claiming that both are acceptable. It may be that the risk of being killed by lightning is not accepted, but tolerated only because of the expense of any remedial strategy. The problem of one-dimensionality is not solved by introducing a distinction between voluntary and involuntary risks, because there is no such thing as completely involuntary risk: all risks can be ameliorated, although the cost of doing so may be prohibitive.

The political decision about which risks are to be reduced, and by how much, ought ideally to be aided by the best possible information available concerning the magnitude of the various risks and the associated costs of marginal reductions, to ensure as far as is possible equity of treatment between the different elements of a totally risk conscious society.

Appendix A. Handling probabilities

A.1 Introduction

There are basic rules to which all probabilities must conform. Thus the manner in which probabilities of compound events are derived from those of simple events is quite invariant and independent of the methods by which the probabilities of the simple events have been initially obtained.

All probabilities are non-negative and expressed on a scale from 0 to 1. (Occasionally the scale is expressed in percentage terms from 0 to 100.) The greatest degree of probability which any future event can have is certainty, and the scale assigns this a probability of 1.00 (or 100%). At the other end of the scale, the lowest degree of probability that a future event can have is 'impossibility' to which is assigned a probability of zero. The next two sections introduce the basic rules for the addition and multiplication of probabilities when compound events are concerned.

A.2 Addition of probabilities

A stationery shop stocks three types of stapling machine. Examination of past records shows that 40% of customers purchase a machine of type A, 35% one of type B, and 25% of type C. Types A and B are made by manufacturer X, type C by manufacturer Y. A customer comes in to buy a stapling machine; what is the probability that he will buy one made by manufacturer X?

Denote by $P(A)$ the probability that a machine of type A is purchased, etc. and by $P(A+B)$ the probability that either type A or type B is purchased. Then

$$P(A) = 0.4, \quad P(B) = 0.35 \quad \text{and} \quad P(A+B) = 0.75$$

This illustrates the simplest form of the addition rule, namely that the probability that any one of several possible, mutually exclusive, uncertain events will occur is the sum of the separate probabilities.

Expressed in formal terms

$$P(A+B+\ldots) = P(A)+P(B)+\ldots \tag{A.1}$$

The term 'mutually exclusive' is important, meaning that the events under consideration cannot occur simultaneously. The next example uses a situation in which the events are not mutually exclusive.

The employees of a large organization include 70% who have passed an examination in English and 50% who have passed in mathematics. An employee is chosen at random; what is the probability that the employee has either one or both of the examination qualifications?

Here $P(A) = 0.7$ and $P(B) = 0.5$, where A represents 'English' and B represents 'mathematics'. But we cannot just add the two probabilities to get $P(A+B)$ as before, since that would mean double counting those who possess both qualifications. The reasoning is clear from Figure A.1, a form of *Venn* diagram, where the rectangle represents the totality of employees. The circle on the right encloses those who have English, that on the left those who have mathematics. The shaded area of overlap represents those who have both examinations and would be included twice in a straight addition of the two circles. (In passing, note that $P(A)+P(B)$ would be 1.2, and hence an impossible probability.) The modified probability expression in this instance to avoid overlap is

$$P(A+B) = P(A)+P(B)-P(AB) \qquad \text{(A.2)}$$

where $P(AB)$ represents the probability of both outcomes occurring simultaneously, i.e. that the individual possesses both English and mathematics qualifications.

In this instance no further progress could be made unless the value of $P(AB)$ were known. Although this probability must be at least 0.2, it could be as high as 0.5 and more information is required to proceed.

Figure A.1. An illustrative Venn diagram

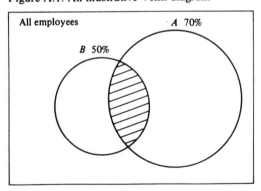

A.3 Multiplication of probabilities

Two business partners, A and B, are 45 and 53 years old respectively. The probability that a person aged 45 will live at least another 20 years is 0.66 while the probability for a person aged 53 is 0.47. What is the probability that both partners will still be alive 20 years hence?

Four mutually exclusive cases can arise in this situation, where two separate and independent happenings, namely whether A lives or dies, and whether B lives or dies are jointly involved. The possible outcomes are:

A lives and B lives, denoted AB

A lives and B dies, denoted $A\bar{B}$

A dies and B lives, denoted $\bar{A}B$

A dies and B dies, denoted $\bar{A}\bar{B}$

These four joint outcomes are mutually exclusive in that *only one* can occur, but they are also 'only possible' in that one of the four *must* occur. Hence the overall probability $P(AB + A\bar{B} + \bar{A}B + \bar{A}\bar{B})$ is equal to 1, given that the four possible events are mutually exclusive and only possible. Now the probability that A lives is 0.66 and, if we know that he lives, the probability that B also lives is 0.47 provided that the outcomes are independent for the two partners (i.e. the death of A does not change the probability of B's death from the original figure of 0.47). The joint probability $P(AB)$ of both events occurring is then the product of the two probabilities, i.e. 0.66×0.47, or 0.31. Another way to look at it is to consider a larger number of situations of this kind. Then in 66% of the cases considered the Mr A will live, and in 47% of *these* cases the Mr B will also live the 20 years. Hence both live in 47% of 66% of cases, which is 31%.

The other three probabilities are calculated on similar lines:

A lives, B lives: probability $P(AB) = 0.31$

A lives, B dies: probability $P(A\bar{B}) = 0.35$

A dies, B lives: probability $P(\bar{A}B) = 0.16$

A dies, B dies: probability $P(\bar{A}\bar{B}) = 0.18$

These four probabilities sum to 1 as expected.

The information and the procedure to be followed is portrayed in the tree diagram given in Figure A.2. From the start point there are two possible outcomes relating to A either living or dying; these are then each allied to a similar bifurcation with regard to B living or dying. The probability at the end of each route is the product of the probabilities lying along the route, with the sum of the end-point

Figure A.2. Probability tree

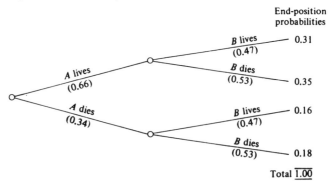

End-position
probabilities

B lives
(0.47) — 0.31

A lives
(0.66)

B dies
(0.53) — 0.35

A dies
(0.34)

B lives
(0.47) — 0.16

B dies
(0.53) — 0.18

Total $\overline{1.00}$

probabilities equal to 1. If $P(A)$ represents the probability of A living for 20 years and $P(B)$ similarly for B, with $P(\overline{A})$ and $P(\overline{B})$ representing their respective probabilities of dying within the 20-year period, then:

$$P(A\overline{B}) = P(A) \times P(\overline{B}) = 0.66 \times 0.53 = 0.35, \text{ etc.}$$

The analysis illustrates the multiplication rule, namely that the probability of the joint occurrence of independent events $A, B, C, \ldots$ is the product of their respective individual probablities. Expressed in formal terms

$$P(ABC \ldots) = P(A) \times P(B) \times P(C) \times \ldots \tag{A.3}$$

A.4   Combination of rules

Chapter 4 gives an illustration concerning accidents to car drivers. The probability of a male driver having an accident in a given year is 0.1; for a female driver it is 0.067. Of the drivers on the insurance company's books, two-thirds are male and one-third are female. The probability of a driver, drawn by lot, having an accident is required. Consider the two-step process: the sex of the chosen driver; whether or not he (or she) has an accident. Symbolically, let M represent male, F represent female, A an accident and $\overline{A}$ no accident. There are two mutually exclusive ways in which the outcome, an accident, can occur. The first is when a male driver is chosen who then has an accident, the second when a female driver is chosen who then has an accident. Hence from formula (A.1)

$$P(A) = P(MA) + P(FA)$$

Now the value of $P(MA)$ is not simply

$$P(MA) = P(M) \times P(A)$$

since $P(A)$ is dependent upon M or F. Instead

$$P(MA) = P(M) \times P(A/M)$$

where the latter term is referred to as the *conditional* probability of an accident, in this case conditional on the driver selected being a male. Thus

$$P(MA) = 0.67 \times 0.1 = 0.067$$

and by similar reasoning

$$P(FA) = 0.33 \times 0.067 = 0.022$$

giving

$$P(A) = P(MA) + P(FA) = 0.067 + 0.022 = 0.089$$

This indicates that, where events are not independent (for example, here the probability of an accident depended upon the sex of the individual) then the previous multiplication theorem (A.3) for probabilities should be amended to read:

$$P(ABC \ldots) = P(A) \times P(B/A) \times P(C/AB) \times \ldots \tag{A.4}$$

As a special case note that while $P(AB) = P(A) \times P(B/A)$, it is also equal to $P(B) \times P(A/B)$.

Suppose a box of ten fuses has five 'duds' indistinguishable by sight. A fuse is picked at random and tested, and the procedure repeated until the fuse selected is a good one. The probability that the first good fuse is found on the fourth attempt is required. Let the four choices in order be represented by the first four letters of the alphabet; A represents a good fuse and $\bar{A}$ a defective fuse, etc. Then the required probability from equation (A.4) is

$$P(\bar{A}\bar{B}\bar{C}D) = P(\bar{A}) \times P(\bar{B}/\bar{A}) \times P(\bar{C}/\bar{A}\bar{B}) \times P(D/\bar{A}\bar{B}\bar{C}) = \tfrac{5}{10} \times \tfrac{4}{9} \times \tfrac{3}{8} \times \tfrac{5}{7} = \tfrac{5}{84}$$

A.5   Fault analysis

Table A.1, based on Brook (1974), gives order of magnitude for the reliability (i.e. probability of failure) for the brakes on a car and, in the event of a failure, the relative severity of the outcome to the car and its driver. The probabilities in column 4, by formula (A.4), are obtained by multiplying the probability of a failure (in column 3) with the probability of the different kinds of outcome from a failure (given one has occurred) from column 1. Column 5 is the *expected* number of cases of each outcome in column 1 that would occur per year among a population of 20 million drivers. This expected number (see Section A.8 below) is the product of the number of drivers (20 mill.) with the appropriate probability from column 4 of each outcome occurring.

A relevant question is how many of those expected to be killed or injured would be saved by fitting cars with a 'back-up' or 'dual-braking' system. Examining this option requires distinguishing between components that are joined together in 'series' as opposed to being in 'parallel'. If there is a series structure, then all components need to work for the system to work. If there is a parallel structure, then some 'redundancy' – an alternative path or set of components – is available as 'back-up'. In the latter case, the system might keep working even though half (or more, depending on the number of back-up systems) of the components failed. In calculating the *overall* reliability of a system the simplest case to take is that

Table A.1. *Outcomes of sudden brake failure without warning*

Possible outcome (1)	Probability of outcome per case of brake failure (2)	Probability of brake failure per year[a] (3)	Probability of outcome per driver year (4)	Expected number of cases per year in a population of 20 million drivers (5)
(a) Car stopped safely on handbrake	0.900		0.0045	90000
(b) Minor damage; no injury	0.080	0.005	0.00040	8000
(c) Injury	0.019		0.000095	1900
(d) Death	0.001		0.000005	100

[a] Assumed to have a probability of 0.005 per driver-year, i.e. to occur once every 200 driver-years

when components and their failures are *independent* of one another. For ease of calculation the reliability R is defined as 1 minus the probability of failure.

If the system has a *series* structure, R is given by multiplying the individual values of reliability of each component, using formula (A.3). At the heart of the car braking system there is a 'master cylinder' M (containing most of the brake fluid which is essential for braking) with a reliability $R(M)$; this is connected to four 'slave cylinders' $C_1, ..., C_4$ (one at each wheel), each of which has a reliability $R(C_i)$. Then the overall reliability is given by

$$R = R(M) \times R(C_1) \times R(C_2) \times R(C_3) \times R(C_4)$$

If $R(M)$ and $R(C)$ are both 0.9 for a ten-year-old car, then $R = 0.59$. We can thus expect only 59 such cars in every 100 not to have a brake failure during the next year. The overall reliability is less than the reliability of any individual component in the system.

For a *parallel* structure, the overall reliability will on the other hand be much higher as the system 'has more than one life'. It survives as long as just one component keeps working (there is built-in *redundancy* or 'insurance' against failure). Suppose that a car has a dual-braking system (two braking systems in parallel), and that these have independent reliabilities of $R(A)$ and $R(B)$ respectively. The total reliability R is then given by the formula:

$$R = 1 - \{[1 - R(A)] \times [1 - R(B)]\} \tag{A.5}$$

Putting numbers into (A.5), with the two braking systems each having a reliability of 0.59 (as in the series example), the total reliability increases to about 0.83.

A.6 Bayes' approach

Many problems involve re-calculating initial probabilities in the light of fresh relevant information. This is done through Bayes' theorem. A patient admitted to hospital with abdominal pain may have appendicitis (A) or not ($\overline{A}$). The proportion of patients admitted to hospital with abdominal pain who actually turn out to have appendicitis is 25% (i.e. $P(A) = 0.25$). Patients are examined by the doctor and given either a positive appendicitis diagnosis (D) or not ($\overline{D}$). The percentage of patients with appendicitis who are diagnosed positively (the true positive rate) is 60% (i.e. $P(D/A) = 0.6$), while the percentage of patients who are diagnosed as having appendicitis but don't have it (the false positive rate) is 25% (i.e. $P(D/\overline{A}) = 0.25$).

From formula (A.4) above

$$P(AD) = P(A) \times P(D/A)$$

or alternatively

$$P(AD) = P(D) \times P(A/D)$$

Thus

$$P(D) \times P(A/D) = P(A) \times P(D/A) \tag{A.6a}$$

Similarly it can be shown that

$$P(D) \times P(\overline{A}/D) = P(\overline{A}) \times P(D/\overline{A}) \tag{A.6b}$$

Next consider the ratio of the two expressions (A.6*a*) and (A.6*b*)

$$\frac{P(A/D)}{P(\overline{A}/D)} = \frac{P(A)}{P(\overline{A})} \times \frac{P(D/A)}{P(D/\overline{A})}$$ (A.7)

(i)   (ii)   (iii)

giving one particular formulation of Bayes' theorem. Item (ii) is the ratio of the prior probabilities of having an appendicitis (i.e. the assessed chances before any diagnosis is made). Item (iii) is the ratio of the conditional probabilities of diagnosing an appendicitis; the numerator if the patient really has appendicitis, the denominator if he hasn't. The product of items (ii) and (iii) gives (i), the ratio of the posterior (or revised) probability after further information from the doctor's diagnosis) of having, or not having, appendicitis.

In this instance the relevant values gives

$$\frac{P(A/D)}{P(\overline{A}/D)} = \frac{0.25}{0.75} \times \frac{0.60}{0.25} = \frac{4}{5}$$

Since $P(A/D) + P(\overline{A}/D)$ must equal 1 it follows that

$$P(A/D) = \tfrac{4}{9} \quad \text{and} \quad P(\overline{A}/D) = \tfrac{5}{9}$$

Thus the probability of having appendicitis, even if the doctor has diagnosed it, is less than a half. (The figures used here are based on experience at a northern UK hospital.) This example only had two possible outcomes (i.e. you do or do not have appendicitis). Bayes' theorem is more general than this and can be applied to any number of outcomes as the next section demonstrates.

A.7   Bayes' theorem

The general form of Bayes' theorem, which is not proved here, runs as follows:

If $E_i(i = 1, 2, \ldots, r)$ are r mutually exclusive and only possible occurrences, such that an event F can occur only if one of these r results has occurred, then the probability that E_i occurred when F is known to have occurred is:

$$P(E_i/F) = \frac{P(E_i)P(F/E_i)}{\Sigma^r_{i-1}P(E_i)P(F/E_i)}$$ (A.8)

where $P(E_i)$ represents the prior probability of outcome E_i,
$P(F/E_i)$ represents the conditional probability that event F occurs, given that result E_i has occurred, and
$P(E_i/F)$ represents the posterior or revised probability of outcome E_i given that event F has occurred.

The following example concerns the oil wildcatter who has to decide whether or not to drill for oil before his option on a site expires. He is uncertain about the extent of the oil deposits at the site. The records of similar, and not quite so similar, drillings in the same area are available and he has already discussed the features peculiar to this particular site with his geologist, his geophysicist and his land agent. He could gain further information (but not necessarily perfect information) about the underlying geophysical structure at the site by arranging for seismic soundings. Such information is costly and, while indicative, is not of direct stratigraphical nature (i.e. does not indicate the kind of rock, sandstone, limestone, etc.). Only drilling can precisely determine this, and the wildcatter has to decide whether or not to purchase this information before he makes his basic decision whether to drill (D) or not ($\overline{D}$).

In formal terms suppose a well sunk on the site can be either dry (w_1), or wet (w_2), or soaking (w_3). Outcome w_1 is bad, outcome w_2 is so-so, while outcome w_3 is very good. After appropriate discussions, but without taking any seismic soundings, the oil wildcatter estimates that the probabilities for the three possible outcomes, if he should drill now, are 0.5 for w_1, 0.25 for w_2 and 0.25 for w_3.

Seismic soundings will give a result in the form of a 'good' or 'not so good' indication. A 'good' indication (G) is broadly linked to the presence of oil (i.e. to outcomes w_2 and w_3), while a 'not so good' indication ($\overline{G}$) is broadly linked to the absence of oil (i.e. to outcome w_1). Past experience of seismic soundings, in this and other sites, suggests that the probabilities given in Table A.2 are a fair summary of the relationship between the results of seismic soundings and subsequent drilled-well results.

Thus if a drilled well at a site were wet (w_2), then a seismic survey carried out at the site before drilling would have a probability of 0.6 of giving a positive result, with a probability of 0.4 of giving a negative result. Similarly for the other two possible drilling outcomes. Note that the seismic sounding results do discriminate, albeit not very precisely, between good and bad situations.

A seismic sounding is taken and gives a positive response (G). The oil wildcatter requires the revised or posterior probabilities for w_1, w_2 and w_3 respectively.

The information available can be itemized as follows:

Prior probabilities:

$$P(w_1) = 0.5$$
$$P(w_2) = 0.25$$
$$P(w_3) = 0.25$$

Conditional probabilities from Table A.2:

$$P(G/w_1) = 0.2, \quad P(\overline{G}/w_1) = 0.8$$
$$P(G/w_2) = 0.6, \quad P(\overline{G}/w_2) = 0.4$$
$$P(G/w_3) = 0.8, \quad P(\overline{G}/w_3) = 0.2$$

Table A.2. *Seismic sounding probabilities*

| Drilled well | Seismic sounding | | |
	G (positive)	$\overline{G}$ (negative)	Total
w_1 dry	0.2	0.8	1.0
w_2 wet	0.6	0.4	1.0
w_3 soaking	0.8	0.2	1.0

From formula (A.8)

$$P(w_1/G) = \frac{P(w_1)P(G/w_1)}{P(w_1)P(G/w_1)+P(w_2)P(G/w_2)+P(w_3)P(G/w_3)}$$
$$= \frac{0.5 \times 0.2}{0.5 \times 0.2+0.25 \times 0.6+0.25 \times 0.8} = \frac{2}{9}$$

Similar calculations for w_2 and w_3 give $\frac{3}{9}$ and $\frac{4}{9}$ respectively. These three probabilities sum to 1, the three results being mutually exclusive and only possible. Note that a result G from the seismic sounding has, not surprisingly, raised the probabilities for w_2 and w_3, but diminished that for w_1.

A.8   Expectation

The concept of an expected value has already been briefly introduced in Section A.6. Put more formally, if a course of action can result in r different outcomes with values $v_1, v_2, \ldots, v_r$ having probabilities $p_1, p_2, \ldots, p_r$ respectively ($\Sigma p_i = 1$) then the expected value of the action is

$$E = v_1 p_1 + v_2 p_2 + \ldots + v_r p_r = \Sigma_{i-1}^{r} v_i p_i \tag{A.9}$$

To illustrate this result consider a shop which stocks a weekly magazine, *Autodriver*. The shopkeeper pays 50p per copy and sells it for 70p per copy. Copies unsold at the end of the week cannot be returned and have no value. An assessment made of past demands per week is as follows:

Demand (copies per week)	Probability
10	0.05
12	0.10
14	0.15
16	0.30
18	0.20
20	0.15
22	0.05

The shopkeeper decides in future to stock 18 copies per week and requires his expected net income for this course of action.

If the demand in the week is 18 or more, only 18 copies are sold; whereas if it is below 18 the demand is met, and the spare copies are wasted. Hence his expected income from (A.9) above will be:

$$0.05 \times 10 \times 70+0.10 \times 12 \times 70+0.15 \times 14 \times 70+0.30 \times 16 \times 70+$$
$$0.20 \times 18 \times 70+0.15 \times 18 \times 70+0.05 \times 18 \times 70 = 1106.$$

The expenditure will be 18×50, or 900, each week and hence the expected net income will be $1106-900 = 206$. This expected net income is commonly referred to as EMV (expected monetary value).

Appendix B. Decision-making procedures

B.1   Introduction

Decisions can be crudely split into two kinds. The first relates to decisions connected with current problems that have an immediacy of application, many of which are colloquially referred to as 'patch-up jobs'. The payoff from each individual decision of this kind is likely to be fairly low, but the frequency of such decisions in any organization is commonly high. The second kind of decision is the search for new opportunities and the making of decisions that will influence the organization's fortunes over the longer term. Managers are generally concerned with both types of decision, the mix for an individual manager depending very broadly on his seniority and level of management. Most junior and middle managers are primarily concerned with the former type of problem-solving situations; senior managers are primarily concerned with the latter type of strategic decisions. Risk enters both types of decision, although in rather different ways. The balance between what is termed (Chapter 3) 'risk' as opposed to 'uncertainty' is generally different in the two cases, the latter being rather more prominent in strategic decisions. The definition of objectives, however, is commonly rather precise and specific in short-term decisions. Section B.2 looks at problem-solving situations, Section B.3 at the longer-term strategic decisions.

B.2   Problem solving

Once an immediate problem has been recognized, three major kinds of action may be taken:

(a) interim
(b) adaptive
(c) corrective

The first, *interim action*, is generally taken before the cause of the problem has been found. It is in the nature of a stopgap operation to keep some process going. It might involve temporary actions such as slowing a production line, introducing extra inspection at a crucial point, or taking special care with the orders for specific customers. These are stopgap actions, alerting all concerned to the problem,

205

allowing for the collection of additional information and providing time for a full analysis to be made, which will lead to a long-term solution.

Adaptive action is initiated by a manager once he has located the cause of a problem and finds, either that he can't do anything to eliminate the cause, or that action to correct the deviation directly is infeasible. Adaptive action aims to enable him to live with the effects of a problem and to minimize the effects. In some instances this may be more worthwhile than to take full corrective action to eliminate the problem. Alternatively, a full corrective solution may lie beyond the manager's own sphere of control. As an example intensive inspection may be maintained for raw material going into certain products to obtain higher-grade items, rather than carrying out full corrective raw material action aimed at producing only high-grade items.

Corrective action aims to eliminate the problem or deviation by removing the cause that produced it. As a general rule, corrective action is the most efficient and economical option in the long run. But such action is only possible when the cause is known and this may require careful, systematic and painstaking investigation. An illustration of this kind of situation occurred in the plant of a large paper manufacturer. A pulping plant was arranged in series with a paper machine, softwood logs being chipped and boiled with chemicals to the correct consistency, and then fed as pulp to the papermaking machine. The plant was working well until small splinters of wood were discovered coming through to the finished rolls of paper. It was initially assumed that something was wrong in the pulping process and that one of the stainless steel screens had broken. Interim action in this direction proved ineffective. An inspector then carefully examined the wood splinters in the finished paper and found these were not softwood but hardwood; moreover they had never been cooked or chemically treated. Looking around the plant he noticed a hardwood pipe that was being used to transfer the pulp to the paper machine. Although there had never been a case of a hardwood pipe breaking up on the inside, it was checked and indeed found to have broken up. Replacement of the pipe solved the problem.

B.3   Choice of action

Decision making of the second kind is essentially the choice of a course of action. Seven alternative approaches that have been suggested for choosing between a number of alternative courses of action are:

(*a*) intuitive

(*b*) minimax cost (or maximin gain)

(*c*) minimax regret (or opportunity loss)

(*d*) satisficing

(*e*) Kepner–Tregoe approach

(*f*) decision analysis

(*g*) decision analysis modified

(a)   *Intuitive*

Intuitive decision making involves no formal analysis, although most decision makers would seek to establish as much relevant information as possible in the time available. Many will argue that the pressure of events and the shortage of time frequently rules out any systematic decision making approach, and hence they must necessarily rely upon intuition to guide them to the best solution. To them the use of a systematic approach is slow and laborious and not suited to the demands of modern society. Yet the dangers of poor decision making are commonly greater when a manager is under stress than at other times: the very conditions used to justify intuitive decision making are indeed those which demand a systematic approach. It is precisely when information and resources are short, and time is at a premium, that a manager most desperately needs an effective method for handling decisions. Indeed, a method that doesn't work under such pressures is itself rather lacking, a situation that has been well recognized by the military with their standard battle drills and standard procedures for military appreciations. Moreover, the familiarity of an effective and systematic approach applied regularly can substantially reduce the time involved.

There are always some decisions which defy formal analysis and invite intuitive approaches. A famous example in the military field was the evacuation of the Gallipoli peninsula at the end of 1915. The generals on the spot recommended evacuation, but estimated that this would involve about 40000 casualties. Lord Kitchener came out from London to see for himself. As he left for home, confirming the decision to evacuate, he confided that he believed it could be done with no casualties, and he was proved correct. More generally, however, a manager without a systematic approach to decision making is not likely to produce consistently the best possible results. Either time will be wasted chasing up blind alleys, or important elements of the decision will be overlooked or ignored.

(b)   *Minimax cost*

The principle involved is first to ascertain the maximum loss that can occur under each alternative course of action and then, secondly, to select that action for which the maximum possible loss is minimized. As a simple illustration, consider a problem concerning the purchase of admission tickets for a swimming pool. A ticket allowing the bearer to use the swimming pool all weekend costs £1.40 if purchased during the preceding week, but a single day's admission costs £1.00, paid on the day itself. The alternative actions are, therefore, to buy a weekend ticket, or to buy daily tickets. Suppose I intend to go swimming whenever the weather is fine, but not otherwise. During the weekend that can be 0, 1 or 2 fine days and these outcomes are denoted by b_1, b_2 and b_3. The payoff matrix displaying the costs of each action/outcome combinations takes the form:

			Event (outcome)			
			0	1	2	fine days
			b_1	b_2	b_3	
Action	Weekend ticket	a_1	1.40	1.40	1.40	
	Daily tickets	a_2	0	1.00	2.00	

The figures in the table represent the amount paid out (£) for each action against the various outcomes. Under a_1 the cost is always 1.40; under a_2, it can be 0, 1.00 or 2.00.

Applying the minimax loss principle the first step would be to take the maximum (or worst) cost for each action, and then to select the action whose maximum is the minimum (i.e. the best among the maxima) for which the appropriate figures are

		Maximum loss for this action	Minimum of these maxima
Action	a_1	-1.40	-1.40
	a_2	-2.00	

Hence action a_1 should be selected and a weekend ticket bought. By this action the maximum possible expenditure is limited to 1.40; while with action a_2 the expenditure could be as high as 2.00. This rule is simple and straightforward, leading to an unequivocal solution, but it has certain snags in that it clearly follows a pessimistic line of approach and ignores completely any information that might be available concerning the relative likelihood of the various outcomes (i.e. weather) occurring. The principle can, of course, be adjusted to gains (instead of costs) by considering the maximum of the minimum gains to be obtained from each action (i.e. maxim in gain).

(c)   *Minimax regret*

In most situations it is too pessimistic to assume that the worst will always happen. If such an attitude were consistently adopted, the decision maker would look back with *regret* at lost opportunities. The regret for any action/outcome combination in this connection is defined as being the difference between (i) the maximum possible payoff that could have been achieved for that outcome, and (ii) the payoff resulting from the action actually taken. Thus it is the amount of payoff lost by not taking the optimal action for the (subsequently known) outcome concerned. In the swimming pool problem, the payoff under the combination a_1/b_1 is -1.40. On the other hand, if outcome b_1 did in fact occur but action a_2 had been taken, the payoff would be 0. Hence the subsequent regret at choosing a_1 rather than a_2 is $0 - (-1.40)$ or 1.40. A table (or matrix) can now be written in which all the entries are not costs as before, but regrets, as follows:

		Outcome			Maximum of row	Minimum of maxima
		b_1	b_2	b_3		
Action	a_1	1.40	1.40	0	1.40	
	a_2	0	0	0.60	0.60	0.60

To select the best action the maximum (greatest) regret is tabulated for each action, and the action chosen for which the maximum regret is a minimum. Under this rule action a_2 to buy daily tickets would be selected, on the grounds that this minimizes the maximum possible regret. The action selected is thus different from that in (b) above. This demonstrates, not surprisingly, that the choice of criterion for decision can affect the decision reached. If this were not the case, the ultimate consequence would be that the decision made was independent of the criteria used – a clear absurdity!

(*d*) *Satisficing*

Satisficing is to make a decision that satisfies one or more minimum criteria. This is usually achieved through examining alternatives sequentially and stopping at the first alternative that meets all the minimal criteria. For example, in choosing a house one cannot possibly look at and assess every house on the market. Hence we may stipulate certain minimum criteria such as maximum distance from a railway station, or from certain schools or shops, at least four bedrooms, maximum price level, minimum (or possibly maximum) size of garden, etc. This list enables the vast bulk of available houses to be disregarded and the choice narrowed to a few that merit further considerations. Again, consider a student preparing for an examination that involves four papers in different subjects. Passing the examination requires 40% in each paper, no special credit being given for extra good performance on one paper against a marginal failure in another. The student's approach to study and revision is likely, therefore, to be a time allocation that ensures a basic level of achievement, rather than aiming at superlative performances in one or more of the papers at the expense of doubts elsewhere.

Time can force a form of satisficing on the decision maker. In choosing a house there may be a strict limit on the time available for search and viewing and hence satisficing is the only way a decision can reasonably be reached in the time available. It must be recognized, however, that satisficing is not the same as optimizing. There can be a danger that, if satisficing becomes too easily the norm rather than an exceptional expedient, it is done at the expense of lowered long-term overall quality of decision making.

(*e*) *The Kepner–Tregoe approach*

Under this approach the objectives are divided into two categories: the *must* objectives and the *want* objectives. A proposed course of action that does not meet one or more of the must objectives is eliminated. After this initial pruning of alternative courses of action, the decision maker establishes the relative weights of the want objectives using a scale, say, of 1 to 10 with the most important want receiving a score 10. It is possible for a must objective to appear also in the want objective list; for example, a minimum return of 20% per annum could be a must, although the company also wants the returns to be as high as possible. Each objective is screened and re-assessed until the decision maker is satisfied that the weights allocated reflect the relative importance to be placed on each objective.

The decision maker next examines the remaining actions in turn, scoring them against each want objective on a 1 to 10 scale, 10 representing perfection and 1 the opposite. By multiplying the score for each want objective with the original weight given to the objective and summing over all want objectives an overall action score is computed. This process is repeated for each of the actions and the one with the highest overall score selected.

The following simple illustration of the procedure involves five want objectives, with two possible courses of action A and B left after the must objectives have been considered. The weights and scores are shown in Table B.1. The weights are relative to 10 for the most important want. The scores are based on a scale of 10 for an action that meets perfectly the particular want objective. The overall weighted total scores are 131 for action A and 139 for action B, thus making B the preferred course of action.

The major advantage of the procedure is that it systematizes the relative import-ance of various objectives, as well as the anticipated level of satisfaction expected from every course of action for each objective. The major disadvantages lie in the formulation of the weights to be given to each objective, and assessing the satisfaction scores. Since the score has to be a single number (from 1 to 10) it will in practice tend to be based on the most probable results from taking the action concerned. Changes in scores could be based on percentage improvements or absolute improvements from some norm, and assessors may not be consistent in their approach to the scoring system, particularly where different assessors have to be used for the various objectives. Hence the procedure disguises the risks involved and, although once the choice is made steps can then be taken to minimize the risks involved, it can be argued that the correct place for these to be exposed is before the choice is made, not after. Moreover, there are also difficulties in deciding how to weight the various objectives; for example, what does a change in the pollution weight of 3 in place of 2 really mean.

Table B.1. *Calculation of overall weighted scores*

		Action scores	
Want objective	Weight	A	B
Profit	10	7	6
Pollution	2	2	3
Technical difficulties	2	6	4
Customer relations	5	5	10
Employee relations	3	6	4
Overall weighted scores		131	139

(*f*)   *Decision analysis*

The basic principles of decision analysis are outlined in Chapter 1. The method requires a complete enumeration of all possible alternative courses of action and considerable effort should be made to achieve such a list before formal analysis begins. For this purpose group meetings can be held with all those involved to ensure that the feasible set is indeed complete. To confine consideration just to those involved in a planning or executive group may omit useful creative suggestions from analysis.

(g)   *Adjusted decision analysis*

The probabilities required for the decision analysis approach in the previous section are commonly split by many decision makers into the categories of *risk* where past information is regarded as directly relevant, and *uncertainty* where this is not the case (although this can be a difficult polarization to make and often not very meaningful in practice). Such a dichotomy suggests a modified approach of analysing the problem, using risk only initially and ranking the alternative options first on this basis. A further analysis is then made on the basis of the uncertainty items, and the ranked order of alternatives adjusted as thought desirable in the light of these extra factors. The difficulty is that to obtain the basic ranking some assumption has commonly to be made about the uncertainty issues themselves. If an optimistic outcome is assumed, then the analysis tends to be forced back into the same kind of debate that would have had to be held to obtain the assumed probabilities for the basic form of decision analysis. Hence this modified method is only likely to be of assistance where there are one or more peripheral risks to the main analysis whose assessed probability is likely to be fairly low, but whose effect is possibly very large. Thus an international investment project might contain a whole range of relatively normal commercial risks, together with an element of uncertainty regarding the nationalization of the plant in some foreign country. This situation could be then treated in the manner just described, possibly in relation to the total portfolio of such uncertainties held by the organization concerned.

The principal merit of the approach is that it explicitly indicates the lost expectation if the ranking is changed because of some particular item of uncertainty, i.e. the minimum cost of changing the ranking because of a particular uncertainty. In this sense the so-called unquantifiable items are, in effect, quantified.

B.4   Comparison of methods

Table B.2 summarizes the eight approaches that have been outlined. Only by maximizing expected utility (or value) for each decision will the greatest long-term gain in utility be achieved. Other methods do not achieve this goal and fall short in various ways, so that it is desirable for the decision maker to be aware of the dangers that may be incurred. The reason commonly given for using alternatives is that time is not available to undertake a full analysis and hence some short-cut method should be used. This is tantamount to saying that the opportunity cost of the time available for further analysis in depth is such that any possible increased expectation is too low. When this is the case, the short-cut approach can be justified, whether it be by rule of thumb, intuition or otherwise.

Finally it is necessary to draw a distinction between the making of a decision and its implementation (Williams, 1982). Naturally, even though a decision taken may involve some risk, all efforts should be made to reduce or eliminate this risk in the implementation stage. These possibilities ought to have been fully explored in coming to the particular decision concerned in the first place. Under decision analysis the whole decision space remaining is in effect re-examined each time the

Table B.2. *Comparison of decision-making procedures*

Procedure (1)	Search for alternatives (2)	Handling of risk (3)	Optimization basis (4)	Choice procedure (5)	Handling of multi-attribute objectives (6)	Implementation procedure (7)
(a) Intuitive	No formal search	Not formalized	Can be explicit	Not formalized	Possible	Normal project management
(b) Minimax cost	Formal search desirable	No consideration	Specified	Minimizing maximum cost	Impracticable	Normal project management
(c) Minimax regret	Formal search desirable	No consideration	Specified	Minimizing maximum regret	Impracticable	Normal project management
(d) Satisficing	Formal search unnecessary	Not formalized	Series of minima	First option to meet minimum criteria	Yes	Normal project management
(e) Kepner–Tregoe	Formal search important	Ignored for (5) considered in (7)	Not specified	Eliminate on musts, choose on wants	Possible	Normal project management with efforts to eliminate risk
(f) Decision Analysis	Formal search essential	Formalized	Specified	Maximize expected value	Yes, but difficult	Review at each decision point
(g) Decision Analysis modified	Formal search essential	Formalized with modifications	Specified	Maximize expected risk values with uncertainty adjustments	Yes, but difficult	Review at each decision point

decision maker comes to a decision point in his implementation. Even though the original strategy may have implied action X at this point, the data should be re-examined in the light of fresh information (if any) and the remaining decisions re-worked to verify whether X is, or is not, still the preferred option.

Appendix C. Reduction of risks

C.1   Introduction

This appendix summarizes some of the methods available for risk reduction. Two general points need to be made. First, any measures taken for the reduction or elimination of risk involve some cost, and the gain to be expected from risk reduction measures must be balanced against the cost of achieving that risk reduction. In general it is worthwhile to carry out a risk reduction programme for a project involving some element of risk provided that

expected gain after risk reduction minus the cost involved

exceeds

expected gain without the risk reduction programme.

This concept, illustrated by the decision whether or not to drill for oil on a block of land, was discussed in Section A.4 of Appendix A. Initial assessments had been made of the likely oil yield if drilling is carried out, but there was also the option of obtaining extra information at a cost. This information would be purchased if the rule just enunciated held, i.e. the expected monetary value after purchasing the information is greater than it would be after making such a purchase. Risk must be measured against the expected gain for which it is run.

Table C.1. *Approaches to risk reduction*

Ensuring choices made minimize the risk	Reducing the risk of a project	Pooling the effects of risk once decision choice is made
Market research	Reappraisal of proposition	Insurance
Step-wise decision procedures	Legislation	Self-insurance
	Diversification	Pooling or sharing risks
		Re-arranging costs

The second point is the need to distinguish between risk reduction and the amelioration of the effects of risk. An example here would be deciding whether or not to increase the amount of reservoir capacity to hold water in the UK. The risk of running dry in a long hot summer could be reduced at substantial capital cost and some extra running costs. On the other hand the risk could be left as now and further steps taken to ameliorate the occasional hardship that would be caused by a severe drought. The first option reduces the risk itself; the second leaves the risk at its current level, but ameliorates its effect. This appendix is primarily concerned with the former rather than the latter.

Table C.1 tabulates the main avenues of risk reduction, arranged under three broad but overlapping headings. The first relates to situations where effort is made to ensure that action choices are those where the risk is appropriately minimized: the second to situations where the risk is reduced; and the third when the effects of risk are pooled. The three groups are discussed in turn.

C.2 Minimum risk choice

Market research is primarily concerned with estimating the market demand for new (or existing) products through observational methods such as surveys. The researcher himself has no direct control over the products in the market, he merely seeks to measure current attitudes about them to draw inferences about the market as a whole. Since market research is a statistical form of fact finding based on a sub-set of the total universe of concern, the results of necessity contain a probabilistic element. Risk as to the level of market demand for some product can be reduced, but not in practice eliminated, and to meet our original criterion the costs involved in carrying out the market research should not exceed the extra expected net gain by using the market research information.

Figure C.1 illustrates this diagrammatically. The broken line represents the cost of obtaining the market research information. The unbroken line represents the value of the information thus obtained in terms of the expected *extra* gain to be

Figure C.1. Optimum value of information

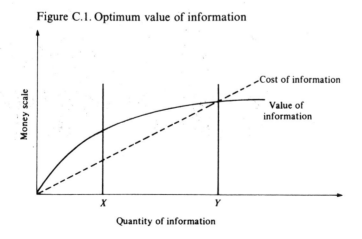

expected from a decision made with the aid of the market research information. The difference between the two lines represents the expected extra net gain when the costs are taken into account. The difference is positive at first rising to a maximum around point X; it then decreases until it becomes zero at point Y, and is thereafter negative. Hence for any additional information obtained beyond point X, the marginal gain in expected value from the optimal decision falls short of the marginal extra cost of the information. Beyond Y, it would indeed be better not to undertake any research at all. The value of information line is steep at first but flattens out and would eventually be virtually horizontal in that the extra market research has decreasing marginal utility. It is difficult to devise a general method for determining the precise form of Figure C.1 for individual problems, but attempts have been made for particular situations. Green and Frank (1966) used Bayes' theorem to evaluate whether or not a new label on a consumer product would have a beneficial effect, and the desirable level of market research to undertake before reaching a conclusion. The choice involved the possibility of four levels of market research; an exhaustively large survey at one extreme and no survey at all at the other extreme. In-between there were two further types of survey; one that cost about one-third of the exhaustive survey and the other a two-stage procedure with a moderate survey as the first stage, and a follow-up if it appeared worthwhile. On the various assumptions made the authors come down in favour of the survey that costs about one-third of the exhaustive survey, but it must be stressed that this is the 'right' answer for the particular problem posed, not necessarily for all such problems.

A step-wise decision procedure likewise involves splitting a project up into a series of sequential steps and only proceeding to the next part if satisfactory results have been obtained from the previous part. The aim is to limit any possible losses by investing the minimum capital sums required on a stage by stage basis. An example of such a procedure arises in exploration work for minerals. A large firm estimates that, having taken an initial concession on a particular piece of land after a rough geological, economic and political survey, the initial odds against a profitable mine being established on that area are 5000 to 1. Geochemical work is now done and, if these results are promising, the odds then improve to 1000 to 1 against. If promising, the next stage is to carry out preliminary drilling, otherwise exploration is abandoned at this point. If this stage is successful the odds improve further to 25 to 1 against and the project proceeds to the next stage. If not, the project is abandoned. If the final project stage of detailed drilling is successful the odds narrow yet further to 4 to 1 against. (For a fuller discussion see Cheesewright, 1978.) This is a situation where the risk is cumulatively reduced on a stage by stage basis, but not entirely eliminated, before full commitment to commercial drilling has to be made. The general position is not quite so clear cut as suggested here, in that there are really four possible decisions at each stage: stop the exploration, hold the property being worked as a possible future resource, continue exploration work in the normal fashion or, finally, accelerate the effort. Formalizing the procedure in the way described not only speeds up the exploration process by defining rules and timetables, but is a means of planning and communicating cash flow more effectively.

C.3   Reducing project risk

A *re-appraisal of a proposition* can sometimes be made with a view to changes that will lower the risks involved. Such changes fall broadly in three fields; the physical means of manufacturing or producing the product; the financial backing mechanisms to enable the project to be brought to fruition; and the markets sought for the project. The first can be helped by activities such as the building of prototype models, a more detailed examination of equipment proposed, a re-study of the formulated design, of the materials to be used in manufacture, of alternative processes used in other countries, etc. Such activities can often reduce the risk, in that the action taken has a lower maximum loss and/or a higher expected gain than before, but such activities cannot usually eliminate risk entirely.

The financing methods to be used for the project can be re-examined to ensure they will not leave the project starved of necessary cash at some critical point, for example if the development work takes longer than expected. The third form of study may either be by more elaborate forms of desk research or by market research (see section C.2) aimed at determining the optimum way in which the product should be produced and sold, or by a combination of market research with changes in design and manufacture.

Legislation provides another means by which risk reduction can be enforced, as demonstrated in Chapter 12. For example, fire precautions can be made more stringent by legislation. There will be extra costs to be offset against the saving of lives and injuries and the use of fire services. Hence it may be a balancing reduction not a 'free' reduction in risk. Likewise legislation can be used to impose speed limits on roads. For example a restriction on motorways to 80 kilometres (50 miles) per hour would undoubtedly cut down the risk of accidents, but would also put up the time required for many journeys and might thereby raise costs, for example for the transport of goods that commonly go by road. Thus legislation can reduce risks, but there is normally a cost to be paid for such reductions, and the costs are not always borne by those who benefit directly.

Another approach to risk reduction in commercial firms involves vertical integration or diversification. Under the former, a corrugated case manufacturer could own or control a paper mill as well as his corrugated case plant, and also possibly some forests to provide timber for the pulp used in the paper mill. A manufacturer of cars could own various component manufacturers and a steel mill as well as the car plant. Clearly such forms of integration lower certain types of risk, such as outside suppliers putting up prices for raw materials or component parts in light of competition for their products from elsewhere. It may, however, heighten other risks by effectively putting too many eggs into one basket. For example, the efficiency of the different supplying units could be affected by their not being obliged to compete in the open market. Or a stoppage in one part of the organization could spread elsewhere and make its effect more extensive than it might have been with a series of independent suppliers.

Diversification, on the other hand, implies that the firm carries on activities that bear different and relatively independent risks, so that the chance of any one part of the organization failing and dragging down the whole firm is minimized. For the advantages to accrue, the separate parts of the diversification should be genuinely independent. In as much as they are associated (correlated) as regards their risks, then the beneficial effects of diversification are lowered. This is directly related to the converse concept of diversifiable risk in Stock Exchange investments discussed in Chapter 8. A diversified company may pose severe managerial problems in having available a wide range of expertise to deal with the differing parts of the diversified parts of the organization. Against this, successful diversification allows the risks of one part of the business to be fruitfully offset against the differing risks of the other parts.

C.4   Pooling risks

There are many types of risk, such as fire, loss of profits, consequential losses, public liability, employee liability, cars, etc., where insurance is commonly used as a means of indemnification. The risk is not thereby reduced or eliminated as such, but its effects transferred elsewhere for a mutually acceptable fee. Even here alternatives need to be examined; for example is it economical to install sprinklers in a factory given the saving in insurance premiums? An examination needs to be made to see whether judicious expenditure or re-arrangements can save costs by reducing the insurance premiums otherwise payable sufficiently to offset the costs of the re-arrangement. However, while insurance can cover many risks such as the above, and the well-developed risk management activities of many organizations seek to codify such possibilities, firms will not pay the premiums demanded on many other types of risk if self-insurance is cheaper than insurance in the long run. (One need only note that expenditure on motor claims accounts for about half the motor premium income of insurance companies to realize the scope for self-insurance.) Hence, while insurance may be appropriate for smaller firms where the cash strain on any occurrence of loss could be heavy relative to free assets, it is not automatically appropriate for a larger firm which can carry the ups and downs of losses from a variety of smaller risks (small in consequence, rather than necessarily small in probability terms). In general, insurance tends to be used to cover risks where the probability is small but the consequence is relatively large, or alternatively where there is some form of legal liability. This attitude coincides with the corporate utility function which is normally of a risk-aversion form when possible losses are large relative to net assets. Moreover, insurance deals primarily with the areas labelled 'risk' rather than with those labelled 'uncertainty'. The quoted costs of insurance in the latter may be so high as to make insurance infeasible to the putative insured.

Industrialists can combine self-insurance with arrangements for sharing or pooling the risk with other organizations or individuals. This can be done in a number of ways, for example by an issue of special equity shares, by partial government aid, or by some form of joint venture undertaken by a consortium of companies. The aim is to ensure that, should the project go sour, the sponsoring organization is less crippled than it would otherwise have been. Normally this can only be achieved at a price that creams off some of the potential gains to the original sponsors. Moreover, the project risk itself has not been eliminated as such, but transferred to a greater number of stakeholders so that any consequential financial losses are shared. North Sea Assets is an example of a company pooling financial risks on a consortium basis, albeit in an industry-based context.

The life insurance industry provides a further example of pooling financial risks where the fit pay for the unfit. The risk, i.e. the maximum payoff, is generally small in relation to the total assets of the insurance company so that it can carry the risk itself. In general insurance this may not always be wise, for example when insuring a major ship. For this situation re-insurance is appropriate whereby somebody who has taken the whole risk gives part over to a re-insurer. It may be a defined proportion of the whole risk, or it may be part of the claim above a basic level that is fully carried by the original insurer. The desirable level of re-insurance is a derivative of the utility function of the insurer who took on the risk in the first instance, combined with the rates he is quoted for re-insurance.

Another possibility that reduces the financial risk, but not the project risk, is to re-arrange some of the costs involved, such as the capital costs. Thus equipment could be leased rather than purchased outright. In the UK the volume of equipment leasing in 1979 was estimated to be approximately £1800 million, equivalent to about 12% of the total industrial capital expenditure. The figure is rising rapidly. Although regarded as an expensive form of financing it has advantages of timing and the containment of commitments. The extra cost involved is effectively the price paid to lower the financial sums at risk, which has the consequential effect of lowering the expected gain from the project as a whole.

Another form of re-arrangement is to build initially a smaller manufacturing facility than would seem to be warranted, with the option of expanding it later. This will generally lower the financial risk. It may also lower the expected gain from the project as a whole, because of diminished sales potential in the early years, suggesting that, if the project is successful, there will be greater opportunities for competitors to move in. The re-arrangement of the project may thus provide an acceptable trade-off between the lowered expected gain and a reduction in the probability of loss. Different actions taken by various individual decision makers in such a situation is not necessarily because they disagree on the risk assessments, but primarily because of varying attitudes towards risk.

Situations such as these illustrate how the decision maker may be working (either intuitively or formally) on expected utilities rather than expected monetary value, and be anxious to avoid consequences that are low or even negative. Risk *avoidance*, as distinct from risk *management*, may be desirable in some senses, but it also carries the consequence that the total level of economic activity undertaken under such a policy is likely to be lowered in comparison with a policy of maximizing expected gain. To side-step the non-linearity of the corporate utility function can be counter productive and, to quote a former chairman of Unilever, Sir Ernest Woodroofe (1974); 'It follows that all levels of management must understand the level of risk that the enterprise is prepared to take.' Only in this way can a large organization maximize its overall expected return on the capital it has available for investment.

Exercises

1 A factory produces nuts and bolts on separate processes in packets of six. If satisfactory, the nuts and bolts can be matched in pairs. The number of defective nuts and bolts varies from packet to packet. Past experience has shown that reasonable estimates of the probability distribution of the number of defectives per packet, x and y respectively, are as shown in the table.

Nuts	x	0	1	2	3	4	5	6
	$p(x)$	0.83	0.12	0.03	0.02	0	0	0
Bolts	y	0	1	2	3	4	5	6
	$p(y)$	0.89	0.05	0.03	0.02	0.01	0	0

A customer purchases one packet of nuts and one packet of bolts. What are the probabilities:
   (i) That the packet will provide six satisfactory nut–bolt combinations;
   (ii) That the packet will provide at least four satisfactory nut–bolt combinations;
   (iii) That there will only be one unsatisfactory nut–bolt combination in the packet?

2 The number of defects (x) on first assembly in a certain model of television set is distributed as shown in the table.

x	0	1	2	3	4	5
$p(x)$	0.60	0.22	0.10	0.05	0.02	0.01

If the production cost of a set is $100 and the average cost of removing each defect found is $10, what is the expected cost of producing a defect-free set? Find also the expected cost for producing ten defect-free sets. (Assume sets are independent as regards occurrence of faults.)

3 A married couple, both aged 65, make a proposal to an insurance company for a policy with the undermentioned benefits. The benefits are
(i) £2000 if the wife, but not the husband, dies within five years,
(ii) £4000 if the husband, but not the wife, dies within five years,
(iii) £1000 if both die within five years. The company assesses from life tables the independent probabilities of the proposers dying as shown in the table.

	Husband	Wife
Dying within five years	0.15	0.10
Surviving at least five years	0.85	0.90

Estimate a suitable premium for the insurance company to charge for this policy. Assume that the office expenses are £8 per policy written, and that it aims to make a profit per policy equal to 25% of the premium charged. (Ignore any discounting of the sums of money involved.)

4 A large restaurant, for costing purposes, is developing a probability model to describe the lifetime of the cups it uses. For this purpose, it assumes that, at each serving where the cup is used, there is a constant probability p of the cup being damaged and that servings are independent. Once damaged, a cup is thrown away.
(i) On this model what is the probability that a cup newly purchased
    (a) is damaged before the fifth serving;
    (b) is damaged on the fifth serving;
    (c) survives its first five servings?
(ii) If x is the number of servings before a newly purchased cup is scrapped, what is the expected value of x?

5 In a community of 20 households, five of whom take the magazine *Punch*, what is the probability of finding that, in a random sample of ten households, exactly two take the magazine? What is the probability of more than two households in the sample having the magazine? How would the former probability be affected if the sample of ten households came from a larger community of 20 000 households, of whom 5000 took *Punch*?

6 A certain process turns out articles of which a proportion θ are defective. The process is inspected by choosing randomly over a period of time a large number of samples of four articles and inspecting them. The following information is known: in 60% of the samples selected, none of the four was defective, while in 30% of the samples just one of the four was defective. What fraction of the articles produced by this process would you estimate to be defective, i.e. estimate θ?

7 One of the publications carried by a certain store is the weekly magazine *Sharetips*. The dealer pays 30 cents per copy and sells it for 50 cents per copy. Copies unsold at the end of the week cannot be returned and thus have no value. The probability distribution for demand is shown below:

Demand (number per week)	Probability
20	0.10
30	0.15
40	0.25
50	0.20
60	0.15
70	0.10
80	0.05

Use each of the following decision criteria to determine the optimal number of magazines to stock:

   (i) maximin gain;

   (ii) minimax regret criterion;

   (iii) EMV criterion.

Which criterion do you consider the most sensible one for the dealer to adopt?

8 A card-shop owner is trying to decide how many boxes of a special Mother's Day card to stock. The cards carry a high profit margin and come in boxes of 20 cards; they cost $4.80 and retail for $8.10 per box. Each box unsold by Mother's Day can be sold afterwards for $3.60. Customers will not demand the special card if it is out of stock, as they look at the selection available and choose from it. The owner has, however, limited capital and does not like to invest in items that he will not sell because he could earn more by not tying up his capital in such a way. The owner feels that for each $4.80 invested in a box of these cards that are not subsequently sold in the season, he could have earned $1.20 profit by investing in other cards. He also estimates that the probability density function for the number of boxes of cards demanded will be:

$p(0) = 0.03$	$p(4) = 0.20$	$p(8) = 0.05$
$p(1) = 0.04$	$p(5) = 0.20$	$p(9) = 0.03$
$p(2) = 0.08$	$p(6) = 0.15$	$p(10) = 0.02$
$p(3) = 0.15$	$p(7) = 0.05$	

How many boxes should the owner stock at the beginning of the season if it is impossible to place reorders? (Ignore the possibility of the owner only selling part of a box of cards.)

9 My car is rather old and I am considering whether to replace it now or keep it for a further year. If if do not replace it I estimate that there is a probability of 0.5 that repair bills will be $800 (moderate), 0.2 that they will be $400 (low) and 0.3 that they will be $2000 (high).

   If I do replace the car now my newer car will incur me a fixed cost of $800 to own over a year plus a repair cost of $200 (small) (with probability 0.7) or $400 (large) (with probability 0.3).

   (i) What should my decision be if my objective is to minimize expected total annual cost?

   (ii) I could ask for an inspection to be carried out on either my current car or the potential replacement or both. A single car inspection would cost $80 and after such an inspection I would be certain as to which of my cost estimates was correct. If I elect to have both cars inspected then I would receive the two inspection reports at the same time and the cost would be $150. Should I avail myself of one or other (or both) of the inspections offered?

10 The purchasing manager of Transatlantic Fruit Ltd (TF) in London has to decide what to do about forward dealings in grapefruit. TF knows of only two cargoes of grapefruit due to be landed in London in January next year, one of 1000 tonnes and one of 700 tonnes. The purchasing manager can purchase either at £200 a tonne, but he cannot afford to buy both, and he must sign a contract of purchase immediately. Smaller quantities of up to 400 tonnes can usually be purchased at any time for immediate delivery, at a price of £220 a tonne.

   The two big customers for grapefruit are British Produce (BP) and National Fruit (NF). Their requirements for January are 1000 tonnes and 600 tonnes respectively, and they are usually prepared to pay £260 a tonne. They will place contracts for the whole of their requirements with a single supplier next month, and TF feels that it stands a good chance of winning these contracts. If TF fails to win either, it can sell small quantities (up to say 100 tonnes) at £240 a tonne, but larger quantities would all have to be sold at clearance prices, probably £200 a tonne. TF does not have any space to store grapefruit.

   TF's sales manager has been thinking about the chances of winning either the BP or NF contracts. He cannot bid for both because the two companies insist on not more than one supplier. If TF purchases the 1000 tonne cargo, the sales manager feels he has a 50% chance of winning the BP contract. Competition in this market is rarely in terms of price, and great emphasis is placed on security of supply. So if TF buys the large cargo, and bids for the smaller NF contract, the sales manager feels that he has an 80% chance of winning, whereas if he buys the smaller cargo, he has only a 70% chance of winning. It would be possible to buy a small cargo and then bid for the BP contract, relying on day-to-day purchases to make up the difference. But he feels that BP would be rather wary of his ability to supply, and his chance of winning would fall to 40%. Use a decision tree to show TF's alternative decisions, and select the optimal strategy. (Based on material supplied by P. Morris.)

11 You have acquired a good deal of experience in sales forecasting, and you forecast that one of your company's new products will sell 4000 units next year. Your superior asks what you can say about the degrees of uncertainty in your forecast. To answer this you examine your forecast performance in the past and feel that:
   (i) In the long run sales would turn out to be greater than your forecast about as often as they would turn out to be less.
   (ii) On about half of all occasions, sales would be between 20% below and 30% above forecast, and that when they did fall outside this range, they would be equally likely to fall above it as below it.
   (iii) On only about one occasion in 100 would sales be less than half your forecast, and only about one occasion in 100 would they be more than twice your forecast.
Construct a suitable form of distribution to demonstrate to your superior the degree of uncertainty inherent in your forecast.

12   (i) Assess prior probability distributions in cumulative density form for the following:
     (*a*) the price of ICI ordinary shares in the UK or General Electric in the USA six months hence;
     (*b*) the percentage change in the cost of living index over the next twelve months;
     (*c*) the price of gold ($ US per ounce) six months hence;
     (*d*) the number of new car registrations in your country over the next twelve months;
     (*e*) the number of months to the next general election in Great Britain.
   (ii) Compare the prior distributions you obtain in (i) with those obtained by two or three colleagues, and reach a group agreement as to a single prior distribution for each item. Is there any pattern of relationship between the combined prior distributions and the individual distributions from which they were formed?

13 The following is an extract from a leading article in *The Guardian* newspaper of 21 April 1979: *Is there mullet still for tee?*

It is reported that a fish weighing 1.5 lb was dropped by a seagull 300 feet on to a golfer on the 15th green at Melbourne, costing him a winning position in an important open championship. The fish was a mullet and the golfer was knocked out. Although sympathy is due to the golfer, it should be pointed out that a mullet of that weight dropped from that height will inevitably cause a fairly painful blow.

The golfer, a Mr Staatz, is particularly unfortunate in that 1.5 lb is approaching the maximum weight of mullet that a seagull can reasonably carry, although fish of 3 lb and more are not unknown in Australian waters. He is unfortunate again in that had the mullet been only slightly smaller the seagull would probably have been able to hang on to it and the regrettable incident would not have occurred. (Not only would it not have occurred: no one would have given any thought to the possibility of its occurrence.) Mr Staatz therefore appears to have had the worst of both worlds. It is true that his chances of being struck by a falling mullet a second time are so small as to be, for practical purposes, negligible, but that can have been of only small comfort to him at the moment of collision.

A subsequent correspondent wrote: 'Since the probability of Mr Staatz (the golfer in question) being struck once by a falling mullet has increased to a certainty (it has happened), it follows that his chances of being struck twice or more have also increased.'

Do you agree? If not, why not?

14 *The Times* of 11 August 1982 quoted Dr L as saying that having an anaesthetic was safer than driving a car 10 000 miles. Dr B, on 24 August 1982, pointed out that it takes an average person a year to drive this distance but the average time of an anaesthetic is a matter of hours. Looked at another way, said Dr B, a better comparison is that one car trip in 4 million leads to a fatality compared with one in 10 000 anaesthetics. Do you accept this latter comparison, or can you suggest a better way of comparing the relative likelihoods of dying from these two hazards of modern life?

15 In the experience of a certain insurance company, customers who have sufficient funds in their bank postdate a cheque by mistake once in 100 times, while customers who write cheques on insufficient funds invariably postdate them. The latter group constitutes 1% of the total cheques received by the insurance company. The company receives a postdated cheque from a policyholder. What is the probability that the customer has insufficient funds?

16 An insurance company classifies drivers as class A (good risks), class B (medium risks) and class C (poor risks). The company believes that class A risks constitute 30% of the drivers who apply for insurance, class B 50% and class C 20%. The probability that a class A driver has an accident in any twelve month period is 0.01; for a class B driver the probability is 0.03; and for a class C driver it is 0.10. Assume that the probability of more than one accident in a year is negligible.

   (i) Mr Jones takes out an insurance policy and within twelve months he has an accident. What is the probability that he is a class C risk?

   (ii) If a policyholder goes five years without an accident, and we assume years to be statistically independent, what is the probability that he belongs to class A?

17 The Great European Hotel Association is about to poll its members on whether or not the association should accept a certain credit card. The Secretary of the association attaches the probabilities shown in the table to various percentages of members in favour.

Percentage of member hotels in favour	Prior probability of exactly that percentage in favour
30	0.10
40	0.30
50	0.40
60	0.20

(i) On this information only, would you, as Secretary, expect a vote for the credit card to be carried?

(ii) Suppose a random sample of fifteen hotels were drawn and eight were in favour and seven opposed. What probabilities would you now assign to the various percentages of hotels in favour?

(iii) After the sample in (ii) has been taken, what is the expected proportion of hotels in favour?

18 A simplified version of the way the law relating to drunken driving operates in a number of countries is as follows. A motorist can be stopped by a police officer and asked to take a breath test. If this is negative, no further action ensures. If the test is positive the motorist is taken to a police station where a second test based on a blood specimen is given. If this second test is negative the motorist is released, if positive the motorist is automatically charged and convicted of drunken driving.

The two tests concerned are not entirely precise in their operation and their accuracy has been investigated with a large scale controlled trial on a probabilistic basis with the results shown in the table.

Test	Motorist's true state		Test result
	Drunk	Sober	
First test	$\left.\begin{array}{l}0.8\\0.2\end{array}\right\}$ 1.0	$\left.\begin{array}{l}0.2\\0.8\end{array}\right\}$ 1.0	+ −
Second test	$\left.\begin{array}{l}0.9\\0.1\end{array}\right\}$ 1.0	$\left.\begin{array}{l}0.05\\0.95\end{array}\right\}$ 1.0	+ −

(i) What is the probability that a motorist stopped who is, in reality, drunk will be convicted under this law? Conversely what is the probability that a stopped motorist who is, in reality, sober will be convicted?

(ii) Past information suggests that the proportion, P, of those stopped for the first test who are in reality drunk is 0.6. A motorist is stopped for testing and subsequently convicted. What is the probability that he was actually drunk? What is the probability that he was sober? Comment on how the latter probability varies with changes in P.

19 A computer software consultancy company, with initial net assets of £15000 (£15k), has a contract to develop either of two new program packages, A and B. Package A would yield a net profit (i.e. an addition to net assets) of £8000, and package B would yield a net profit of £3000.

In addition, there is a possibility that a second client will decide to buy whichever package has been developed, which would yield an *additional* profit of £20000 on package A, or £35000 on package B. The company estimate that the probability of making a sale to the second client is 0.1 for either package, but that this could be increased to 0.7 for either package by making it compatible with an existing package. This would involve buying the existing package, at a cost of £x, before developing the new package.

(i) Construct a decision tree for the company.

(ii) The company's utility function for net assets of £y thousand is given by $u(y) = y/(y+10)$ for $y \geq 0$. Which strategy maximizes the expected utility for (a) $x = 3$, (b) $x = 8$ and (c) $x = 13$?

20 A fund of $1 million may be invested in either or both of two financial securities, X and Y.

Security X will give a net profit of 10% for certain. Security Y will give either a net profit of 100% with probability p, or a net loss of 50% with probability $(1-p)$. The fund has a utility function

$u(s) = 1 - e^{-s}$ for net assets of £s million.

(i) For $p = 0.5$, what proportion of the fund should be invested in security X?

(ii) For what values of p should at least part of the fund be invested in security Y?

21 As part of an attempt to ascribe a utility function to a certain company, the following prospects (assuming a specified initial wealth) were considered (one at a time) by the managing director:

Prospect A:	a loss of £2 mill.	with probability 0.4
or	no loss	with probability 0.6
Prospect B:	a loss of £1 mill.	with probability 0.9
or	a loss of £4 mill.	with probability 0.1
Prospect C:	a gain of £2 mill.	with probability p_C
or	a loss of £1 mill.	with probability $(1-p_C)$

Prospect D:	a gain of £2 mill.	with probability p_D
or	a loss of £4 mill.	with probability $(1 - p_D)$
Prospect E:	a loss of £2 mill.	with probability 0.9
or	a loss of £4 mill.	with probability 0.1

He stated that:

(a) If he was faced with prospect A (only), he would be prepared to pay a maximum of £1 million to be insured against it.

(b) If he was faced with prospect B (only), he would be prepared to pay a maximum of £2 million to be insured against it.

(c) If he were offered prospect C (only), the smallest value of p_C for which he would accept it is 0.6.

(i) Assign utilities to all possible outcomes of the above prospects. (Hint: You are free to choose values to represent the best and worst of these suggested outcomes.)

(ii) Using these utilities, find the largest value of p_D for which the managing director should be prepared to pay £1 million to be relieved of prospect D.

(iii) If he were faced with either prospect E only, or two (independent) prospects of type A, which should he prefer?

22 Miss Starway has invested 60% of her money in stock A and the remainder in stock B. She assesses their prospects as follows:

	A	B
Expected return (%)	15	20
Standard deviation (%)	20	22

(i) What is the expected return and standard deviation of return on her portfolio if the correlation between returns is 0.5?

(ii) How would (i) change if the correlation were (a) zero or (b) −0.5?

(iii) Is Miss Starway's portfolio better or worse than one invested entirely in stock A, or is it not possible to say?

23 For each of the following pairs of investments, state which would always be preferred by a rational investor (assuming that these are the only investments that are available to him):

(i) Portfolio A	$r = 18\%$	$s = 20\%$
Portfolio B	$r = 14\%$	$s = 20\%$
(ii) Portfolio C	$r = 15\%$	$s = 18\%$
Portfolio D	$r = 13\%$	$s = 8\%$
(iii) Portfolio E	$r = 14\%$	$s = 16\%$
Portfolio F	$r = 14\%$	$s = 10\%$

(r is the expected return and s is the standard deviation of the expected return.)

24 Mr Bullbear proposes to invest in two shares, X and Y. He expects a return of 12% from X and 8% from Y. The standard deviation of the returns

is 8% for X and 5% for Y. The correlation coefficient between the returns is 0.2.

(i) Compute the expected return and standard deviation of the following portfolios:

Portfolio	X (%)	Y (%)
1	50	50
2	25	75
3	75	25

(ii) Sketch the set of portfolios composed of X and Y.

(iii) Suppose that Mr Bullbear can also borrow or lend at an interest rate of 5%. Show on your sketch how this alters his opportunities. Given that he can borrow or lend, what proportions of the common stock portfolio should be invested in X and Y?

25 A company prospecting for minerals divides their exploration area into ten plots, intending to drill to a depth of 300 metres near the centre of each plot. Geological data suggest that the ten plots are either wholly within a large mineral field discovered in a neighbouring area or wholly outside the field, and that there is a 50:50 chance of either. Drilling to 300 metres within the field would give a 50% chance of a strike, whereas outside the field there would be virtually no chance of a strike.

On striking minerals the total operating profit can be expected to be $100 million, excluding the cost of exploratory drilling, the cost of which is $200000 per hole.

After each hole has been drilled a decision is made whether or not to continue drilling with the next hole. The criterion used for this decision is whether the expected drilling cost, not including the holes already drilled, exceeds the expected operating profit.

(i) What is the probability that the plots lie within the field, given that no successful holes have been drilled?

(ii) How many unsuccessful holes will the company drill before abandoning the search, and what is the expected drilling cost before the operation starts?

26 A chemical firm is about to invest in a plant for producing a plastic. The firm has a choice of two methods of producing this plastic. The first method involves the use of an established process and the cost of the plant using this manufacturing process is $2.4 million. The plant for producing the plastic by the second method would cost $2 million and involves using a process which has not been tested commercially. The firm's chief chemical engineer feels that there is a 70% chance of the new process being successful commercially and a 30% chance of the process being unsuccessful. If the process is unsuccessful commercially the plant would have to be modified at a cost of $2 million to produce the plastic by the established process.

In view of the uncertainty about the new process, the chief chemical engineer has suggested that the firm could build a pilot plant, at a cost of $100000, to provide the further information on the commercial viability of the new process. The chemical engineer feels that there is an 80% chance of the pilot plant being successful and a 20% chance of it being unsuccessful. If the pilot plant does prove successful, the chemical engineer feels that there is a 90% chance of the commercial plant being successful and a 10% chance that it will be unsuccessful. If the pilot plant is unsuccessful, then the commercial plant using the new process would definitely be unsuccessful.

Use a decision tree approach to help management with their investment decision.

27 A company is faced with the problem of deciding whether it should build a small or a large plant when there is uncertainty about future demand. Management assess that the probability of high demand is 0.3 and that of low demand 0.7.

Currently the company is considering using a detailed market survey to assist in determining demand. The *a priori* assessment is that there is a 0.4 probability that a market survey will indicate high demand.

On the basis of surveys of a similar kind conducted in the past it is reckoned that if the survey were actually carried out and the result were to indicate high demand, then the probability of this high demand occurring would be 0.8. On the other hand, if the result were to indicate low demand then the probability of this low demand occurring would be 0.9.

The cost of the market survey would be £0.5 million. The payoffs (excluding the cost of the market survey) in present value terms are given in the table below.

		Demand	
		High	Low
Plant	Large	£19 mill.	£2 mill.
	Small	£9 mill.	£7 mill.

Draw a decision tree for this problem and hence determine the optimal strategy for the company to maximize expected monetary value. What is the expected monetary value of this optimal strategy?

28 (i) Mill Hill Equipment (MHE) is currently developing a new model in its typewriter range with which it expects to make a significant impact on the UK market and also hopes to penetrate the European market. They are confident of total sales of 20000 units, but success in Europe, which they rate at a 50:50 chance, would raise this total sales figure to 50000.

A decision must shortly be made on production facilities. It is possible to manufacture the new model essentially using the existing plant with modification costs of £0.25 million; alternatively a new production line costing £2.5 million could be set up (capacity is not seen as a problem). It is expected that production costs per unit utilizing the existing plant would be £520, while this figure would be reduced to £460 on the new line. The typewriter is intended to sell at £600 in both markets. Show how decision analysis could guide MHE in its decision between the two options.

(ii) As MHE have had only limited experience in the European market, they are also considering commissioning a market analysis by a firm of marketing consultants. The analysis would contain a prediction of either success or failure in the European market. A quotation of £50000 for this work has been received. The consultants concerned have a high reputation, and the probabilities of their predictions being correct, based on MHE's previous experiences with them and their initial comments on the European typewriter market, have been summarized in the table below:

	Prediction	
Actual conditions in Europe	Success	Failure
Excellent: product would succeed	0.6	0.4
Poor: product would fail	0.2	0.8

Should MHE commission the analysis and, if so, how should they react to the possible predictions?

29 A company sells welding supplies to industrial customers and maintains an extensive distribution network throughout the USA with its 250 sales representatives. The company has been in existence for about twenty-five years and sells only the most traditional types of welding supplies. In recent years a fairly new welding method, tungsten inert gas welding (TIG) has been making some inroads into the sales of this company. There is, however, still a vast untapped market of potential customers estimated to be equivalent to at least 100000 units.

Recently, the company has been given an opportunity to market a new inexpensive and very flexible TIG torch which could be used as an adaptor for a traditional arc welder. The marketing of this product would involve a fixed investment of approximately $100000, consisting mostly of sales literature and advertising. Net profit, that is the sales price less the manufacturer's royalties and sales representative's commissions, was conservatively estimated to be $50 per sale. The management of the company has to decide whether or not to market the product.

The product planning committee has met in emergency session and agreed that an appropriate prior distribution for π, the proportion of the potential market who would buy the torch, was given by an exponential distribution with a mean of 0.025, i.e. $p(\pi) = 40e^{-40\pi}$.

There is just time to carry out a small test marketing of the product. This would be done by selecting a simple random sample of 100 potential customers at a cost of $8000, including the purchase of the torches likely to be sold on such a test marketing.

What should be the company's choice of initial strategy: accept the offer, carry out a test market, or reject the offer? If you recommend a test market, give the decision rule for acceptance or rejection of the offer that would be followed. (Note that the suggested prior distribution actually allows π to be greater than 1, but the probability of such a value is effectively zero.)

30 A company manufactures and installs a type of machine. It has been found that a proportion p of the machines manufactured have a certain kind of fault, and the rest are satisfactory. If a satisfactory machine is installed, the company makes a return of £500; if a faulty machine is installed, the company makes a loss of £1000.

Machines can be overhauled before installation, at a cost of £300, and this ensures that they are satisfactory.

Each machine can be tested, at a cost of £100, and if a fault is present there is a 50% chance that it will be detected (the test never indicates a fault when none is present).

It is required to maximize the expected net return, using p as an estimate of the prior probability that a machine is faulty.

    (i) Give a decision tree for the company, and find the optimal strategies, and expressions for the corresponding optimal expected returns, for all possible values of p.

       Suppose that it is also possible to carry out a cheaper test, at £50, provided the other test has not been carried out first; this cheaper test will detect a fault with estimated probability s, and would not affect the result of the other test if this were subsequently carried out.

    (ii) Find the optimal strategy for $p = 0.2$ and $s = 0.3$,

    (iii) Using your results for part (i), or otherwise, show that for values of p less than $1/6$ it would never be optimal to use both tests, whatever the value of s.

Bibliography

(Items marked with an asterisk are cited directly in the text.)

Chapter 1

Ayer, A. J. (1965). Chance. *Scientific America*, **213**, 44–54.

Brown, R. V., Kahr, A. S. and Peterson, C. R. (1974). *Decision Analysis for the Manager*. New York, Holt Rinehart & Winston.

Bunn, D. W., Hampton, J., Moore, P. G. and Thomas, H. (1976). *Case Studies in Decision Analysis*. London, Penguin.

*Coyle, R. G. (1981). A model of the dynamics of the third world war. *Journal of Operations Research Society*, **22**, 755–65.

Devereux, E. C. (1968). Gambling, in *International Encylopaedia of the Social Sciences*, Macmillan, Vol. 6, pp. 53–62.

Lindley, D. V. (1971). *Making Decisions*. London, Wiley–Interscience.

*Moore, P. G. and Thomas, H. (1976). *The Anatomy of Decisions*. London, Penguin.

*Raiffa, H. (1968). *Decision Analysis: Introductory Lectures on Choices under Uncertainty*. New York, Addison-Wesley.

Rowe, W. D. (1977). *An Anatomy of Risk*. New York, Wiley.

Chapter 2

Benjamin, B. and Pollard, J. H. (1977). *Analysis of Mortality and Other Actuarial Statistics*. London, Heinemann.

Cox, P. R. (1975). *Demography*. Cambridge University Press.

*de Moivre, A. (1718). *The Doctrine of Chances*. W. Pearson. Reprinted in 1967 by F. Cass, London.

*General Register Office (1965). *English Life Table No. 12*. Decennial Supplement England and Wales for 1961. London, HMSO.

Jeffreys, H. (1939) *Theory of Probability*. Oxford University Press, Ch. 1.

*Jewell, W. S. (1980). *Generalised Models of an Insurance Business*. 20th International Actuarial Congress, Lausanne.

Johnson, P. D. and Hey, G. B. (1971). Statistical studies in motor insurance. *Journal of Institute of Actuaries*, **97**, 199–249.

Levy H. and Roth, L., (1936). *Elements of Probability*. Oxford University Press, Chs. 1–3.

Mises, R. von (1939). *Probability, Statistics and Truth*. London, W. Hodge.

*Whitworth, W. A. (1897). *Choice and Chance*. Hafner, New York.

*Zeisel, H. (1978). Statistics as legal evidence, in *International Encyclopedia of Statistics*. London, Collier–Macmillan.

234

Chapter 3

*Balthasar, H. W., Bosch, R. A. A. and Menke, M. M. (1978). Calling the long shots in R & D. *Harvard Business Review*, **56**, 151–60.

*Barclay, S. and Peterson, C. (1973). Two Methods for Assessing Probability. Working Paper, Decisions & Designs Inc., Washington.

*Battersby, A. (1965). *Network Analysis for Planning and Scheduling*. London, Macmillan.

*Brown, B. and Helmer, O. (1962). *Improving the Reliability of Estimates Obtained from a Consensus of Experts*. California, Rand.

*Downton, F. (1982). Legal probability and statistics. *Journal of Royal Statistical Society* A, **145**, 400–7.

*Gustafson, D. (1971). Behavioural Decision Theory in Medical Care. Working Paper, Department of Industrial Engineering, University of Wisconsin.

*Hoerl, A. E. and Fallin, H. K. (1974). Reliability of subjective evaluations in a high incentive situation. *Journal of the Royal Statistical Society* A, **137**, 227–30.

*Kabus, I. (1976). You can bank on uncertainty. *Harvard Business Review*, May–June, pp. 95–105.

*Lindley, D. V., Tversky, A. and Brown, R. V. (1979). Reconciliation of probability assessments. *Journal of Royal Statistical Society* A, **142**, 146–80.

*Linstone, N. A. and Turoff, M. (Eds.) (1975). *The Delphi Method: Techniques and Applications*. Massachusetts, Addison-Wesley.

*Murphy, A. H. and Winkler, R. L. (1977). Reliability of subjective probability forecasts of precipitation and temperature. *Applied Statistics*, **26**, 41–7.

*Raiffa, H. (1968). *Decision Analysis:* Introductory Lectures on Choices under Uncertainty. Addison-Wesley.

*Souder, W. I. (1969). The validity of subjective probability of success forecasts by R & D project managers. *IEEE Transactions of Engineering Management*, EM-16, February.

*Winkler, R. L. (1968). The consensus of subjective probability estimates. *Management Science* B, **15** (2), B61–75.

Chapter 4

Hampton, J., Moore, P. G. and Thomas, H. (1973). Subjective probability and its measurement. *Journal of the Royal Statistical Society* A, **136**, 21–42.

Hogarth, R. M. and Makridakis, S. (1981). *Forecasting and planning: an evaluation*. *Management Science*, **27**, no. 2, 115–38.

Lindley, D. V. (1982). The improvement of probability judgments. *Journal of Royal Statistical Society* A, **145**, 117–26.

Moore, P. G. (1972). *Risk in Business Decisions*, London, Longman.

Moore, P. G. and Thomas, H. (1973). Measurement problems in decision analysis. *Journal of Management Studies*, **10**, no. 2, 168–93.

*Morlock, H. (1967). The effect of outcome desirability on information required for decisions. *Behavioural Science*, **12**, no. 4, 296–300.

*Raiffa, H. and Alpert, M. (1969). A Progress Report on the Training of Probability Assessors. Unpublished report, Harvard Business School.

*Tversky, A. (1974a). Assessing uncertainty. *Journal of the Royal Statistical Society* B, **36**, 148–59.

Tversky, A. (1974b). Judgments under uncertainty: heuristics and biases. *Science*, **185**, 1124–31.

*Wallace, J. B. (1975). Subjective estimation bias and PERT statistical procedures. *Omega*, **3** (1), 79–85.

Winkler, R. L. (1967). The assessment of prior distributions in Bayesian analysis. *Journal of The American Statistical Society*, **62**, 776–800.

Chapter 5

*Beard, R. E., Pentikainen, T. and Pesonen, E. (1969). *Risk Theory*. London, Methuen.

*Borch, K. (1967). The theory of risk. *Journal of the Royal Statistical Society B*, **29**, 432–60.

*Brown, R. V. (1970). Do managers find decision theory useful? *Harvard Business Review*, May, 78–9.

*Committee on Policy Optimisation (1978). Command 7148. London, HMSO.

*De Neufville, R. and Keeney, R. L. (1974). Use of decision analysis in airport development for Mexico City. In *Systems, Planning and Design* (ed. R. De Neufville and D. H. Marks). New York, Prentice-Hall.

Harrison, F. L. (1977). Decision making in conditions of extreme uncertainty. *Journal of Management Science*, **14**, 169–78.

Hull, J. C., Moore, P. G., and Thomas, H. (1973). Utility and its measurement. *Journal of the Royal Statistical Society A*, **136**, 226–47.

Keeney, R. L. (1972). Utility functions for multi-attributed consequences. *Management Science* **18**, 276–287.

Keeney, R. L. and Raiffa, H. (1976). *Decisions with Multiple Objectives*. London, Wiley.

*Moore, P. G. (1977). The manager's struggles with uncertainty. *Journal of the Royal Statistical Society A*, **140**, 129–65.

Moore, P. G. and Thomas, H. (1975). Measuring uncertainty. *Omega*, **3**, 657–72.

Moore, P. G., Thomas H., Bunn, D. E. and Hampton, J. M. (1976). *Case Studies in Decision Analysis*. London, Penguin.

Pratt, J. W. (1964). Risk aversion in the small and in the large. *Econometrica*, **32**, 122–136.

*Report of a Study of Rail Links with Heathrow Airport (1970). Parts I and II. London, HMSO.

*Roskill Commission (1971) Report on the third London airport. London, HMSO.

Savage, L. J. (1971). Elicitation of personal probabilities and expectations. *Journal of the American Statistical Association*, **66**, 783–801.

*Simon, H. A. (1957). *Administrative Behaviour*, 2nd edn. London, The Free Press.

*Spetzler, C. S. (1968). The development of a corporate risk policy for capital investment decisions. *IEEE Transactions on Systems Science and Cybernetics*, September, 279–300.

*Swalm, R. O. (1966). *Utility theory – insights into risk taking*. *Harvard Business Review* December, 123–6.

Tversky, A. and Kahneman, D. (1971). The belief in the law of small numbers. *Psychology Bulletin*, **76**, 105–10.

Wallach, M. A., Kogan, N. and Bern, D. J. (1962). Group influence on individual risk-taking. *Journal of Abnormal and Social Psychology*, **65**, 75–86.

Watson, S. R. and Brown, R. V. (1978). The valuation of decision analysis. *Journal of the Royal Statistical Society A*, **141**, 69–78.

Chapter 6

*Broyles, J. E. and Franks, J. R. (1973). Capital project appraisal: A modern approach. *Managerial Finance*, **2**, 86–96.

*Hertz, D. B. (1964). Risk analysis in capital investment. *Harvard Business Review*, **42**(2), 95–106.

*Higgins, J. C. (1982). Decision-making at board level. *Journal of the Operational Research Society*, **33**, 319–26.

*Hoskins, W. R. (1970). How to counter expropriation. *Harvard Business Review*, September, 102–12.

*Jodice, D. A. (1980). Sources of change in Third World regimes for foreign direct investment, 1968–76. *International Organisation*, **34**,(2), 177–206.

*Meisner, J. and Demiren, F. (1981). The creaming method: A Bayesian procedure to forecast future oil and gas discoveries in mature exploration provinces. *Journal of the Royal Statistical Society* A, **144**, 1–22.

Rummel, R. J. and Heenan, D. A. (1978). How multinationals analyse political risk. *Harvard Business Review*, January, 67–76.

*Wilson Committee (1978). North Sea Oil. Research Report No. 2 London, HMSO.

Wilson Committee (1979a). Studies of Small Firms' Financing. Research Report No. 3. London, HMSO.

*Wilson Committee (1979b). The Financing of Small Firms. Interim Report. London, HMSO, Command 7503.

Chapter 7

*Einham, H. J. and Hogarth, R. M. (1978). Confidence in Judgment: Persistence in the Illusion of Validity. *Psychology Review*, **85**(5), 395–416.

*HMSO (1979). *The ownership of company shares: a survey for* 1975. London.

Moore, P. G. (1981). Some Financial Implications of Risk in the UK. *Omega*, **9**, 113–25.

*Moyle, J. P. (1971). *The Pattern of Ordinary Share Ownership, 1957–70*. Cambridge University Press.

*Wilkie, A. D. (1981). Indexing long term contracts. *Journal of Institute of Actuaries*, **108**, 299–341.

Chapter 8

Brealey, R. A. and Myers, S. (1981). *Principles of Corporate Finance*. New York and London, McGraw Hill.

*Clarkson, R. S. (1981). A market equilibrium model for the management of ordinary share portfolios. *Transactions of the Faculty of Actuaries* **39**, 1–133.

*Dimson, E., Hodges, S. D. and Marsh P. (1980). Systematic international diversification in the light of modern portfolio theory. Paper presented to 19th Advanced Seminar on Portfolio Investment and Finance.

*Fama, E. F. and Macbeth, J. D. (1973). Risk, return and equilibrium: empirical tests. *Journal of Political Economy*, **81**, 607–36.

*Kendall, M. G. (1953). The analysis of economic time-series, part I, prices. *Journal of the Royal Statistical Society* A, **96**, 11–25.

*Markowitz, H. M. (1952). Portfolio selection. *Journal of Finance*, **7**, 77–81.

Modigliani, F. and Pogue, G. A. (1974). An introduction to risk and return. *Financial Analysts Journal*, **30**, March, 68–80; and May, 69–88.

*Sharpe, W. F. (1964). Capital asset prices: a theory of market equilibrium under conditions of risk. *Journal of Finance*, **19**, 425–42.

Sharpe, W. F. (1978). *Investments*. Englewood Cliffs, New Jersey, Prentice-Hall.

*Sharpe, W. F. and Cooper, G. M. (1972). Risk return classes of New York Stock Exchange common stocks 1931–67. *Financial Analysts Journal*, **28**, 46–54.

*Wagner, H. M. (1969). *Principles of Operations Research*. Englewood Cliffs, New Jersey, Prentice-Hall.

*Wagner, W. H. and Lau, S. C. (1971). The effect of diversification on risk. *Financial Analysts Journal*, **26**, 7–13.

Chapter 9

*Ashe, T. M. (1976). Insider dealing – what can and should be done? *Accountancy*, **87**, no. 994, 50–2.

*Barr, D. (1976). Gambling on drought. *Country Life*, 9 September.

Fama, E. F. (1965). Random walks in stock market prices. *Financial Analysts Journal*, **21**, 55–9.

*Fielding, X. (1977). *The Money Spinner: Monte Carlo Casino*. London, Weidenfeld and Nicholson.

*Hoerl, A. É. and Fallin H. K. (1974). Reliability of subjective evaluations in a high incentive situation. *Journal of the Royal Statistical Society* A, **137**, 227–30.

Manne, H. G. (1966). In defence of insider trading. *Harvard Business Review*, **44**, 113–22.

*Report of the Royal Commission on Gambling (1978). Chairman Lord Rothschild. London, HMSO.

Weaver, Warren (1977). *Lady Luck, the Theory of Probability*. London, Pelican.

Chapter 10

Ashby, Lord (1977). The subjective side of assessing risks. *New Scientist*, 19 May, 399–400.

*Combs, B. and Slovic, P. (1979). Causes of death: biases in newspaper coverage. *Journalism Quarterly*, **56**, 837–43.

Green, A. E. and Bourne, A. J. (1972). *Reliability Technology*. New York, Wiley.

Kahneman, D., Slovic P., and Tversky, A. (Ed.) (1982). *Judgment under Uncertainty: Heuristics and Biases*. Cambridge University Press.

Kletz, T. A. (1977). What risks should we run? *New Scientist*, 12 May, 320–2.

*Lockett, J. E. (1980). Catastrophes and catastrophe insurance. *Journal of Institute of Actuaries Students Society*, **24**, 91–134.

*Rothschild, Lord (1977). Risk. The Dimbleby Lecture of the British Broadcasting Corporation.

Slovic, P., Fischhoff, B. and Lichtenstein, S. (1980). Fact versus fears: understanding perceived risk. In *Societal Risk assessment: How Safe is Safe Enough?* (ed. R. Schwing and W. A. Albers) New York, Plenum Publishing.

*Slovic, P., Fischhoff, B. and Lichtenstein, S. (1981). Perceived risk: psychological factors and social implications. *Proceedings of Royal Society of London* A, **376**, 17–34.

*Starr, Chauncey (1979). General philosophy of risk-benefit analysis. In Perspectives on Benefit-Risk Decision Making. US National Academy of Engineering Report and Stanford University.

*Upton, A. C. (1982). The biological effects of low-level ionizing radiation. *Scientific America*, **246**, no. 2, 29–37.

Chapter 11

*Card W. I. (1980). Rational justification for therapeutic decisions. *Metamedicine*, **1**, 11–28.

*Doll, R. and Bradford Hill, A. (1956). Lung cancer and other causes of death in relation to smoking. *British Medical Journal*, **2**, 1071–101.

*Girdwood R. H. (1974). Death after taking medicaments. *British Medical Journal*, **1**, 501–4.

*Inhaber, H. (1981). The risk of producing energy. *Proceedings of the Royal Society of London* A, **376**, 121–8.

*Office of Health Economics (1976). Report No. 55 on Anaesthesia. London, HMSO.

*Office of Population Census and Surveys (1979). *Birth Statistics* FM1, no. 3. London, HMSO.

Pochin, E. E. (1981). Quantification of risk in medical procedures. *Proceedings of the Royal Society of London* A, **376**, 87–101.

*Siddall, E. (1980). Control of spending on nuclear safety. *Nuclear Safety*, **21**(4), 451.

*Social Trends (1979). Vol. 9, Government Statistical Service. London, HMSO,

United Nations Scientific Committee on the Effects of Atomic Radiation (1977). Report to the General Assembly, New York, United Nations.

Chapter 12

*Card, W. I. and Mooney, G. H. (1977). What is the monetary value of a human life? *British Medical Journal*, Part 2, 1627–9.

*Jones, R. V. (1965). *The Secret War*. London, Hamish Hamilton.

*Report of the Committee of Enquiry on the Structure of the Electricity Supply Industry (1976). Chairman, Lord Plowden. London, HMSO.

*Starr, C. (1976). General philosophy of risk-benefit analysis. Extract from *Energy and the Environment: a Risk-benefit Approach*, edited by Ashley, H., Rudman, R. L. and Whipple, C. London, Pergamon Press.

*Stork, W. (1973). The cost effectiveness of international vehicle regulations. *Automotive Engineering*, **81**, no. 3, 30–40.

*Thompson, A. (1976). Two British errors; their probable size and some possible lessons. Inaugural lecture, University College, London.

Appendix A

*Brook, R. H. W. (1974). How safe is safe? *Chartered Mechanical Engineer*, **21**, no. 10, 75–8.

Cass, T. (1980). *Statistical Methods in Management*, Books 1 and 2. London, Cassell.

Feller, W. (1953). *Probability Theory and its Applications*, Volume 1. New York, Wiley.

Moore, P. G. (1979). *Principles of Statistical Techniques*. Cambridge University Press.

Wadsworth, G. P. and Bryan, J. G. (1960). *Introduction to Probability and Random Variables*. New York, McGraw-Hill.

Wonnacott, T. H. and R. J. (1969). *Introductory Statistics*. Wiley, New York.

Appendix B

Kepner, C. H. & Tregoe, B. S. (1965). *The Rational Manager*. New York and London, McGraw-Hill.

Simon, H. A. (1965). The new science of management decision. In *The shape of Automation for Men and Management*. New York, Harper & Row, pp. 57–79.

Welsch, L. A. & Cyert, R. M. (eds.) (1970). *Management Decision Making*. London, Penguin Modern Management Readings.

*Williams, A. J. (1982). Project management. *Journal of Institute of Actuaries*, **105**, 100–40.

Appendix C

*Cheesewright, P. (1978). Mineral exploration: pay now and hope to collect later. *Financial Times*, Tuesday 7 February, p. 13.

Doherty, N. A. (1975). Some fundamental theorems of risk management. *Journal of Risk and Insurance*, **5**, 447–60.

*Green, P. E. and Frank R. E. (1966). Bayesian statistics and market research. *Applied Statistics*, **15**, 173–90.

Moore, P. G. (1976). The shackles of risk. *The Statistician*, **28**, no. 4, 281–93.

*Woodroofe, E. G. (1974). Catering for uncertainty. Haldane Memorial Lecture. London, Birkbeck College.

Index